T0323009

NEGOTIATING INTERNET GOVERNANCE

Negotiating Internet Governance

ROXANA RADU

OXFORD
UNIVERSITY PRESS

OXFORD
UNIVERSITY PRESS

Great Clarendon Street, Oxford, OX2 6DP,
United Kingdom

Oxford University Press is a department of the University of Oxford.
It furthers the University's objective of excellence in research, scholarship,
and education by publishing worldwide. Oxford is a registered trade mark of
Oxford University Press in the UK and in certain other countries

Published with the support of the Swiss National Science Foundation

First Edition published in 2019

Impression: 1

Published in the United States of America by Oxford University Press
198 Madison Avenue, New York, NY 10016, United States of America

British Library Cataloguing in Publication Data
Data available

Library of Congress Control Number: 2018961478

ISBN (HARDBACK): 978–0–19–883307–9
ISBN (ONLINE): 978–0–19–187140–5
ISBN (UPDF): 978–0–19–256948–6
ISBN (EPUB): 978–0–19–256949–3

DOI: https://doi.org/10.1093/oso/9780198833079.001.0001

Printed and bound by
CPI Group (UK) Ltd, Croydon, CR0 4YY

To my mom, with infinite love.

Foreword

The global governance of the Internet is an ongoing, complex, contested, and unfinished project. In its early days, Internet governance could be characterized as a classic example of private authority in global governance, but as this book masterfully demonstrates, as the Internet's commercial and political salience increased over time, its governance evolved into a composite arrangement of public and private actors interacting in different multi-stakeholder initiatives. The governance of the Internet is more analogous to the global governance of the environment than it is to the governance of global trade. It is a regime complex with different governance and institutional arrangements in different issue domains and with no clear hierarchy among them. While the domain has become increasingly securitized in recent years, the emerging and highly imperfect governance of cybersecurity is only one aspect of contemporary Internet governance. In a regime complex like Internet governance, the nascent governance in one issue domain such as cybersecurity will invariably have implications for the governance of other important issue domains, such as freedom of expression and liberty, privacy and surveillance, fair access, and the global digital divide.

In this important new book, Roxana Radu situates the global governance of the Internet historically and traces its origins from the seemingly ad hoc assignment of domain names by private actors in the 1980s through its commercialization in the 1990s to the ongoing series of global multi-stakeholder governance arrangements over the past two decades. As a participant in many key, formative meetings, she not only describes the historical development of governance arrangements, but also contributes to current policy debates on Internet regulation and digital developments. She identifies watershed moments defining power dynamics in Internet governance, proposes an original framework of analysis for mechanisms of governance at work across time in Internet policy, and offers a detailed analysis of the praxis of governance and how it evolves over time in light of the interaction between various instruments, actors, and logics at work. In that sense, the book translates global governance theory ideas and operationalizes core concepts, offering the first comprehensive study of Internet governance mechanisms at the global level.

The book shows how steering mechanisms come into being through various channels and individuals operating within a transnational policy network, and it also reveals shifts in governance patterns over a relatively long period of time (more than forty years). It also adds a new dimension to the investigation of governance articulation by examining anchoring practices in Internet governance. As such, it provides an important building block for a broader research agenda dedicated to the emergence of governance in new issue domains, refining our understanding of the genesis and structuration processes involved.

The current governance of the Internet is far from ideal from many different vantage points, but that does not mean that it is ungoverned or ungovernable. It simply means that the normative quality of the existing governance arrangements is deficient in some important respects, whether we are concerned with inclusivity, transparency, effectiveness, efficiency, adaptability, or fundamental fairness. This book makes a significant contribution to the ongoing debate about how the Internet should be governed. We need to understand the history of Internet governance, its evolution, its constant experimentation, and its past failures in order to participate in an informed way in the project of improving the quality of Internet governance today. With its historical overview, its comprehensive treatment of the subject, and its analytical framework for understanding the mechanisms of governance at work, this book provides a critical first step in this important project.

Thomas Biersteker
The Graduate Institute, Geneva

Acknowledgements

Negotiating Internet Governance follows directly from my doctoral dissertation. I would like to express my deep gratitude to my supervisor, Professor Thomas J. Biersteker, for his invaluable guidance throughout the PhD process and for his unchanged enthusiasm for my project since 2011. Precious contributions to this work also came from Professors Liliana Andonova and Nanette Levinson, whose comments helped me revise and update the content. Dr Nicole Stemlau at the Centre for Socio-Legal Studies in Oxford welcomed the book project and offered crucial space and support to finalize it: an improved version of the book is available today as a result!

To my colleagues and friends at DiploFoundation and the Geneva Internet Platform: thank you for setting an excellent example of collaboration and for the steep learning curve I went through while working together. I am intellectually indebted to all the Internet governance experts I interacted with in the past seven years, during the many meetings attended, as well as during my research stays at the Hertie School of Governance in Berlin and the Institute for Technology and Society in Rio de Janeiro.

This project would not have been possible without the financial support of the Swiss National Science Foundation, which I gratefully acknowledge.

My family's support and encouragement was essential in completing this book, at a distance and in Geneva. Eugenia, Paola, and Piero were there when I needed it the most. I am extremely thankful for having been surrounded, at all times, by amazing friends, who made this journey as exciting as it could possibly be: Alex, Aura, Ezgi, Ioana P., Ioana T., Merih, and Rishabh.

Special thanks go to my partner, Alberto, always patient, loving, and inspiring.

Table of Contents

List of Abbreviations

ACM	Association for Computing Machinery
ACTA	Anti-Counterfeiting Trade Agreement
AI	artificial intelligence
ARPA	US Advanced Research Projects Agency
ARPANET	Advanced Research Projects Agency Network
ASEAN	Association of Southeast Asian Nations
BAT	Baidu, Tencent, and Alibaba
BBN	Bolt, Beranek, and Newman
BRICS	Brazil, Russia, India, China, and South Africa
BSBN	Beijing-Shanghai Backbone Network
CBMs	confidence building measures
CCBI	Coordinating Committee of Business Interlocutors
CCITT	International Telegraph and Telephone Consultative Committee
cc-TLDs	country-code top-level domains
CCWG-Accountability	Cross-Community Working Group on Enhancing ICANN Accountability
CDA	Communications Decency Act
CERN	European Organization for Nuclear Research
CERTs	Computer Emergency Response Teams
CIRP	UN Committee for Internet-related Policies
CJEU	Court of Justice of the European Union
CNRI	Corporation for National Research Initiatives
CoE	Council of Europe
CORE	Council of Registrars
CREN	Corporation for Research and Educational Networking
CSIRTs	Computer Security Incident Response Teams
CSNET	Computer Science Network
CSTD	UN Commission on Science and Technology for Development
DARPA	Defense Advanced Research Projects Agency

DCA	Defense Communications Agency
DNS	domain name system
DNSO	Domain Name Supporting Organisation
DoC	Department of Commerce
DoD	Department of Defense
DOT Force	Digital Opportunities Task Force
ECHR	European Court of Human Rights
ECOSOC	UN Economic and Social Council
EU	European Union
FCC	Federal Communications Commission
FNC	Federal Networking Council
G8	Group of 8
GAC	Governmental Advisory Committee
GDDI	Global Digital Divide Initiative
GDP	Gross Domestic Product
GDPR	General Data Protection Regulation
GFCE	Global Forum on Cyber Expertise
GIC	Global Internet Council
GIP	Global Internet Project
GNSO	Generic Names Supporting Organisation
gTLDs	generic top-level domains
gTLDs-MoU	Generic Top-Level Domain Memorandum of Understanding
HTTP	Hypertext Transfer Protocol
IAB	Internet Activities Board
IAHC	International Ad Hoc Committee
IANA	Internet Assigned Numbers Authority
ICANN	Internet Corporation for Assigned Names and Numbers
ICCB	Internet Configuration Control Board
ICG	IANA Stewardship Transition Cooperation Group
ICPC	International Cable Protection Committee
ICTs	information and communication technologies
ICT4D	ICT for development
IEG	Informal Experts Group
IENs	Internet Experiment Notes

IETF	Internet Engineering Task Force
IFWP	International Forum for the White Paper
IG	Internet governance
IGF	Internet Governance Forum
ILO	International Labour Organization
IMPs	Interface Message Processors
InterNIC	Internet Network Information Center
INWG	International Packet Network Working Group
IOs	international organizations
IoT	Internet of Things
IP	Internet Protocol
IPTO	Information Processing Techniques Office
IR	international relations
ISF	Internet Social Forum
ISO	International Organization for Standardization
ISOC	Internet Society
ISPs	Internet Service Providers
ITAA	Information Technology Association of America
ITAG	IANA Transition Advisory Group
ITRs	International Telecommunication Regulations
ITU	International Telecommunication Union
IUF	Internet Ungovernance Forum
LAWS	lethal autonomous weapon systems
LRO	Legal Rights Objections
MAG	Multistakeholder Advisory Group
MDG	Millennium Development Goal
MILNET	military network
NASA	National Aeronautics and Space Administration
NATO	North Atlantic Treaty Organization
NCP	Network Control Protocol
NCSG	Non-Commercial Stakeholder Group
NEPAD	New Partnership for Africa's Development
NIC	Network Information Center
NIPRNET	Non-classified Internet Protocol Router Network
NPL	National Physical Laboratory

NRO	Number Resource Organization
NSA	US National Security Agency
NSF	US National Science Foundation
NSFNET	National Science Foundation Network
NSI	Network Solutions, Inc.
NTIA	National Telecommunication and Information Administration
NWICO	New World Information and Communication Order
NWG	Network Working Group
OAS	Organization of American States
OECD	Organisation for Economic Co-operation and Development
OSCE	Organization for Security and Co-operation in Europe
OSI	Open Systems Interconnection
PC	personal computer
PIPA	Protect IP Act
PrepCom	Preparatory Committee
PTT	post, telephone, and telegraph organizations
RFC	Request for Comments
RIRs	Regional Internet Registries
SCO	Shanghai Cooperation Organisation
SDG	Sustainable Development Goal
SIPRNET	Secret [formerly Secure] Internet Protocol Router Network
SOPA	Stop Online Piracy Act
STS	science and technology studies
TCP	Transmission Control Protocol
TLDs	top level domains
UAE	United Arab Emirates
UDRP	Universal Domain Name Dispute Resolution Policy
UN	United Nations
UNCTAD	UN Conference on Trade and Development
UNDP	United Nations Development Programme
UNESCO	UN Educational, Scientific and Cultural Organization
UNGA	UN General Assembly
UNGIS	UN Group on the Information Society

UNICTTF	UN ICT Task Force
W3C	World Wide Web Consortium
WB	World Bank
WCIT-12	World Conference on International Telecommunications 2012
WEF	World Economic Forum
WGEC	Working Group on Enhanced Cooperation
WGIG	Working Group on Internet Governance
WIPO	World Intellectual Property Organization
WITSA	World Information and Telecommunication Association
WSF	World Social Forum
WSIS	World Summit on Information Society
WSIS + 10	decennial review of the World Summit on Information Society
WTO	World Trade Organization
WWW	World Wide Web

1

Introduction

On the Internet, everything we love and everything we hate has a name. It also has a number or a string of 0s and 1s making it technically viable. And, more often than not, it comes with a price tag, whether visible or disguised as data value. Since the 1980s, the infrastructure for our digital traces and digital legacies has continued to grow, scientifically and politically. In a few decades, it evolved from the purview of one government to the globalizing world to become the most influential means of communication, the biggest global market, but also the largest mass-surveillance tool ever devised. Digital flows are estimated to add about 15 to 20 per cent of the global GDP annually (WIPO 2015) and data-driven businesses have made Internet companies the most profitable in the world. Indisputably, the Internet is now a global domain of power.

Hundreds of governance instruments are at work to regulate the digital aspects of our lives, from connectivity to online behaviour on social networks. Our well-being, our relationships, our health, and our labour are all affected by the billions of Internet-connected tools around the world. Recent discussions around algorithms and artificial intelligence (AI), the 'Internet of Things', and smart cities refocus attention on device-to-device communication, as in the early days of networking. Some of the current debates are reminiscent of the struggles to find a legal and ethical framework for technical advancements in the early 1990s. Understanding the answers given then and the continuous contestation will help us better respond to the dilemmas we are confronted with today.

The governance of the Internet transcends the conventional boundaries among state, market, and user interests. Alongside formalized efforts that can be easily categorized, 'complicated, little understood and often improvised processes of governance' (Schmitter 2010, 85–6) characterize the field. How these two types of processes emerge, develop, and coexist in Internet governance (IG) is the focus of this book. In this exploration, the Internet is analysed as a nascent policy domain around which political commitments, business models, user preferences, and moral predispositions amalgamate.

Negotiating Internet Governance. Roxana Radu © Roxana Radu 2019. Published 2019 by Oxford University Press.

Drawing on international relations (IR) and Internet governance scholarship, I explore how rule-making is achieved for a field in constant evolution. To dissect the complex arrangements of global policies, norms, and standards in the making, power dynamics are analysed along three axes: mechanisms, actors, and practices of governance. Each one of these presents tacit or explicit power differentials and tensions that structure ongoing negotiations. In this study, they are put in perspective through a periodization exercise, which runs from the early days of networking experiments in the 1970s to 2018.

Today, most Internet users are located in China (772 million) and India (481 million). Combined, the two countries have almost 40 per cent of the world's youth online and lead the smartphone market (Nilekani 2018). Although nearly half of the globe's population is now online, important variations in the patterns of access and use persist: the large majority of people in the world's forty-six poorest nations remains unconnected and only 5 per cent of the world's estimated 7,100 languages are currently represented on the Internet (Broadband Commission for Digital Development 2018; 2015). To become the global backbone for political, legal, commercial, and social life, the network underwent transformations in scope, size, and scale, setting into motion the greatest technical collaboration in modern history and transforming into an authoritative policy space ever more crowded.

Currently, one in three Internet users is under eighteen (Livingstone et al. 2015), experiencing the broad societal changes triggered by the widespread use of the Internet: new patterns of communication (instant delivery, (micro) blogging, citizen journalism, automatic translation tools, etc.), tele-work, autonomous driving, social networking, sharing culture (Benkler 2006), or crowdsourcing. Novel art forms, business models (largely based on big data analytics and behavioural targeting), e-participation, digital currencies, and smart wearables reconfigure the relationship we have with technology. Independent of our age, the everyday Internet use is concentrated around the visible components of the World Wide Web: social media, email, file transfers, peer-to-peer sharing, dating apps, or online transactions. In these interactions, the functioning of the Internet remains invisible; 'for hundreds of millions of users around the world, the Internet is indeed governed without governors' (Sylvan 2014, 36).

But this is no longer the case for policymakers, as the salience of IG grew exponentially. Network controls, cybersecurity and privacy concerns, the increased power of private intermediaries, and an emerging cyber-diplomacy agenda have raised the profile of this field to a scale comparable to environmental politics or global health. A 'political construct in progress' (Brousseau and Marzouki 2013, 371), the Internet was understood as a mechanism for the projection of power, both hard and soft (Carr 2015), but also as a technology of disruption (Demchak 2003; Milan 2013; Dencik and Leistert 2015). Because of its dual use, the Internet presents, on the one hand, opportunities for strengthening governance mechanisms using digitization, non-stop communication, ease of access to information, online delivery, as well as through the potential nurturing of communities of practice. On the other hand, it can undermine or interfere with efforts by different actors to govern, via the use of extensive surveillance, real-time information leaking, fraudulent and criminal activities, or cyber-attacks. This tension—juxtaposing personal freedoms and empowerment, societal well-being, and destabilizing practices—remains at the core of the various visions put forward for governing the network.

But as more and more of the Internet technical specifications come under the spotlight with global debates on universal access, net neutrality, or encryption, the societal changes they bring about are also called into question. Developed and developing countries alike are confronted with processes of Internet-induced adjustment and complexity management. As discussed throughout this book, a number of governance arrangements emerged spontaneously, out of informal interactions, but consolidated into institutional mandates, practices, and shared expectations, showing hybridity at work across *modi operandi* and across time. Moreover, rapid technological advances and specific sets of local issues have permeated the global sphere, continuously transforming the meaning of IG.

The global governance literature, with its diverse research traditions, provides a useful starting point for unpacking the complexity of global Internet arrangements. Parallel to analyses of new policy dilemmas (Fyfe and Crookall 2010) and 'super wicked' issues (Levin et al. 2009), complex governance systems are understood in IR as embedded in and entangled with societal values and power positions that they reinforce, mediate, or contest. While this has not translated directly into a research agenda on the governance of new technologies, it has inspired a number of IG studies to pursue a holistic understanding. Alongside the focus on formal attributes of institutions,[1] more emphasis has been placed in recent years on studying informality in IG processes, with an increasing degree of empirical and theoretical sophistication (Flyverbom 2011; Epstein 2013; Chenou 2014).

Adding to the transformations in governance, the digital age restructured global governance and the *problematique* of power in a two-fold manner. Not only has it created new loci of power outside the purview of a powerful hegemon, but it has created and perpetuated a transnational policy network

---

[1] Ziewitz and Pentzold (2014, 311) note that IG research is 'closely tied to policy discourses and has developed a corresponding focus on the role of more or less institutionalised stakeholders at the national or transnational level'.

(Biersteker 2014) comprising experts from different fields, countries, and backgrounds acting both formally and informally. The relations among international organizations, their constituencies, and other stakeholders have altered as the Internet fostered the development of horizontal networks (Castells 1996, 469), which have supplemented, rather than replaced, the existing hierarchies.

Navigating Global Governance

The reality of governance existed *avant la lettre*. More than two decades after its popularization in IR studies, the 'global governance' concept remains rather permissive and broad. It was mainstreamed in the early 1990s with the establishment of the United Nations Commission on Global Governance and the strong academic impetus to move away from the narrow analysis of the interstate system to broader interactions between governance actors, spaces, and mechanisms (Rosenau and Czempiel 1992; Osborne and Gaebler 1992). For policymakers, it was closely linked to the 'good governance' priorities spearheaded by the World Bank (Weiss 2000; Gisselquist 2012). 'Internet governance' is among the newest topics added to the international agenda, for which global governance scholarship provides the most extensive, but also the most diverse, set of perspectives. I take this as the starting point for the analysis of emerging issue areas for which an institutional architecture is not entirely solidified, but rather continuously negotiated and contested. Normative dimensions at the core of contemporary governance—responsibility, legitimacy, and accountability—extend to IG naturally, making the reflection on the mechanisms at work more enticing.

Historically, new technologies played an essential role in shifting governance debates from the domestic to the international level. With the laying of the first transatlantic connection of copper cables for telegraphic signals in 1858, cross-border communication and collaboration became a permanent feature of international relations (Thiemeyer 2013). By the mid-twentieth century, the Frankfurt School placed a central emphasis on the use of technology for the subjugation of the masses by the modern state and opened the door for critical theories that account for the transformation driven by information and communication technologies (ICTs). In the words of Kranzberg (1986, 545), technology is 'neither good nor bad; nor is it neutral … technology's interaction with the social ecology is such that technical developments frequently have environmental, social, and human consequences that go far beyond the immediate purposes of the technical devices and practices themselves'. Debates in science and technology studies (STS)[2] neatly parallel predicaments in IG, as technological determinism and social constructivism tenets surface regularly in the discourses of politicians, business leaders, civil society, or technical community representatives.

In this study, global governance is understood as 'a set of authoritative rules aimed at defining, constraining, and shaping actor expectations in a purposive order, generally implemented through a set of mechanisms recognized as legitimate by relevant actors' (Biersteker 2010).[3] This goal is accomplished through a plethora of laws and regulations, but also through institutional dialogue, transnational policy networks, social practices, and informal ways of bargaining and negotiation. When applied to the Internet, the global governance framework presents us with a 'bricolage' picture: this emerging issue domain is currently run through a combination of frameworks of coordination, rhetoric and modelling, constraints and inducements, as well as routine interactions (Sylvan 2014). Authoritative decision-making for this domain may come as part of intergovernmental processes, yet not exclusively: it is often implemented through technical standards and protocols, business practices, legal precedents, and everyday routines.

Since the 1920s radio connection revolution, the spaces, objects, and subjects of international governance have mutated continuously. As a substantial preoccupation, the Internet became an object of governance around 1983, when the Internet protocol suite—the Transmission Control Protocol (TCP) and the Internet Protocol (IP)—started to be implemented widely. Concerned with the changes in state-based institutions, global governance scholars have—at the time of the Internet boom—paid little attention to the way in which the Internet gets to be governed and generates an institutional architecture as a global domain. Yet the constitution of a system of rules for the Internet is not only relevant for how the field evolves, but also for understanding the global ordering that emerges with it.

Internet Governance under the Magnifying Glass

As an emerging field of study (deNardis et al. 2013), IG can be easily circumscribed to the fragmented global governance architecture, understood to be 'an overarching system of public and private institutions that are valid or

---

[2] STS designates a branch of information science investigating the relationship between scientific knowledge, technological systems, and society, and its social, political, and cultural implications. Sismondo (2010) offers an expansive introduction to the field.

[3] The emphasis on authority and legitimacy is also strong in Cutler et al. (1999) and in Gupta and Pahl-Wostl (2013), who assess that 'only a small part of the governance spectrum' can make regulatory decisions (p. 54).

active in a given issue area of world politics, comprising organisations, regimes, and other forms of principles, norms, regulations and decision-making procedures' (Biermann et al. 2009, 15). But this delineation remains incomplete without an in-depth look at the specificities of this new domain in international affairs, built around the core tension of power-sharing arrangements. So far, IR theories have dealt primarily with power contests in physical spaces and have not yet provided satisfactory answers to the challenges posed by virtual spaces (Choucri 2012, 5).

The Internet encompasses both narrow and broad questions of governance (Solum 2009). The former refers to the management of technical aspects and basic infrastructure, whereas the latter covers public policy and ethics. Understood broadly, 'Internet governance would be more or less equivalent to "law and politics" at least in the "wired" and "wireless" (or more developed) nations' (Solum 2009, 49). For a long time, a strong emphasis was placed on studying the institutions governing the Internet standards and protocols, as well as the domain name system, with their specific organizational processes and functioning. Yet framing Internet governance as 'technical only' obliviates related socio-political implications and minimizes the latent political stakes.

Adopting a broad understanding of the Internet is thus a prerequisite for studying its evolution. Throughout this book, I refer exclusively to the visible part of the Internet, which most users know, access, and use daily. The non-indexed section of the Internet, also referred to as the 'deepweb'—a term coined by computer scientist Mike Bergman in 2000—or 'darkweb', remains relatively obscure to the majority of users, although it is assumed to be several times bigger than the searchable web.[4] This hidden side of the World Wide Web is not covered by regular search engines, and access to it generally requires the use of circumvention and anonymity technology. The darkweb is a space of self-regulation, where state control is rather limited.

Encapsulating different approaches, 'Internet governance', just like the governance concept before, became a catchword that denotes a plethora of actions ranging from legal provisions to routine practices. While most IG scholars recognize the complexity and heterogeneity of the field, the majority focus on specific processes such as co-regulation, standard-setting, or cybersecurity governance (Marsden 2011; DeNardis 2014). In the IR literature, there has been an overwhelming focus on the myriad manifestations of

---

[4] The non-indexed web includes: dynamic web pages, blocked sites, unlinked sites, private sites (with access via login credentials), non-HTML/-contextual/-scripted content, and limited-access networks. The latter generally use sites with domain names that are not managed by the Internet Corporation for Assigned Names and Numbers (ICANN) and may employ non-standard top-level domains requiring specific Domain Name System (DNS) servers to resolve adequately.

new forms of governance. This had been pursued at the expense of calling into question the emergence of governance and grounding its articulation historically. This trend has not only overshadowed explanations of continuity and change in key processes, but also questions of agency, as pointed out by Biersteker (2014), Bulkeley et al. (2014), Nolke and Graz (2008), or Whitman (2005). A similar tendency could be observed among the scholars of Internet governance; very few have engaged with longitudinal studies that reveal dynamic interactions. The Bourdieu-inspired 'turn to practice' outlined the significant role of routines and thus helped open up the universe of silent power dynamics. Praxeological approaches recast the agency debate in empirical terms, rather than conceptual only.

To navigate this space theoretically, the following chapters revisit key underexplored concepts such as governance emergence and articulation, discussed as fundamental phases in the constitution of a new domain of power, which appears as decentralized, in flux, and cross-sectoral. Being a field under construction, the Internet poses two main challenges to the researcher: the conceptual understanding of how governance comes into being and becomes articulated, and the observation of governance patterns and power dynamics as they present themselves in practice. IG is thus constituted as a field of action that has specific praxis, structuring the positional and dispositional logics of its actors.[5] Theorized this way, it offers clues for understanding the ambiguities and tensions driving its evolution.

Global Governance—The Enactment Thesis

Governance does not exist *in abstracto*. With the partial exception of normative inquiries, discussions about governance cannot elude the relational and the practical side of it, that is actions and outcomes. In that sense, governance is not simply happening in the background; it is enacted. When people act, events and structures that would not have existed otherwise are set in motion. Enactment reconfirms a direction of action or breaks away from an established perspective. Interactions are thus key: it is through them that both meanings and actions are formed. At the global level, such interactions structure the space and the activities in which actors engage.

Governance theories encompass relational and societal facets of power. At the macro-level, there is often an implicit reference to 'power over' (control,

---

[5] Bourdieu (2000) asserts that one's position does not cause action necessarily, but occupying a position over time tends to leave some dispositional traces that help make sense of certain practices.

dominance) à la Nye (2011), whereas in micro-interactions the 'power-to' aspect is brought forward, enabling individual autonomy and freedom. Outside the nation-state structure, power is modelled through ideas, values, and expertise that shape the context, conditions, and nature of social interactions and actions. These create systems of rule in which formal and informal governance can be exercised. Barnett and Finnemore (2005, 179) present power not only as the ability to regulate behaviour, but also to constitute the world in particular ways and to define the problems to be solved. The 'power to' and 'power with' (Slaughter 2011) approach—dominant in constructivist studies—highlights sources of authority such as knowledge, stamina, or intellect. The Internet is a field of power that cuts across these analytical distinctions: the creation of authoritative technical standards and protocols is one such example of simultaneous 'power over' and 'power to' instances.

The central focus of global governance studies—the growing capacity of non-state actors to permeate and challenge the inter-governmental structure(s)—showed its limitations in the marked absence of a systematic understanding of how governance worked in practice for a new domain such as the Internet. Nye talked about 'cyber governance' (2014), using the regime complex theories for mapping related activities. Levinson (2015) applied De Burca's et al. (2014) global experimental governance framework to Internet governance, highlighting the difficulty of finding an appropriate conceptual framework for integrating developments in this emerging field. Despite the important contribution of Bourdieu and of scholars following in his footsteps, very little cumulative progress can be reported on the study of global fields of action in international relations. In focus for regime theorists, the structuration[6] of new issue domains remains a theoretical concern, rarely anchored empirically.

Understood as relational, the act of governing focuses on associations and interplay, rather than on separate units. If 'entities are already entities before they enter into social relations with other entities' (Jackson and Nexon 1999, 293), the perspective remains static. To conceive of them as dynamic requires an implicit acceptance of 'enactment', the act of bringing structures and events into existence and setting them in action, while simultaneously designing 'limitations' to avoid unwanted directions (Weick 1988). The Bourdieu-inspired preoccupation with capturing everyday activities initiated the so-called 'turn to practice' in IR. More than simple actions or behaviours, practices embody social organization and hierarchy and render communities cohesive. Dominant practices thus represent enactments of 'constitutive rules', defining conduct and basic rules of thumb. They are performed by

---

[6] Structuration is understood here as the formation and articulation of an issue domain, different from the terminology used by Giddens in his post-empiricist 'structuration theory' (1984).

individuals and by networks recursively and obtain structural meaning in time, through their insertion in a sociopolitical context. As such, habits shape discourses and activities, shifting the focus of attention beyond individual agency to systems of meaning embedded in structures and reproduced regularly without questioning the rationale behind.

So far, IR studies dedicated to new issue domains remained by and large abstruse regarding the emergence of governance and how it is achieved in practical terms as both actors and instruments of governance proliferate. The general tendency was to study one approach in isolation from the others with a focus on the 'novelty' of interactions and, in particular, on an emergent institutional characteristic (Biersteker 2014). Despite the consensus around the density and diversification of policy formation and implementation mechanisms, our tools for empirical investigation are slow to adapt to (better) capturing this reality.

Amidst ongoing policy debates regarding the future of the Internet, it is timely to revisit the origins and evolution of this fast-developing policy domain that Levinson describes as an 'ecosystem', a setting where 'multiple stakeholders can interact and where conflicting interests and even contentious collaborations can arise' (2008, 1). This study opens up an important agenda for discussing emerging issue domains such as Internet governance by combining analyses of governance mechanisms and actors with dominant practices.

Research Focus, Central Question, and Argument

What is at stake for how the Internet continues to evolve is the preservation of its integrity as a single network. In practice, however, its governance is neither centralized nor unitary. It is piecemeal and decentralized, with authoritative decision-making coming from different sources simultaneously. Historically, the conditions of their interaction were rarely defined beyond basic technical coordination, due at first to the academic freedom granted to the researchers developing the Internet and, later, to the sheer impossibility of controlling mushrooming Internet initiatives. In 2018, more than 160 organizations and entities contributed to creating rules for the global Internet. Cutting across sectoral interests, Internet governance is (re)negotiated in numerous fora by a variety of players, including governments, UN bodies, civil society organizations, businesses, technical and academic experts, as well as end-users.

The research question asked here aims to elucidate these relations in order to locate authority and identify decision-making channels: How does governance emerge and get articulated globally in new issue domains? This inquiry is both theory- and practice-oriented. Its first objective is to present governance structures in interaction, rather than as static. In doing so, it responds to calls for understanding dynamic systems of rule as they come into place in dense global governance configurations. It draws on an ulterior problematization of enacting governance in hybrid contexts, while unpacking the historical origins of contemporary global arrangements beyond 'an idealised and constructed past' (Biersteker 2014, 3). Providing an empirically grounded analysis of Internet governance in a longitudinal perspective is the second objective of this study and a key contribution to the IR literature.

IG is neither a homogenous object of governance, nor of study. It can be—and in fact is, in daily coordination activities—decomposed along a number of dimensions, be they institutional mandates or thematic clusters, with specific governance arrangements for each. The analytical difficulty in breaking apart this umbrella term stems from the constant state of flux, the vast scope of inquiry, and the high socioeconomic and politico-military stakes associated with this field. The association of the two terms, 'Internet' and 'governance' has been a subject of contention from the outset. Long negotiations around definitional issues, such as the principle of common, but differentiated responsibilities and high-impact disclosures (2013 Snowden revelations, the 2010 WikiLeaks), merged with rapid technological developments to make the complexity of the field reach new heights.

This book takes an initial inroad to a novel research agenda which translates global governance theory into praxis for a highly contested power domain. The increasing density of Internet governance arrangements presents a number of analytical challenges and opportunities for IR theory. On the one hand, it pushes for an interdisciplinary understanding of nascent issue domains reflecting cross-sectoral concerns and global positioning struggles, in particular between the developed and developing countries. On the other hand, it opens the door for re-assessing underexplored dimensions for the enactment of governance, namely its emergence and articulation. With this in mind, I aim, in what follows, to provide a convincing account of the way in which Internet governance emerged and is continuously articulated via different mechanisms by an increasing number of stakeholders enacting dominant practices. To achieve this, I deconstruct the evolution of the Internet from its early days to date, exploring the meaning of governance at different points in time and its effect on the structuration of a new global field. Based on an in-depth historical and empirical analysis of the governance patterns observed, I argue that the specificities of IG give us critical insights for theorizing about the lifecycle of new issue domains.

Present dynamics have a historical dimension, the study of which is essential for a holistic understanding of the field. With Bourdieusian inspiration, I explore the genesis and structuration of a global domain in a dynamic manner. Constituted, at a minimum, by a set of issues, mechanisms, and practices, discursive and non-discursive, a field brings together actors in distinctive interaction modes. Analysing its evolution over time gives us a better understanding of how governance is enacted, not least through performativity. In that sense, the 'reality of governance' is not given, but achieved through instruments, processes, and outcomes, as well as through our studies, presentations, or policy briefs.

Method

To uncover the evolution of Internet governance as a global field of power, the analysis undertaken here starts with the antecedents of the network of networks, situating the 1970s ARPANET developments and the initial group of scientists and governmental employees expanding internetworking under contract with the US Department of Defense. The end-point of the research is September 2018, providing an extensive observation space for the enactment of governance. With more than 311 authoritative instruments of governance at work—ranging from intergovernmental treaties to voluntary codes of conduct—the complex picture that IG presents us with poses a number of methodological challenges to the researcher.

Among these, the cross-sectoral nature of the Internet and the ongoing technical and political developments call for the use of a mixed-method, qualitative approach, relying on an in-depth historical analysis and an exploration of a self-constructed dataset of governance mechanisms spanning 1969–2015. In addition, I make extensive use of textual analysis and participant observation to further explore political tensions, dominant practices, and community formation patterns. Over the last seven years, I was directly involved in more than two dozen global IG processes and meetings and this facilitated detailed discussions and interactions with IG experts, as well as the observation of community practices.

In the constructivist tradition, I take methods to be integral to the normative construction of knowledge. The research design adopted here is adapted to the deconstructive analytical framework I propose in Chapter 2, highlighting three key dimensions of governance that provide a dynamic perspective. Accordingly, the governance actors, mechanisms, and anchoring practices are investigated across three broad periods that reveal distinct governance patterns: (1) the early days of the Internet, dominated by informal governance and governance through technical standards (1969–94); (2) the boom of the commercial Internet, with private actors and business practices flourishing (1995–2004); and (3) the decade of global regulatory arrangements, featuring hybrid configurations (2005–15). For each of these, I explore the interactions between actors and forms of governance as they are formed and consolidated in time.

The dataset of governance instruments provides a unique vantage point, allowing for charting the IG domain and subareas of interest as they emerge. The entries in the dataset are further categorized into mechanisms of governance enactment and compared longitudinally. On this basis, the historical analysis and the relevant insights from participant observation and textual analysis provide a cohesive picture of a rather difficult-to-grasp, evolving domain. This involves tracking modalities of governance and actors in interaction over a long period of time, and mapping the emerging patterns and shifts in a variety of ways. The analysis focuses on governance instruments as outcomes of international processes, reviewing experiences over time in six subdomains constitutive of the field: infrastructure and critical resources, cybersecurity, legal issues, digital economy, ICT for development, and civil liberties.

In addition, a set of grounding practices are investigated in this study as the depiction of governance in everyday activities (what people do). Methodologically, the challenge is to make the invisible visible, namely the anchoring of activities in meanings that are specific to the communities implementing them. Meaning-making thus becomes dependent on the hidden assumptions, underlying logics or courses of action that are power-laden. Just like the choice of governance instruments, the practices that dominate over time represent normative and value expressions. Calling their origin into question is the critical endeavour contributed to here.

Structure of the Book

The analysis of the Internet as a global issue domain is both challenging and enticing. Its politically negotiated system of rules, built on technical features and power sensitivities specific to the field, is explored here in five chapters, followed by concluding remarks. Aiming to shed light on contemporary dynamics of governance, this book addresses both scholars and practitioners. It provides a fresh perspective on the structuration of a nascent field of global governance, a timely addition to the study of international affairs.

The next chapter explores the global governance scholarship and its cross-fertilization with the study of Internet developments. Clustered around three prominent themes in international affairs—varieties of governance, sources of authority, and praxis—the chapter scrutinizes scattered, often implicit proposals on the emergence and articulation of governance. It links these to more recent attempts to study the Internet as part of distinct repertoires, identifying the genesis and structuration of new issue domains as a marginal focus in the literature. Based on a deconstructive approach, it provides a guiding frame that distinguishes between three key dimensions for the enactment of governance: mechanisms, actors, and anchoring practices. Methodologically, this translates into a complex research design combining historical and empirical analysis, subsequently detailed.

Chapters 3, 4, and 5 each investigate a specific period in the evolution of IG as a global domain, starting with the origins. The three phases covered by the dataset are: the 1970s to 1994, 1995–2004, and 2005–15. In the early days the Internet was a rather homogenous domain, closely linked to computer science and networking experiments. The rules designed for its management were function- and efficiency-driven. Starting in 1983, different forms of governance, combining public and private initiatives, begin to profile, largely around an active community of professionals in the Advanced Research Projects Agency (ARPA) network. Until the expansion and commercialization of the Internet in the mid-1990s, the predominant governance route was that of standards and protocols making networks interoperable. In a path-dependent trajectory, Internet services remained exempted from regulation. Chapter 3 thus sets the stage for the long-term analysis of the evolution of the field.

Chapter 4 delves into the salient role of corporate actors in Internet policymaking as the network became private and global. Market dynamics drove the development of the field and the digital economy shifted attention to the potential of the network in the neoliberal understanding. From the mid-1990s to mid-2000, three major shifts occurred in Internet governance arrangements: they grew in size, scale, and scope. A number of rules for the technical management of the network were defined during this period and the bodies in charge consolidated their institutional structure. The emergence of political contestation also dates back to this period, when the positions of developing countries on key IG issues started to consolidate.

The governance of the Internet faced a reflexive turn throughout the World Summit on Information Society (WSIS) decade (2005–15), explored in Chapter 5. Concerns for authority, legitimacy, and accountability—expressed by different stakeholders—became central to the evolution of the field. A number of challenges, stemming from three diverse sources, were embedded therein. First, questions were spawned by the modus operandi of the *sui generis* institutions, such as the international technical bodies exercising public governance functions to ensure the continuous functioning of the Internet. Second, demands resulted from the gradual adaptation of intergovernmental organizations with core or tangential interests in the field. Third, the role of private intermediaries was called into question as their financial and political power rose steeply. Their relation to governments was also probed, particularly after the 2013 Snowden leaks.

Chapter 6 locates authority and agency in Internet governance, thus disentangling the power threads in the field and in the community enacting it. Starting with a longitudinal, comparative perspective of the governance trends identified in previous chapters, it discusses the changing role of Internet companies and influential states in post-2015 developments, zooming in on market dynamics, cyber norm debates, and artificial intelligence strategies. It further analyses community formation patterns in IG, presenting the internal dynamics of decision-making and the perpetuation of core values among newcomer groups. Against the continuous expansion and diversification of the field, this section traces the many continuities that structure a now mature field of power.

The final chapter concludes, highlighting the outcomes and the contributions of this book to IR and IG, theoretically and empirically. It clarifies how the findings of this research fit in the ongoing policy debates and in the global governance scholarship and reflects on the value of the research agenda proposed here. Last but not least, the closing chapter offers analytical directions for future explorations of governance emergence and structuration in new global fields.

2

Deconstructing Internet Governance: A Framework for Analysis

At the core of governance debates is the conceptualization of power, diffused and commanded in novel ways with the advent of new technology and new actors. In one of the shortest definitions ever given, governance is 'order plus intentionality' (Rosenau 1992, 5), representing a political act with forms of inclusion and exclusion and, inherently, an expression of power. Its use with reference to the Internet carries the same meaning, exposing an intricate network of hierarchical and social relations, only comparable to the complex technical architecture on which it relies. Despite the plethora of writings on globalization and technological change, a more refined look at governance is required in order to understand nascent global domains, in particular their genesis and structuration.

Part of broader governance transformations, Internet policy-making remains polycentric and in flux. Metaphorically, Ziewitz and Pentzold refer to Internet governance (IG) as a 'difficult horse to catch' (2014, 306). Studying its institutions, rule systems, and steering mechanisms remains particularly challenging due to an ever-increasing number of processes spanning global and regional levels. The tendency to study modes of governance in isolation partially explains the limited engagement with this in international affairs. Its direct effect on the foundational international relations (IR) scholarship is the false assumption that problem-solving drives institutional interactions in an undifferentiated manner. I propose below an analytical framework that challenges the idea of the Internet as a homogenous object of governance by distinguishing among three key dimensions for observing variation: mechanisms, actors, and practices of governance.

The deconstruction exercise undertaken here serves two purposes: first, it positions central elements required to understand the emergence and articulation of IG and delineates its evolution phases. Second, it underscores how the governance concept is a broad, yet powerful analytical framework for exploring the multifaceted ways in which regulatory arrangements come into

Negotiating Internet Governance. Roxana Radu © Roxana Radu 2019. Published 2019 by Oxford University Press.

being, in addition to decision-making processes and coordination proced-ures. The deconstructive analysis used here strips the concept of its ideo-logical connotations in a first phase and adds the context, power dynamics, and actors in a second phase. After exploring the global governance literature in search of tenets that provide useful insights for the present analysis, this chapter elaborates on the framework of analysis in use and the research design guiding this study.

Global Governance Repertoires and the Internet

The asymmetric concentration of technology in the West, the birth of the Internet in the American context, and the evolving space for regulatory input were at first considered in isolation, rather than as part of broader trans-formations in governance. Until recently, limited attention was paid in IR to the way in which global priorities permeate daily operations, regulatory standards, and action plans. This was partly due to a split in the way govern-ance was conceptualized. Reflecting on this polarization, Graz (2014) dis-tinguished between functional and structural theories of governance. At the core of functional theories is the drive to 'get things done' and find solutions to concrete problems. Focusing on the exercise of power through practices, functional governance theorists generally investigate coordination and com-petition, decision-making processes, and institutional design. They tend to converge around forms of steering and regulation[1] similar to or distinct from governmental operations.

In line with the critical tradition in International Political Economy (Shields et al. 2011; Cohen 2014), structural theories of global governance address complex interconnections, sites of authority, and power relations among actors, analysing underlying ideologies, as well as market and state system transformations; they make normative claims about the reconfiguration of objects and subjects of authority and question governing epistemologies and inclusion/exclusion mechanisms. Accountability, democratic practices, and inclusiveness at the global level are also explored. Interrogations on the role of technology in supporting, advancing, and reinforcing ideologies, while dom-inant in science and technology studies, remain rather limited in IG (excep-tions include Mueller 2004; deNardis 2009; Chenou 2014; Carr 2016).

---

[1] Baldwin et al. (1998) assert that there are three distinct concepts of regulation: (a) authoritative rules; (b) efforts of state agencies to steer the economy; and (c) mechanisms of social control (widest sense). Throughout this book, regulation is predominantly understood as authoritative rules.

The diversity of approaches that attempt to explain contemporary governance processes cannot be disconnected from the modalities employed. Early influential work on global governance focused—almost exclusively—on formal mechanisms; subsequent writings provided a more nuanced approach by integrating informality and everyday practices. Twenty-five years after the seminal work of Rosenau and Czempiel (1992) on 'governance without government', a number of limitations and blind spots constrain the theoretical expansion of this promising agenda. In pointing out how governance is different from government, the majority of studies have been modelled on the state/non-state actor dichotomy (Stoker 1998) and processes that are most visible in a number of issue areas, emphasizing similarities and differences with governmental ordering (Graz 2014, 5).

A granular approach to 'changing modes of governance' emerging in the 2000s (Pierre 2000; Kooiman 2003; Pierre and Peters 2005) revived the debates by introducing a dynamic perspective. It inspired a diversity of approaches: transnational new governance (Abbott and Snidal 2009), 'public–private partnerships' (Boerzel and Risse 2005, 2010; Andonova 2010, 2014), 'multistakeholder initiatives' (Jerbi 2012; Raymond and deNardis 2015; Radu et al. 2015), or transnational policy networks (Biersteker 2014). This added to the complexity of understanding formal mechanisms, and provided a basis for cumulative knowledge on the inner workings of global governance. Importantly, these endeavours also noted the degree of informality within and outside formal decision-making and shifted attention to what is not directly observable and remains largely non-codified in global policymaking. Relying on non-binding forms of cooperation and selected membership (no mandate or formal entitlement), informal governance dominates IG processes, but remains largely understudied.

The mechanisms through which informal governance emerges originate either with networks or with processes. In the first category, elites design and impose or interact strategically to reach the expected outcomes; in the second, decentralized processes with a plethora of actors require coordination mechanisms, one-stop-shops as focal points, bargaining or repeated interactions bargaining (Knight 1992). Guy Peters (2007) proposes to divide informal governance into soft law, networks, partnerships, co-production, multilevel governance, and open method of coordination. Broadly understood, informal governance refers to the 'operation of networks of individual and collective, private and public actors pursuing common goals' (Christiansen et al. 2003, 7). Some of these elements are also employed in the norm-building literature, where human agency, indeterminacy, chance occurrences, and favourable events are generally explored to explain emergence, primarily through process tracing or genealogy.

Building on the work of Finnemore and Sikkink (1998), the norms creation dimension is emphasized in global governance discussions of 'norm entrepreneurs' and 'organizational platforms'. This is consonant with the 'networked governance' approach applied to Internet security by Mueller et al. (2013) for the identification of interdependent actors that opt for collaboration or for unilateral action in the absence of overarching authority. Defining, enforcing, and reproducing norms stands at the basis of governance articulation, which can take numerous forms and shapes. Various governance mechanisms co-exist simultaneously, making the process of designing norms highly complex and oftentimes hybrid, with multiple sources of authority involved. Opening up IG to the conditions of its formation permits an in-depth tracing of the individuals behind influential proposals that later on consolidate into powerful institutional forms.

A useful analytical tool to distil the multidimensional governance concept is the distinction between what is observable through concrete outcomes and what remains invisible to the public eye. Understanding that technology, just like the regulatory infrastructure on which is it built, is not neutral, allows for a methodically sound investigation of formality and informality. The first comprises the mechanisms set in place by decision-makers, be they hard or soft law instruments. The latter captures the role of actors beyond what can be quantified and power dynamics that are reproduced in everyday practices, sometimes without a conscientious acknowledgement of the effects.

This vantage point bridges a number of disciplinary approaches and permits the exploration of key dimensions from the (meta)theoretical repertoires of global governance that best explain how the Internet evolved into a field of global power. These elements inform the analytical framework presented subsequently. For each research stream, I also explore, where available, related, oftentimes implicit hypotheses on the emergence and articulation of governance and assess their relation to IG developments and writings.

Varieties of Governance

Formal outcomes of international negotiation processes, in particular treaties and conventions signed and ratified by states, have been meticulously studied post-Second World War. The focus on transnational cooperation and implementation of international law surfaced early on, exhibiting a plethora of governance means applied outside the domestic sphere. Born out of a military project of the US government at the end of the 1960s, ARPANET, the precursor of the Internet offered little of interest to scholars of global governance, but set in motion the greatest revolution in telecommunications and subsequently in socio-economic affairs. To be understood as a new and influential policy field, the Internet needed to reach a global scale. It now accounts for structural changes in power distribution, power perception, and behaviour shaping, but does not fit swiftly into a single theoretical stream. The many instances of private initiative and cooperation across stakeholder groups stand at odds with the statist perspective, while governance arrangements mixing the formal and the informal escape a streamlined theorization.

The international regime theory, developed in the 1980s, provided new impetus for the analysis of global institutional arrangements. Its contribution to disentangling modalities of governance is significant here for two reasons: first, it pinpointed the complex process around establishing rules, norms, and principles to be adopted by a wide range of actors; second, it provided the terminology for issue-areas, which constitutes a starting point for this study. Krasner defined international regimes as 'sets of implicit or explicit principles, norms, rules and decision-making procedures around which actors' expectations converge in a given area of international relations' (1983, 19). According to him, 'principles are beliefs of fact, causation, and rectitude. Norms are standards of behaviour defined in terms of rights and obligations. Rules are specific prescriptions or proscriptions for action. Decision-making procedures are prevailing practices for making and implementing collective choice' (Krasner 1983, 2). Formally, the members of international regimes were sovereign nations (generally treated as monolith entities), yet implementation of actions governed by international regimes could and often was conducted by private entities (Young 1982) and usually constrained elites within states (Puchala and Hopkins 1982).

Regimes assigned power to collective units, which develop, agree, enforce rules and establish institutions. In early approaches, agency was eluded as emphasis was placed on regime principles, rather than on the role of specific organizations or individuals. Critiques pointed out the degree of 'imprecision and woolliness' (Strange 1983) surrounding the regime theory and the implicit risk of tautology: 'theories about regimes have run into trouble when the same theory explained the origin, as well as the maintenance or the demise of a regime' (Smith 1987).

Newer strands of research, expanded to 'regime complexes', address upfront the role of active leadership (structural, intellectual, charismatic) in promoting cooperation (Keohane and Victor 2010). For Raustiala and Victor (2004), a regime complex represents an 'array of partially overlapping and non-hierarchical institutions governing a particular issue area'. Orsini et al. refine this to understand a regime complex as 'a network of three or more international regimes that relate to a common subject matter; exhibit overlapping membership; and generate substantive, normative or operative interactions recognized as potentially problematic whether or not they are managed effectively' (2013, 29). Mueller, Mathiason, and Klein (2007) and Nye (2011) subsequently applied this understanding to the governance of the Internet.

Mixing norms, institutions, and procedures of both formal and informal nature, Nye (2014) takes this further and reflects on 'the regime complex for managing global cyber activities'. However, his analysis and similar attempts to apply the regime complex framework to IG remain oblivious of organizational infrastructure and stop short of defining the relevant 'nodes' in the networks constituting regime complexes (Levinson and Marzouki 2015). The other major limitation is the difficulty in explaining how regime shifts occur. Helfer suggests that regime shifting works by 'broadening the policy spaces within which decisions are made and rules are adopted' (2009, 39), but it remains unclear how this applies across various IG subfields.

Despite its shortcomings, the regime theory literature needs to be credited for its contribution to the development of the 'issue area' concept as a deliberate cluster of concerns. In early theorization, regimes were originally established to regulate single issues (fishing, money, radio frequencies, etc.) rather than issue domains. As seen earlier in the discussion on regime complexes, the boundaries of an issue domain are rarely clearly delimited, and different groups may disagree on what could be included under a certain label, meaning that the process of contestation is continuous. Changes in an issue domain are rarely tackled convincingly by regime theorists. As any other evolving process, issue development is affected by internal and external factors that cannot be properly captured in a static theory. A dialectic approach is thus more adequate. The tenets discussed above remain incomplete without a clear picture of how they come into play in the constitution of a global field of power. This book sheds light on how such dynamics get established and articulated over time in ruling the Internet.

The complexity of existing orderings gets more difficult to distil as their mixed nature allows for strengthening the public or the private character of organizations in ways that best suit the case at hand. The same entity might be treated as public for some purposes and as private for some other. Moreover, informal governance arrangements, a well-established form of cooperation at the international level, are often obscured in the theorization of governance regimes. For Abbott and Snidal (2000), they represent transitory arrangements on the path to legalization, whereas for Biersteker (2014) and Pauwelyn et al. (2013) they are a permanent feature of contemporary governance. Non-binding forms of governance ('soft law') and sector-specific policy communities foster information exchange, clarify legal and technical matters, have the potential to table solutions and narrow down policy options, as well as extend the reach of agreements that can be rubber-stamped in formal processes. Conversely, they render processes of policy inclusion narrower through selective participation and constraints through pre-decisions, while increasing the potential for rule fluctuation, non-codification abuse, and deficient accountability.

A global policy space is made up of relations that can be observed and those that are hidden to the public eye. In the Bourdieusian tradition, the processes of inclusion and exclusion are intrinsic to the structuration of the field[2] and, thus, to its hierarchical disposition. The IG field is seen here as a setting in which agents situate themselves via social positions. Shaped by the interactions taking place, the field is structured according to rules that are specified in the process of constructing the domain, but also based on the agent's habitus and capital, be it social, economic, or political. For Bourdieu, power and class relations structure internally the system of social positions, thus turning the field into an arena of struggle for the appropriation of different forms of capital.

He makes an important distinction between the vertical and the horizontal organization of a field. While the first is a hierarchical dimension of structuration, the latter is a transversal one, applying across different subfields with equal purchase. Both are forms of power that can be observed in the constitution of new issue domains, in particular as they undergo differentiation to become independent or autonomous spaces of rule-making. To situate these dynamics, a broader perspective on the IG shifts is needed, revealing the extent to which this new domain is influenced by global ordering trends, regulatory or deregulatory.

As a sociopolitical, hybrid space, the Internet we know today comprises different modes of governance instituted at the global level, including technical decisions, private business policies, and international regulatory arrangements, as well as formal and informal mechanisms and practices that become authoritative in the everyday operation of the network. Having clarified the varieties of governance presented in the literature, authority sources and practices are discussed next as concrete ways to develop and implement norms and principles for regulating a new issue domain.

State and Private Authority

Conceptualized either as a unitary actor or as an elaborate network, the state re-surfaces at junction points in IG discussions. Contrary to dynamics in other international domains, state control is highly contested in the Internet

---

[2] Bourdieu's field concept is used in this analysis interchangeably with 'domain' to refer to the relations established for creating a global system of rules for the governance of the Internet.

arena, where new governance arrangements emerged in quasi-private setups like the Internet technical standards and protocols or the allocation of domain names. Operations critical to the functioning of the Internet remain exclusively in private hands, including submarine cable production and deployment, Internet access provision, and the majority of services and products available on the web. Alongside the public Internet, many private Internet spaces developed, such as Intranets, estimated to be ten times larger than the public network (Brown and Marsden 2013).

The 'hollowing out of the state' (Rhodes 1994) predicted a complex process through which state functions were privatized, devolved, eroded, or transferred at supra-national (EU) or international levels. In such situations, governments engaged in cross-sector partnerships, entering constellations of actors and decision-making processes in which they were not endowed with final authority, though they could (re)turn to the position of regulators (Majone 1996; Higgott et al. 2000; Moran 2002). The 'retreat of the state' (Strange 1996) suggested the enabling cooperative mechanisms of meta-coordination, namely rules, frameworks, and regulation of externalities. Closely related was the thesis of 'state orchestration', with governments acting as incentivizers, initiators, or implementers (Abbott et al. 2015; Jerbi 2015).

Internet governance studies have long been explicitly concerned with the role of the state and its multiple transformations in a hybrid environment. Celebrating the multiplicity of regulatory frameworks and mechanisms in place, their novelty and the characteristics of the actors involved in these processes oftentimes eluded the substance of governance debates and power positionings. Institutional design—and later on the focus on broadly defined stakeholder participation in decision-making—shifted attention towards the state as a catalyst, funder, or partner (van Eeten et al. 2014). Novel, yet fragmented governance arrangements are generally preferred as a focus of research: voluntary schemes such as the Global Network Initiative (Jerbi 2015), institutional innovations like the Internet Corporation for Assigned Names and Numbers (ICANN) or the Internet Governance Forum (IGF) (Mueller 2004; Antonova 2007; Malcolm 2008), transnational state networks on cybersecurity or child online protection (Livingston 2013), multistakeholder initiatives and public–private partnerships (Schmidt 2014), or crowdsourcing initiatives (Radu et al. 2015).

Territoriality, a key concept for state-centric approaches, saw a gradual shift in meaning, from exercising control over hard borders to controlling networks and soft borders (Biersteker 2014). Unlike what early cyber-libertarians proclaimed, the Internet was not 'unbound with respect to geography' (Goldsmith and Wu 2006, 58) and sovereign principles dominated technical specifications, in particular through the laying of cables and the use of location-sensitive software. Examples abound: complete Internet shutdowns occurred in 2011 at the request of governments amidst mass protests in Egypt, Libya, and Syria; 'cyber-sovereign' China created its own version of the network; and the United States only ended its oversight over the ICANN in September 2016.

At the other end of the spectrum, private rule-making processes were studied, among others, by Risse (2006), Boerzel and Risse (2005), Pattberg (2005), Kirton and Trebilcock (2004), who laid the foundations for a pluralistic understanding of spheres of authority, with insights from sociology, history, political science, and economics. Forms of private governance discussed in the literature range from corporate social responsibility (Vogel 2005), voluntary instruments (Ruggie 2004), and industry self-regulation (Webb 2002) to user-generated or Web 2.0 content regulation (O'Reilly 2005). Non-state actors actively involved in world politics may be motivated by 'universal values or factional greed, by profit and efficiency considerations, or the search for salvation' (Ruggie 2004, 509).

As a key *problematique* in contemporary governance studies, the proliferation of private actors and the diversification of their means of action is also relevant for this study. Private initiative is a dominant causal explanation for how governance comes into being, as well as for the structuring of particular configurations of governance (Cutler et al. 1999; Hall and Biersteker 2002; Bjola and Kornprobst 2010), generally perceived as more flexible and innovation-fostering. Originally, Cutler et al. (1999), Haufler (2001), and Hall and Biersteker (2002) investigated how governance functions formerly performed by states became privatized and outsourced to private actors. Hall and Biersteker identified three types of private authority—market-based, moral, and illicit—through which 'non-state actors cooperate across borders to establish rules and standards of behaviour accepted as legitimate by agents not involved in their definition' (Nolke and Graz 2008, 2).

Hall and Biersteker also draw attention to the 'the reversibility of private authority' (2002, 213), discussing how the state might supersede the private arrangements and how authority might be undermined in a salient political situation. Their book does not offer a single answer to the question of when reversibility occurs, noting that allowing or limiting private authority depends on the case at hand. What the contributors to the volume agree on is that a reversal of authority has long-term consequences and becomes costlier over time. Internet policymaking, notably in the last decade, offers many instances of authority being transferred back to governments, with closer supervision imposed, in particular on matters of cybersecurity and data protection.

Today, global governance scholars agree that authority is diffused, decision-making is in part privatized, and the nature of global challenges requires a multiplicity of structures and means of implementation. Among these, semi-private, quasi-public initiatives such as the Global Environmental Facility, Global Alliance for Vaccines and Immunization, Global Water partnership, or the Anti-Spam Alliance bring together businesses, governments, civil society groups, and international organizations (IOs) from the outset. Standardization bodies performing global roles of accreditation and coordination are sometimes privately owned. Law-like arrangements with private institutions are not uncommon, in particular in dispute resolution in IG. The legitimacy of these configurations rests with the work of communities, who reiterate their practices and routines to bring about contestation or acceptance and buy-in.

Praxis

Understanding how processes and actions are shaped on a daily basis required a change of perspective and that came about with the praxeological turn. The concrete observation of discourses and routines had a long tradition in sociology and anthropology (Geertz 1973; Cetina 1981; Adler 2013; Autesserre 2014), but only recently captured the attention of IG scholars (Flyverbom 2011; Epstein 2013). Global governance-focused contributions in this tradition emphasized shared practices as part of daily habits, dissecting the tacit understandings and knowledge that make such interactions meaningful (Neumann and Sending 2010; Eagleton-Pierce 2013; Best and Gheciu 2014; Bueger 2016; Pouliot 2016).

In world politics, routines explain actions that seem spontaneous and guide us through the translation of what is invisible, but authoritative (Bourdieu 1976). They demarcate the inclusion/exclusion lines and embedded power mechanisms, providing insight into organizational logics. Oftentimes, they become visible through the dichotomies and oppositions used: sane versus mad (Foucault 1965), dominant versus dominated. In line with Bourdieu's work, a practice approach pushes for identifying the *modus operandi* of 'the field' before defining the actors. A field is structured according to a system of binary oppositions (orthodox/heterodox, sacred/profane) and is socially constructed, with broadly defined limits 'situated at the point where effects of the field cease' (Bourdieu and Wacquant 1992, 100).

Practice theory insists on the mutual constitution of social structure and action. It shifts the realm of investigation from the ideational level to the physical and the habitual (Swidler 2001). But how do they come into place, if not formulated directly as such? Bourdieu (1976) provides a partial answer to this: in his view, people replicate the constitutive rules not with the intention of doing so explicitly, but by acting strategically in a space dominated by those rules. The role of individuals and their personal motivations are thus key to the exploration of nascent issue domains. Without this dimension, our understanding of governance emergence and articulation is incomplete.

Through praxis, regulation itself is collectively mediated and legitimized by the key communities whose buy-in is necessary. Functioning as socially negotiated realities, anchoring practices are foundational for the constitution of a global domain of action when their enactment is public and when specific communities identify with their embodiment. As rules change, dominant practices can be perpetuated, replaced, or supplemented by others. For the latter, a similar process of initiation is set in place, so that the addressees of such practices can see that 'everyone else has seen that things have changed' (Swidler 2001, 87). In explaining continuity in governance mechanisms, the perpetuation of routines is essential.

The research clusters discussed earlier—varieties of governance, state and private authority, and praxis—form a strong theoretical basis for examining Internet policymaking, combining analyses of power with hypotheses for governance emergence and articulation. The insights they provide offer clues for critically reviewing the evolution of the field from the early day until today. To do that in a structured manner, a complex, original framework of analysis is proposed below, followed by a methodological discussion.

Deconstructive Lens

This research situates the evolution of IG amidst global governance processes. In doing so, it decentres IR scholarship as all-encompassing and breaks down the construction of governance mechanisms and power dynamics at the global level. The deconstructive lens applied here opens up global processes to the conditions of their construction, disentangling inherent ambiguities and social positioning over time. It also unpacks processes of meaning-making within communities via dominant practices, taking into account the distribution of power and related discontinuities, as well as contradictions and equivalents in the inner workings of the field.

Initially investigating the relationship between text and meaning, deconstructive approaches tackle the simultaneous process of undoing and affirming. Dismantling conceptual oppositions and systems of thought is at its core. Deconstruction comes to IR from linguistics, but has subsequently been applied across a wide number of disciplines, from anthropology to legal studies. In this expansion, deconstruction acquired a much broader meaning;

its use was also refined to reflect the many ways in which conceptual boundaries are drawn when applied to new contexts. At its core, this approach challenges assumptions of universality, ahistoricity, and stability.

Thinking about IG in deconstructive terms helps us to identify and trace tensions at the macro level, while acknowledging the fundamental ways in which our understanding is dependent on the visible side of governance, captured in formalized processes. Moving beyond that, this is an exercise in analysing how the social space for political struggles is structured, how outcome documents are produced and by whom. Such a reading of events and meanings is necessarily a work in progress, in particular as the constitution of the IG field is ongoing.

Evolution of Concerns over Time

In spite of the regular reference to the 'Internet' as a single unit in everyday speech, this complex network is made up of a number of subfields of governance, ranging from highly technical specifications to socio-economic elements. The fast evolution towards understanding the Internet as a policy field meant that issues related to infrastructure and standards soon came to be regarded as matters of public interest, independent of the sphere of authority under which they were placed. While there is still a functional separation in the work of relevant institutions, it has become difficult to provide a discrete analysis of the Internet without a close investigation of its composite structure.

As a first step in the deconstructive approach taken here, the singling out of subfields of governance allows for a topical separation of the issues under discussion in IG. Growing from a small network to a global political arena took a number of developments that were mirrored in the policy debates of the time, be it for protocols, digital divide, or connectivity in developing countries. The multiple uses of technology also forced a diversification of approaches and, recently, a cross-sectoral understanding of the issues, given that a strict segmentation was no longer possible in a digitized space.

Chartering the field represents a first stage in the situated analysis of actors, issues, institutional mandates, or key developments. Mapping exercises have been particularly prevalent in IG. On the academic level, the most comprehensive mapping exercise was done by Jovan Kurbalija (2005) in his book, *Introduction to Internet Governance*, currently in its seventh edition. His classification of Internet-related issues, divided originally into five baskets (infrastructure and standardization, security, legal, economic, and socio-cultural), evolved over time to include two additional ones: human rights and development. This has been closely mirrored in the United Nations Commission on Science and Technology for Development (CSTD) Mapping exercise in late 2014, which provided an opportunity for stakeholders to comment and review.

Here, I take a historical perspective of the evolution of concerns over time and, with inspiration from the study mentioned earlier, I provide a classification along six dimensions. In a nutshell, the topics covered in Internet-related global discussions advanced from the preoccupation for interconnecting computers to ensuring the security of information flows. Once the Internet expanded globally, legal issues came under the spotlight, starting with a focus on protecting intellectual property rights and, later, on clarifying jurisdictional issues. The e-commerce boom at the end of the 1990s launched what came to be referred to as the 'digital economy', in which the largest proportion of the market had an online component. In the mid-2000s, global attention shifted to development issues in connection with access to the Internet, which led to the formulation of an 'ICT for development' (ICT4D) agenda. Civil liberties also gained stronger ground during the last decade, including a push for considering Internet access a fundamental right and for affording the same protection online as offline for human rights. An overview of the various clusters of concern for IG is provided below.

Infrastructure and Critical Internet Resources

Technical resources were originally in focus as the TCP/IP protocol, the domain name system, and the root zone came under discussion by an international group, beyond the original team at ARPANET. Instant connectivity is what makes the Internet so valuable, and that relies on the submarine cable infrastructure, the technical standards and protocols ensuring interoperability, and the content and applications layer that users come into contact with daily. Historically, a large part of the critical Internet resources was placed on the American territory and control was retained by the US government over a number of key network functions, generating important controversies leading to the structuration of the field.

The prerogative of the technical community working for ARPA was the development of open standards and protocols for improving the network, but as soon as this became a dominant activity for the flourishing of the private sector, a few technical limitations were imposed. Recently, this prolific area of policymaking has seen debates in three new areas: (1) network neutrality—the principle that all data should be treated in a non-discriminatory way on the Internet pipes without a differentiated price tag per service; (2) cloud computing—the server farms enabling users to access and synchronize data and programs over the internet beyond their local computing and storage; and (3) Internet of Things—the omnipresent connectivity of devices and appliances able to exchange with one another, whether in the form of smart watches or smart cities. Last, but not least, regulators have shown a renewed interest in infrastructure and critical resources and started observing code for their regulatory practices. A so-called 'turn to infrastructure' in public policymaking has been recently documented by IG scholars (deNardis 2009; Brown and Marsden 2013; Musiani et al. 2015).

Cybersecurity

Computer security concerns attracted public attention in the early 1980s, when the first cyber viruses were developed (Nye 2011, 3); by the mid-1990s, 'recreational hackers' made the phenomenon more widespread (Sommer and Brown 2011). Yet, cybersecurity discussions have only been placed on global agendas in the post-Cold War context (Hansen and Nissenbaum 2009), gaining prominence in the late 1990s. The availability, integrity, authentication, or confidentiality of information systems was subsequently tested via malware, cyberattacks, probes, and even physical shutdowns, moving the public debates from spam to mass-surveillance.

The debate over ensuring protection online has also underlined that the current infrastructure of the Internet does not contain embedded security guarantees since, due to its original design, it was built as a network to facilitate access and information sharing (Markoff 2012). The rules and behaviour cues embedded in the written computer code did not prevent the misuse of such information for illicit or extortive purposes. The dangers posed by the virtual environment remain a major source of contention in international affairs; journalists and researchers highlight either the menace of a 'digital Pearl Harbor' (Bendrath 2003) or the 'unsubstantiated nature of cyber threats' (Dunn Cavelty and Rolofs 2010). A number of related subfields have thus come into being, such as critical infrastructure protection, cybercrime and cyberespionage, and child online protection.

Legal Issues

Legal issues came to be discussed on the international regulatory agenda when the practice of cybersquatting domain name registrations became pervasive at the end of the 1990s (Litman 2000). Primarily oriented towards the protection of intellectual property rights in the early days, the legal concerns expanded to regulatory mechanisms for Internet transactions, jurisdictional disputes, and arbitration. As a prosperous market was developing, the importance afforded to legal aspects grew. Alongside copyright and trademark issues, the focus included the liability of private intermediaries and the delegation of legal responsibilities to non-state actors.

The role of the courts surfaced in recent years as a counterbalancing act to the myriad of private developments supported by an ever-more powerful underlying infrastructure. New technologies built on top of the Internet, ranging from the Internet of Things to artificial intelligence (AI), have challenged traditional understanding of laws in the offline environment and continue to raise concern about the ability of the current global system to respond effectively to novel challenges.

Digital Economy

From the mid-1990s' e-commerce boom to the full-fledged development of the digital economy, a consolidation of public trust in online services was essential, in part ensured technically through the use of encryption and e-signatures for securing transactions, but also through a number of consumer protection measures and competition policies. Beyond the move of commercial products and services online, the Internet also facilitated the creation of new markets such as those for domain names, software development, or cyber insurance, for which specific regulation is discussed, for example in taxation. The most significant change in the new economy has been in digital advertising and the biggest Internet companies are currently leading in terms of market capitalization.

Technical innovation also gave way to decentralized economic models that bypass the authority of a credible intermediary or a central bank, be it in the operation of the famous cryptocurrency Bitcoin or in the automated execution of digital contracts. 'Sharing economy' business models thriving on ease of access and network effects now compete with traditionally regulated services such as the taxi, hospitality, or delivery services. These novel business models enabled by digital platforms feature a great dependence on user data as the most valuable asset, with their strengths residing in the real-time analysis of tremendous amount of (mainly cross-border) data. The new economics is as much about digital information as it is about building monopolies on top of it.

Information and Communication Technology for Development (ICT4D)

Ever since the early debates on connectivity, the role of ICTs in international development continued to be mainstreamed. The ideal of an inclusive information society was met in practice with highly uneven patterns of access to technologies, only diminished via the massive adoption of mobile Internet across developing countries. From the early days of telecentres to the empowerment of communities of innovators outside of the developed world, the digital revolution was closely linked to developments in e-government, education, agriculture, or health, also highlighted in the Millennium Development Goals.

When the ICT agenda came to be discussed in tandem with the situation of developing countries at the World Summit on the Information Society (2003–05), the digital divide was singled out as the main concern. Access to the Internet was still unevenly distributed across countries and its content did not reflect the world's cultural diversity. Promotion and training for developing e-skills, as well as multilingual, localized content became a priority. The global network enabled online education, but did not fully reach the vulnerable communities. The mixed impact of capacity building and technical assistance programmes, as well as the plethora of unsuccessful private sector-led connectivity experiments led to renewed calls for prioritizing marginalized groups and areas in the 2030 Sustainable Development agenda.

Civil Liberties

Civil liberties, among the thorniest issues of the last decade in Internet-related discussions, became more difficult to disentangle from other issues as it became mainstreamed in Internet-related activities. It incorporates topics such as privacy and data protection, freedom of expression, and identity politics. A 'rights' framing has been adopted across the board for addressing substantive issues (deNardis 2010), also supported by the unanimous recognition, in the UN General Assembly, that the same rights that people have offline must also be protected online.

The decentralized structure of the Internet allows for mobilization in favour of democratic ideals and civil liberties at various levels. The possibility to document, communicate in real-time, and share information about human rights entitlements and abuses has altered the way in which we conceive of the digital environment. On various occasions, though, surveillance, deliberate distortions and disruptions, malicious interference, and the undermining of liberties-driven processes were enabled by the network. New safeguards and digital rights are currently under discussion, as civil liberties continue to lead the civil society global agenda.

Chronicling the evolution of Internet-related subtopics raises an important question: how do these subfields come together to form an autonomous field of IG? For a long time perceived as an ungoverned space, the Internet is increasingly regulated by a multitude of actors, though high-impact decisions at different levels. The strong push to agree on specific principles, norms, and regulations for e-commerce or cybersecurity is indicative of broader power struggles that influence the social positioning in the field and beyond. While different trajectories are possible for the evolution of a field, rule-creation practices and their subsequent redefinition or readjustment are at the core of governance articulation and constitute the focus of this book, based on the framework proposed below.

An Analytical Framework for Internet Governance

Operating at the level of setting the rules of the game, global governance systematically combines various dimensions of state and non-state regulation and different modalities to achieve that. Various mechanisms—formal or informal—are deployed to create a new ordering that shapes and defines expectations for the actors in the field, be it by controlling, directing, or regulating influence (Biersteker 2010). Drawing on three key themes ensuing from the review of IR and IG repertoires, I conclude that insufficient attention has been paid to how governance comes into being across different issue domains. In the absence of a systematic investigation of the genesis, the scattered explanations put forward support one of the four main assumptions: functional needs, powerful state thesis, private initiative, or informal mechanisms. Taking origins for granted has direct consequences on the way in which the articulation of governance is understood. This second critique is also pertinent here: the minimal attention paid to comprehensive, long-term, empirically grounded studies of issue domains only gives us a patchy, oftentimes static view of the enactment of governance.

In the creation of a global field of action, the patterns of governance and shifts in priorities are illustrative of the extent to which global rule-making generates debates, requires joint effort, or relies on targeted action (e.g. specific regulatory responses). Where political decisions are required, the choice between equally viable alternatives will determine the main actors to position themselves in relation to the governance space and the object of ruling. Unlike the rather narrow technical or business decisions, which may or may not be the result of negotiation across a set of institutions, the global rules decided in collective arenas become constitutive of the domain and (re)define the field-specific interplay.

The characteristics of an issue area will define the type of rules set in place at different points in time. As the discussion above shows, the multiple topic areas covered in IG discussions require differentiated approaches, resulting from the pursuit of different objectives, strategies, and instruments of governance. For the Internet, technical specificities determine the extent to which action can be taken on the network. To move packets of data from one computer to another, standards and protocols are essential. Developing in parallel or intersecting and evolving over time, various mechanisms of governance applicable to the Internet take the technical delimitations as their starting point. Two other dimensions are integrated throughout: actors and anchoring practices of governance.

Mechanisms of Governance

Despite its wide appeal, the concept of 'mechanism of governance' poses formidable difficulties to the researcher. To pin it down, I use the soft–hard law continuum, recognizing that not all rules carry the same obligations or have the same effect. The diversity of mechanisms pursued to steer processes essentially describe attachments to one of the dominant features of global ordering, which may involve formal and informal institutions or networks, already in place or newly formed. Importantly, different mechanisms of governance have funding attached to them, ranging from minimal to substantive. The study of mechanisms of governance presented here is based on an *ex-post* analysis of 311 authoritative governance instruments set in place between 1969 and 2015, complemented by an analysis of current trends in Chapter 6.

To understand which mechanisms are at work for particular subfields, I take governance instruments as my entry point, relying on formalized outcomes only. This gives me a uniform proxy for the approaches undertaken to creating rules for governing the Internet, be they legally enshrined or not. I subsequently cluster and categorize them to reveal the mechanisms they illustrate. The database thus constructed allows for exploring the governance patterns, shifts, and variation over time. One of the salient differences between the global structuring and the mechanisms of governance specific to the Internet is that the former defines, constrains, and shapes the environment of the latter. In this study, the global context is not taken for granted; it is problematized to reveal the external shocks and critical junctures that influence the field.

A second important difference is that mechanisms operate differently with respect to intentionality. Technical rules serve a functional purpose: ensuring that the network is functional and that it remains stable over time. Related decisions might comprise international standards, protocols, agreements, and contracts for delegating particular functions to various entities. Private corporate policies and practices, on the other hand, embed a profit-driven logic and are generally based on a contractual relationship. Peer-to-peer agreements, exchange contracts, the management of big data, content development, business plans and strategies, corporate policies, and end-user contracts, firmly regulate interactions among various actors and have long-term effects. However, unlike standards, most of these remained concealed by confidentiality provisions and are generally not available in the public domain.

The contentious, reputational, and benefactor actions that companies and technical bodies tackle in the public domain are the upshot of a core interest in participating in defining the 'rules of the game'. The result of shorter or longer negotiation processes, such steering mechanisms are fundamental for the constitution of an issue domain. On a continuum from hard (treaties and conventions) to soft (declarations, non-binding resolutions, codes of conduct) law, the resulting mechanisms generally pertain to public policy, community formation, and field constitution.

Rather than providing *ex ante* a theoretical segmentation of potential IG patterns, I give preference in this study to an inductive approach based on the relations revealed by the dataset, further discussed in the research design section. Suffice it to say at this point that this strategy, stressing the functional side of constituting new issue domains, is complemented by insights on power distribution captured in the historical analysis. From the literature review and in combination with the data recorded for this study, a tripartite categorization of mechanisms of governance emerged.

Legal enshrinement, covering:

* *treaties, conventions, and binding agreements*;
* *court judgments, policies, legislation, directives with global or regional effects*.

Institutional solidification, covering:

* *specialized bodies*, ranging from developing a specialized division within an organization to a dedicated procedure or initiative for an emergent Internet-related topic;
* *strategic frameworks/agenda/action plans*;
* *monitoring and benchmarking tools*: benchmarking, ranking, global database, monitoring directory/index).

Modelling, covering:

* *discursive actions*: guiding principles, charters, codes of conduct, principles, dynamic coalitions documents, resolutions, high-level statements, (final) declarations;
* *operative guidance*: recommendations, toolkits, model laws, guidelines, implementation alliances, model frameworks.

Legal enshrinement refers to instruments that have a binding effect on the signatories. They are generally initiated (and subsequently signed) by states or issued by a public authority such as a court or a supra-national body. Given their particular status under international law, treaties, conventions, and related agreements (e.g. protocols) are only open to state actors. In contrast, court judgments, directives, and binding policies and legislation may target private actors too, while preserving the requirement for a compulsory action.

At the other end of the spectrum, modelling is generally associated with non-binding commitments formally announced. Their purpose may range from indicating a stakeholder's position to shaping the behaviour and triggering actions by other actors (e.g. setting a standard for the sector). An important distinction is made here between discursive modelling, relying extensively on statements and declarations, and operative guidance tools, which consist of practical recommendations, guidelines, and model documents. Different from the legal enshrinement mechanisms, modelling instruments offer more flexibility and are the result of shorter negotiation processes. Depending on the degree of sophistication, they might require the participation of multiple actors either at the creation or at the implementation stage or in both. Importantly, mechanisms focusing on modelling are open to all actors, from technical bodies and academia to civil society groups and corporate players.

In between these two broad mechanisms we can place a third one, namely institutional solidification, the result of efforts to render a procedure, working group, or concern (more) permanent. Attaching a form of institutional design to a process leaves a trace on the global governance spectrum. Generally involving at least a person on a payroll, or a small secretariat, instances of institutional solidification can also be divided according to intentionality and scope of actions: specialized bodies refer to expert work coordinated in a structured manner (e.g. Committee for Science and Technology for Development, Article 29 Working Party); strategic frameworks, plans of action, and global agenda set objectives for collective work and, more often than not, have funding attached to them; monitoring and benchmarking tools commonly require iterative processes (annual rankings, global database updates, etc.) and require a longer-term financial commitment. The mechanisms of institutional solidification are open to actors aiming to position themselves uniquely, or at least prominently in the governance space.

Actors

Understanding who the key actors are and their position over time is a prerequisite for grasping governance patterns, resulting from specific interactions among a multitude of actors, from individual to institutional ones. International organizations, states, corporations, technical bodies, and civil society groups, while not necessarily unitary actors, follow their specific logics and interests. In negotiating the global rules for governing the Internet, their intersubjective positioning is essential. The way in which roles are specified has an impact on power distribution and on how other actors locate themselves on the governance spectrum.

The coexistence of various actors in policymaking processes represents a key feature of contemporary governance and this is also the case for the Internet. The diversion of resources towards IG policies all around the globe is a noteworthy transformation, from the early days of the Internet as a scientific project at the US Department of Defense to the myriad of social and political programmes currently in place. The explosion of cyber-activities has been met by an unprecedented financial commitment of all the actors involved. In hybrid governance configurations, however, it is more difficult to establish where the financial power lies and, similarly, to clearly determine the accountability links.

Although participation in public consultation or open mailing lists is customary in IG (Radu et al. 2015), decision-making generally rests with an institutional actor. In technical standardization issues, this might be an organization like the Internet Engineering Task Force or the ITU Telecommunications Standardization Sector (ITU-T); in civil liberties cases, it might be a court decision establishing a precedent or a landmark ruling, or a company with millions of users implementing an authoritative policy; in development, an organization taking the lead on an e-skills programme at the regional level or a public institution monitoring multilingual Internet in areas with many different local languages.

Beyond the exercise of mapping agency in IG, analysing how stakeholders act in new issue domains provides two avenues of inquiry: the first regards whether new stakeholders are given central or marginal roles; the second concerns the extent to which they adopt domain-specific approaches, which may result in the creation of new institutions or in institutional innovations. In many cases, such developments might depend on the leadership and entrepreneurship of key individuals, while in others they might result from specific processes of area differentiation or from reactions to critical junctures or global trends.

Anchoring Practices

Foundational social practices guide the work of the IG communities. They represent an infrastructure of co-creation based on repeated interaction. As the literature highlights, practices remain a stable referent because they standardize procedures and facilitate categorization and action. In emerging issue domains, they constitute meaning-making endeavours without which it is impossible to grasp internal dynamics. Moreover, they pattern interactions between individuals, forcing them to go back to known, yet hidden, assumptions and common denominators.

Yet bringing the 'invisible' out into the visible is not an easy task methodologically. In global fields that cut across issues and institutions, routines are part of political processes involving communication, negotiation, or contestation. A systematic exercise to pin down the authoritative forces at work within the communities operating in complex fields such as IG exposes the daunting task of capturing interactive processes on the move. This is the first time a praxeological lens is applied in a study of IG spanning developments over more than four decades.

In the exploration of practices and communities, the positioning of the researcher is key to the knowledge one has access to. The selection of events and people, as well as our engagement with them (presentations, interactions, sharing of ideas and arguments) is never neutral. It generally interferes with how routines are conducted, be it by reinforcing them or by challenging them. In the tradition of Bourdieu, who perceived knowledge as relational and political, researchers need to engage in a 'sociology of sociology' and inquire about their own position.

Understood as enacted, governance exists through performers. In complex issue domains such as the one under investigation here, it is rarely the case that a handful of individuals can be actively involved in all relevant processes. While individual influence can be identified behind key initiatives, governing practices are important when they are transformative beyond singular agency, for a particular group or community. The inner logic of enduring routines, besides providing the hidden meaning and decoding clues, can also be translated to shed light on how certain actors are empowered and certain activities are legitimized or de-legitimized.

Informed by the theoretical tenets discussed above, the framework of analysis presented here captures various dimensions along which the governance of the Internet can be deconstructed. It explains how the modalities, mechanisms, and anchoring practices of governance can be disentangled in order to grasp the transformations and dominant patterns over time, providing guidance for the empirical analysis. The research design of this study is detailed below.

Research Design and Methods

To address the challenge of interdisciplinary and ongoing development in Internet policymaking, an analytical eclectic approach (Sil and Katzenstein 2010) is adopted in this book, favouring engagement across various research traditions in order to respond to broad research puzzles and real-world complexity. In line with social constructivism, the framework applied here upholds the ontological assumption that no single reality exists, meanings and representations always being shared or collectively formed (Hughes and Sharrock 1997). A single method does not suffice to draw a comprehensive picture of the evolution of a field. An empirically informed analysis of how governance is articulated throughout distinctive periods requires a longitudinal study and a complex research design. Here, this is achieved by combining historical analysis and empirical insights, two approaches that capture sensitively the multiple sociopolitical factors and interactions at work in the expansion of a policy field.

Historical Analysis

Neither the Internet, nor its governance structures emerged in a vacuum. Historical approaches link the nature of governance arrangements with societal and economic shifts, providing insights into the degree to which specific changes are contingent on global transformations. Critical scholarship generally employs chronological research to answer the question of 'how we got here', pointing out the dependency, the paths not taken, and the alternatives. A historical reconstruction is also part of a comprehensive periodization effort, revealing the underpinnings of broad trends usually discussed in the lifecycle of an issue domain.

To situate the analysis and explain the emergence of governance, I reconstruct the early history of the Internet along sociopolitical lines, drawing on a variety of original documents and individual accounts. In contrast to other histories of the Internet, this investigation looked specifically at regulatory configurations, actors, and anchoring practices over time. The historical account reveals that tensions over the development of the Internet have been present from the beginning. The use of multiple sources, including personal testimonies, allowed for the corroboration and correlation of insights from active participants and observers, enriching the perspective presented here and complementing the empirical analysis.

However, such an exercise is by definition partial: there is 'no such thing as a definitive account of any historical episode' (Gaddis 2001, 308). Despite the recent birth of the Internet, our epistemic access to early developments is limited, often fragmentary and more focused on technological aspects, rather than policy considerations. Generally, some Internet paternity claims enjoy greater support than others; my historical overview addresses this through the examination of multiple independent lines of evidence, subsequently compared with testimonies of actors involved in those processes.

Secondary sources have long been used in IR as documentary evidence (Thies 2002), particularly when the type of investigation is suited for combining materials from different sources. The limitations in such analyses—unwarranted selectivity and investigator bias—were overcome in this study by relying on primary sources that were as close to the event as possible (original memoranda of understanding, speeches, event transcripts, etc.). The input and the complementary information around international negotiations and their formal outcomes were just as useful as the texts of the documents themselves, and their interpretation was facilitated by the triangulation of different sources of information.

In the selection of historical material, consideration was given to alternative background narratives, which enable a more rigorous reading of the genesis and structuration of a nascent issue domain. Not only does it allow us to examine the presence or absence of specific attributes, but it also relies on manifest and latent dimensions to explicate the articulation of governance. Observing the underlying credo and ideology is accomplished here through an analysis of dominant practices, whose methodological underpinnings are explained below.

Empirical Analysis

An analysis as comprehensive as the one presented here has not been previously pursued due to the lack of data and the absence of a systematic conceptual framework that permitted a domain-wide scrutiny. With an expanding field of governance, the challenge is twofold: on the one hand, assessing the integration of new issues into discussions as they happen is notoriously difficult, other than for very narrow reporting purposes; on the other hand, such an approach indirectly fixes the boundaries of governance to a specific moment in time. Contrary to this, what this study aims at is building the conceptual toolbox for deconstructing IG by providing an evolutionary perspective.

Dataset and Coding

At the empirical level, the unit of analysis was a governance instrument agreed at the regional or global level with lasting impact in that specific subfield. Among these, the 'soft' governance instruments were the most difficult to disentangle, given that modelling activities could take various forms. Ranging from voluntary codes of conduct to model laws, the modelling of other actors' behaviour was frequently resorted to in a highly sensitive, political context. To avoid the problem of incommensurability, the framework of analysis employed here proposed the exploration of the same dimensions across time and a dialectal basis loyal to the period investigated. The research design put forward here included a mapping of the field based on topical issues, as well as the construction and analysis of the 311 instruments dataset, complemented by insights from daily practices and routines acquired through participant observation. These different aspects thus provide us with possibilities to better theorize the nature and dynamics of governance across time.

To overcome the limitation of present-day categorization applied at a time when certain concepts were not yet in use, I deduced the broad areas of concern historically, investigating the main clusters of issues on which governance efforts were concentrated without pre-empting variation inside these over time. I then combined that with an outcome-oriented, inductive approach that takes all governance instruments on selected topics into account. In constructing the dataset, I was thus guided by two approaches: deductive and inductive. For the latter, I recorded, for each of these sub-areas identified above, formalized instruments of governance ranging from international treaties to voluntary agreements and benchmarking efforts. Cognizant that the 311 governance instruments thus arrived at have a different standing and cannot be treated in the same way, I used the hard–soft law continuum to locate them in broader mechanisms at work.

The extensive data collection exercise was performed between September 2014 and June 2015 and was based on the initial mapping of the Digital Watch observatory and the CSTD mapping exercise. It was later supplemented with information regarding ongoing developments until 2016— relying on primary sources including original texts of the declarations, resolutions, treaties, as well as secondary references to additional materials in press releases, meeting minutes, official documents of different organizations, reports, and homepages. Developments up until September 2018, discussed in Chapter 6, were captured as they happened.

Multiple independent sources were used to cross-validate the relevance of the selected instruments including dedicated websites of specific organizations (European Commission, Council of Europe, OECD, OSCE, etc.), specific webpages for global events (Global Conference on Cyberspace, Freedom Online Coalition, etc.). This information was complemented by selected media reports, both from media outlets (*New York Times*, *The Economist*, *Financial Times*, *The Guardian*, *Washington Post*, BBC, *Le Monde*, RFI, *China Daily*) and IG specific sources, such as the GIP Digital Watch newsletter, CircleID, and IPWatch. This cross-validation ensured that important mechanisms did not fall under the radar. As part of the dataset construction, further operationalization and distinctions were drawn, such as the deliberate exclusion of national policies, except where they influenced courses of action critical for IG. For each instrument, I recorded the year of adoption, instrument and origin, whether it was IG-specific or it tangentially covered Internet aspects, whether it was global or regional, and the type of mechanisms it was an instance of.

Studying a myriad of governance mechanisms amid ongoing, incomplete developments renders some instruments more visible than others. As such, this survey, although authoritative and robust, cannot claim to be exhaustive. Similarly, some of the temporal inter-linkages were lost due to the nature of the exercise: when constructing a database, each instrument was assigned a line, rather than being seen as a process; to compensate for this limitation, dynamic aspects were brought back into the discussion through historical analysis and participant testimonials. The coding process and subsequent categorization shed light on the variation of key governance mechanisms across subfields. Moreover, it provided the tools to study events and conditions at the same time, and thus better capture complexity in the IG field. The clustering of mechanisms according to the issues addressed was particularly useful for providing a longitudinal perspective on the evolution of concerns, as discussed in detail in each of the empirical chapters.

Textual Analysis

In the construction of the dataset, many documents were consulted to clarify provisions, mandates, and institutional origin. Some of these were particularly telling of dominant processes in IG, and were thus classified as key texts. The selection of texts was further expanded based on the historical overview to better understand relevant discourses and narratives explaining how the Internet came into being as a global policy field. Occasionally, the texts included mailing list discussions, and analysis of transcripts of video interviews and meetings conducted by important members of the IG community.

The strategy adopted for textual analysis was a flexible one, zooming in when needed to extract particular information of relevance to the historical narrative or to the argument. Particularly telling were the possibilities to unveil specific language and references to the IG 'community'. Given the long-term perspective of this study, the documents were never analysed in isolation from one other.

Participant Observation

Participating directly in IG discussions over the last seven years was key to grasping the dynamics and interlinks of this nascent field. I used the extensive knowledge acquired in meetings and policy discussions in Geneva and elsewhere to ground this study. My access to these events was facilitated by working closely on IG issues in an academic and professional capacity. As an IG scholar and practitioner, I was partially immersed in the communities I was studying, which allowed me to acquire a broad, evolving understanding of the various processes and relationships hard to capture from formal documents. Beside my participation in conferences, policy meetings, summits, and forums, I also attended social events. These allowed me to observe the articulation of practices and routines, in particular through recurrent participation in global meetings such as the IGF, World Summit on Information Society Forum, or Internet Society and ICANN meetings.

As a member of relevant communities, negotiating access did not pose problems; on the contrary, an internalization of procedures and rules of thumb occurred over time. Dissecting the tacit assumptions and understandings was a strenuous exercise, once I started penetrating the frames of meaning used by those studied. Through their insights, I also gained indirect access to what has happened or was happening in meetings I was not physically present in. Their interpretation, balanced against a thorough reading of relevant outcome documents and numerous meeting minutes and transcripts, guided my analysis.

Throughout this period, I also had numerous in-depth conversations with relevant stakeholders, both formal and informal, around international IG meetings. Many statements disclosed informally provided insights useful for understanding the history of selected practices. Participant observation also allowed me to grasp the internal dynamics and comprehend important details about organizational aspects, both inside and outside the meeting venues. It also aided in locating the positions key players were speaking from and the associated dispositional logics. To limit the potential bias from immersion in the IG community on controversial aspects, I went back to original documents to see the exact wording used, informally asked experts about their opinion, and made an effort to attend a meeting relevant to that discussion, if it was possible.

This prolonged social interaction with members of the IG communities grounded my holistic perspective; it structured the way in which I conceptualized governance as enactment in this book and explains, to a large extent, my focus on anchoring practices spanning more than four decades. In practice theory, the meaning of routines can only be deciphered if they are both alien and native to the interpreter's own system of meaning. As an insider, I gained the practical knowledge and tacit know-how that helped me make sense of their strength, while distancing myself enough for a critical reflection. The critical self-investigation, or 'reflexivity', represented a constant throughout the writing of this book.

Synopsis

Neither fully public nor fully private, neither entirely structured nor ad-hoc, nascent issue areas pose a set of multifaceted analytical and methodological challenges. This chapter proposes an inward journey through the literature, contextualizing the focus of the current research against the highly fragmented global and IG literatures. Although the concept of governance is not uniformly defined across these, the main points of convergence relate to different forms and roles of rule-making, authority, and praxis. Despite its wide engagement with governance concepts across different traditions, existing scholarship offers limited empirical insights on the long-term evolution of issue domains, how they are articulated and constituted in particular contexts, rather than given.

To conceptualize emergent forms of governance, this study proposes a situated analysis that brings together governance shifts, mechanisms, and anchoring practices, based on a novel conceptual and methodological framework. Rather than analysing one institution or a group of stakeholders and defining the *problematique* in advance, this study unpacks broad concepts into the multiple activities that comprise them, observing their emergence, articulation, and displacement or permanentization. Drawing on key tenets from the highly fragmented global and IG scholarship, it singles out the 'what', 'who', and 'how' in the key phases of the development of this field.

Offering a multifaceted exploration of governance, the deconstructive approach adopted here prioritizes the links between governance structures and actors, reflecting on power differentials. The methods used in this exploration include historical and empirical approaches that cover, in a granular manner, the general and the specific aspects of the three key dimensions elaborated in the analytical framework: governing mechanisms, actors, and anchoring practices. This tripartite structure guides the analysis in the next three chapters.

3

Revisiting the Origins: The Internet and its Early Governance

The universe of services, business models, and innovations built on the Internet was—and continues to be—made possible by the technical architecture of the network, as well as the political commitment to its development. Both of these are tightly linked to the early history of the Internet, which is explored in this chapter. The birth of the Internet was the result of a series of relatively informal interactions, as part of an academic effort mainly driven by computer scientists contracted to work for the US Advanced Research Projects Agency (ARPA)[1] in both technical and leadership positions. The early days of the Internet encapsulate much more than *prima facie* efforts to create a physical network of computers able to communicate with each other. They also elucidate the origins of governance activities in this field. Various functions, performed by different coordination bodies, amounted to direct or indirect decision-making with global implications, right from the start. All of these pre-date the very concept of 'Internet governance' (Abbate 1999), and are key to understanding how this field of inquiry emerged.

Contrary to how this may be portrayed nowadays, how the Internet came about is not without controversy. As Bing notes, despite its recent birth, the history of the Internet is 'shrouded in myths and anecdotes' (2009, 8) and partisan accounts have become widespread. Goldsmith and Wu talk about the Internet pioneers 'in effect building strains of American liberalism, even a 1960s idealism, into the Universal language of the Internet' (2006, 23). McCarthy refers to the 'creation of an Internet biased towards a free flow of information as the product of a culturally specific American context' (2015, 92). In this chapter, I explore the lineage of the Internet through constructivist lenses. After outlining the heterogeneity of ideas that stood at the basis

---

[1] The Advanced Research Projects Agency (ARPA) changed its name to Defense Advanced Research Projects Agency (DARPA) in 1971 and again in 1997 and went back to ARPA between 1993 and 1996.

Negotiating Internet Governance. Roxana Radu © Roxana Radu 2019. Published 2019 by Oxford University Press.

of creating an interconnected network of computers, the development of problem-solving working groups is explored, followed by an analysis of the political environment that allowed for this network's expansion. The role of the US government in subsidizing developments and encouraging the privatization of the Internet in the mid-1990s is discussed subsequently. For Abbate, the history of the Internet is 'a tale of collaboration and conflict among a remarkable variety of players' (1999, 3), but it is also a tale of informal governance, with key individuals and networks at the forefront, as presented here.

The global network of networks known as the Internet came out of a subsidized project by (D)ARPA and later by the National Science Foundation (NSF), which funded the 'NSFNET', the basis for the current backbone of the Internet. Essential Internet Protocols still in use today, including File Transfer and TCP/IP, date all the way back to the ARPANET experiment. Developments like the World Wide Web and the Border Control Gateway make the Internet a global network able to connect different types of systems using Internet Protocol datagrams. From laying the infrastructure to the content of web applications, the Internet has, from the start, been subject to various forms of governance, in addition to being an object of contention internationally and domestically. The latter is further illustrated by the competing projects of the different US agencies, in particular DARPA and the NSF.

To reconstruct the political dimensions of the debates around the creation and design of the Internet, I draw on a multiplicity of sources and historical accounts on both sides of the Atlantic (including scholarly publications, original documents, and personal conversations) in an attempt to provide a full(er) picture of the tensions between the different technological camps and the type of action they structured. In this chapter, I divide the Internet's early history into two parts: first, I explore the pre-Internet developments that established the structural conditions necessary for a computer networking experiment. Second, I analyse the TCP/IP-related developments, the distinguishing protocol also known as the 'Internet' and delineate its different phases, from ARPANET to NSFNET, looking at the early governance practices and formalized arrangements.

Setting the Stage: Pre-Internet Developments

In the 1970s, humankind started to fulfil a long-time aspiration: a global communication network sharing, storing, and sorting the largest amount of information ever amassed. Scientists on both sides of the Atlantic were essential to the development of the features that constitute the modern Internet. Military and political support, extensive funding, light touch management, and long-term vision were all required to make this dream a reality. In 1837, the British mathematician Charles Babbage proposed a mechanical general-purpose computer with integrated memory and conditional branching, laying the foundations for modern computers. The invention, which was program-controlled by punched cards, was called the Analytical Engine and raised great interest in Europe, but not enough funding to ever be completed. Working on this with Babbage, Ada Lovelace published in 1862 the first algorithm for implementation on the engine. To show the full potential of the programming capacities of the machine, the algorithm was designed to compute Bernoulli numbers, but it never got tested during her lifetime.

Among the first to envision a central repository of human knowledge was the British futurist and science fiction author H. G. Wells (1866–1946), but the list of pioneer thinkers is long and spans various disciplines. The American librarian and educator Mervil Dewey (1851–1931) proposed a system of classification that revolutionized and unified the cataloguing of books across the network of US libraries. Still widely deployed around the world, the Dewey system uses a topic-based decimal system with further subdivisions. Card indexing for easily finding references in book storage and, later on, the idea of a 'universal book' are credited to the Belgian Paul Otlet (1868–1944), who elaborated on this in his 1934 'Traité de documentation: le livre sur le livre, théorie et pratique'. Together with Henri La Fontaine, he created the Universal Bibliographic Repertory in 1895 and later worked with Robert Goldschmidt to create an encyclopaedia printed on microfilm.

Technical developments during the Second World War also played a crucial role in the birth of the Internet. Considered the father of the modern computer, the English mathematician and cryptanalyst Alan Turing developed the first electromechanical machine capable of performing multiple programmable tasks and learning from the stored information, with inspiration from Babbage. Working independently, the German Konrad Zuse developed the first programmable computer (Z3) in 1938. The Universal Turing Machine was launched in 1939 and laid the foundations for the machine called 'the Bombe' employed by the British to decipher the encrypted messages of the German intelligence.

With the war over in July 1945, Vannevar Bush, then-director of the US Office of Scientific Research and Development of the Defence Nuclear Research Committee (behind the *Manhattan Project*), called for a post-war research agenda in information management. After coordinating the work of more than 6,000 American scientists on transferring advancements from science to warfare, Bush pushed for a concerted effort to make the rapidly growing store of knowledge widely and easily accessible. In his 1945 essay 'As We May Think' published in the *Atlantic Monthly*, he elaborates on his idea of a 'memex', a document management system very similar to today's personal computer.

Consider a future device for individual use, which is a sort of mechanized private file and library. It needs a name, and, to coin one at random, 'memex' will do. A memex is a device in which an individual stores all his books, records, and communications, and which is mechanized so that it may be consulted with exceeding speed and flexibility. It is an enlarged intimate supplement to his memory. (Bush 1945)

To address the concerns of a potential nuclear war, US scientists were preoccupied with finding a solution for long-distance telecommunication within the Department of Defense, primarily for linking launch control facilities to the Strategic Air Command. The Russian launch of Sputnik I in 1957 brought new impetus for funding technological research that could better position the United States in space exploration and military command. In 1958, President Eisenhower authorized the creation of two special agencies for space research under the Department of Defense: the National Aeronautics and Space Administration (NASA) and ARPA. ARPA's original mandate—with an initial budget of $520 million—was 'to prevent technological surprise like the launch of Sputnik, which signalled that the Soviets had beaten the US into space', and thus fund universities and research institutions to conduct complex research on science and technology useful for the defence industry, though not always explicitly linked to military applications.

ARPA, Internetworking, and the Military Agenda

ARPA's focus on space research faded out shortly after its establishment and the agency began working on computer technology. As Stephen J. Lukasik, Deputy Director and Director of DARPA between 1967 and 1974, later explained:

The goal was to exploit new computer technologies to meet the needs of military command and control against nuclear threats, achieve survivable control of US nuclear forces, and improve military tactical and management decision making. (Lukasik 2011)

For the first years in ARPA's operation, efforts were concentrated on computer-simulated war games. This changed when Joseph C. R. ('Lick') Licklider (1915–90) joined ARPA in 1962 to lead its newly established Information Processing Techniques Office (IPTO). Licklider, a Harvard-trained psychologist and computer scientist, published in 1960 his famous paper 'Man–Computer Symbiosis', proposing technology that would 'enable men and computers to cooperate in making decisions and controlling complex situations without inflexible dependence on predetermined programs'. In 1965, Licklider's 'Libraries of the Future' commissioned research introduced the concept of digital libraries as 'procognitive systems'. Building on Bush's memex work, Licklider noted:

the concept of a 'desk' may have changed from passive to active: a desk may be primarily a display-and-control station in a telecommunication—telecomputation system—and its most vital part may be the cable ('umbilical cord') that connects it, via a wall socket, into the procognitive utility net. (Licklider 1965, 33)

Under Licklider's lead at IPTO, the research focus shifted to time-sharing, computer language, and computer graphics, and cooperation with computer research centres around the United States was prioritized. Licklider referred to this cooperation as the 'Intergalactic Computer Network'—later shortened to *InterNet*. For its implementation, he reached out to a private company based in Boston—Bolt, Beranek, and Newman (BBN)—to develop network technology.[2] Within the span of nine months, BBN, under the lead of Frank Heart, built a network of four computers, each operating on a different system and using the Interface Message Processors (IMPs). Licklider knew BBN well, having served as its vice-president in 1957. To a large extent, the digital direction chosen by the BBN was his idea: 'If BBN is going to be an important company in the future, it must be in computers' (Beranek 2005, 10). Frank Heart and Licklider were both emeriti alumni of the Lincoln Laboratory. The successors of Licklider at the IPTO were hand-picked from the same academic environment. The first was Ivan Sutherland (1964–66), who ran the IPTO when its budget was approximately $15 million (National Research Council 1999, 100), between 1964 and 1966. The second was Lawrence Roberts, who came from MIT and the Lincoln Laboratory to IPTO between 1964 and 1966. The third was Robert Taylor, who formerly worked at NASA, taking office with IPTO from 1966 until 1968.

Working independently, in the early 1960s, Paul Baran at the RAND Corporation in the United States and Donald Davies at the National Physical Laboratory (NPL) in the United Kingdom developed the message block system that set the basis of modern packet switching and dynamic routing, the foundation of the Internet infrastructure today. Packet switching allowed for breaking a message into smaller blocks of data that Davies called 'packets'

---

[2] All major telecom and computer companies dismissed the idea when he presented it in front of 100 business representatives.

and for routing them separately ('switch') via the network, yet ready to be recomposed by the computer at the receiving end. The significance of this breakthrough was compared to the advent circuit switching system used in the early days of the telephone, which enabled telephone exchanges—with human operators manually connecting calls—to create a single continuous connection between two telephones.

Baran's three-fold categorization of communications networks—centralized, decentralized, and distributed networks—set the stage for future work. Baran conducted the largest part of this work while employed by RAND from 1959 to roughly 1962. Although his ideas—summarized in eleven reports and supported by mathematical evidence and graphs—were never implemented, they were later picked up by ARPA scientists (Shapiro 1967). A key advancement in computing came from MIT in 1961, when the time-sharing mechanism became operational, allowing several users to share the capacities of a single computer, which were full-room machines at the time. That same year, MIT's Leonard Kleinrock completed his PhD thesis on packet switching, proposing the transmission of data by dividing messages into smaller 'chunks' lined up at the nodes of a communication system based on two principles: demand access and distributed control (Kleinrock 1962). Originally, advanced level work like Kleinrock's was funded through the division of mathematical sciences, yet as of 1970, the theoretical computer science program was born as the NSF established its Office of Computing Activities. By 1980, the NSF already funded around 400 individual projects in computational theory. Alongside DARPA, it became the main source of funding for computing research during that decade.

ARPANET, its Alternatives and Successors

The first operational packet switching network was ARPANET, a project started with a budget of $1 million at ARPA. A plan to experiment with connecting sixteen sites (ARPANET) across the United States was revealed at the 1967 symposium of the Association for Computing Machinery (ACM) in Tennessee. A year later, ARPA funded its first graduate student conference at the University of Illinois, inviting a few students from each university working on computing research to cross-fertilize ideas. By 1968, to document the work undertaken on the ARPANET, a fast-paced experimentation network, the Network Working Group (NWG) was established under the leadership of Steve Crocker from UCLA.[3] On 7 April 1969, Crocker sent the first

---

[3] Among these experiments was also a failed attempt to link computers on the campus at UCLA in 1968 (under the direction of Ivan Sutherland and Bob Taylor).

Request for Comments (RFC) to the other NWG participants using conventional mail. On 2 September 1969, the BBN Interface Message Processor was connected to UCLA.[4] According to Crocker (2012), the RFC was initially thought of as a temporary tool to share information, independent of the level of formality envisioned for each document.

Beyond documentation purposes, the RFCs also embedded a 'hope to promote the exchange and discussion of considerably less than authoritative ideas' (Crocker 1969). In December 1970, the NWG completed the first interconnection protocol, the Network Control Protocol (NCP). The protocols used started to be documented in a series called RFCs, which became the standard decision-making procedure in the Internet Engineering Task Force (IETF), a body created in 1986 to oversee the development of protocols for the first layer of internetworking. Over time, the RFC became an anchoring practice around which the community coalesced, as discussed towards the end of this chapter.

On 29 October 1969, the first ARPANET link was established between UCLA and the Stanford Research Institute. The latter remains central to the history of ARPANET, hosting the first formal coordination body, the Network Information Center (NIC) established in 1971 at the SRI Augmentation Research Center (Engelbart's lab) in Menlo Park, California. Starting in 1972, it was led by Elizabeth J. Feinler, known as 'Jake', who managed it under a contract with the Department of Defense (DoD). In its early days, the NIC handled user services (via phone and conventional mail at first) and maintained a directory of people ('white pages'), resources ('yellow pages'), and protocols. Once the network expanded, the NIC started registering terminals and financial information, such as auditing and billing.

A number of Internet pioneers discussed the open, relaxed atmosphere of work at the outset,[5] rather unusual under contracts with the DoD. The involvement of young graduates on par with military staff indicated the importance given to the experiment. As only a small number of people had access to this project, no in-built security was prioritized in the early days of the network. Notably, ARPANET was not restricted to military use. Access to the network was limited to ARPA contractors, yet those who had permission to work were not under rigorous scrutiny. Nonetheless, there was a clear recognition among researchers and especially among managers that what was

---

[4] Kleinrock's early development of packet switching theory determined the choice for the first node on the ARPANET: his Network Measurement Center at UCLA.

[5] As Crocker (2012) recalled: 'We were a group of young graduates ... we were handed the task of trying to see what to do with this network that was going to be given to us, or imposed on us, depending on your point of view, so we had to organize from scratch. And it was an interesting technical challenge, open field, I mean no direction.'

at stake was more than the development of a research network, as Lukasik revealed:

So in that environment, I would have been hard pressed to plow a lot of money into the network just to improve the productivity of the researchers. The rationale just wouldn't have been strong enough. What was strong enough was this idea that packet switching would be more survivable, more robust under damage to the network ... So I can assure you, to the extent that I was signing the checks, which I was from 1967 on, I was signing them because that was the need I was convinced of. (Waldrop 2001, 279–80)

Despite its heavy DoD funding, ARPANET never functioned as a military network in the strict sense, with the exception of a few international connections, such as the one with Norway, limited to defence use. As Townes (2012) shows, some elements of the research conducted at the time on ARPANET were kept outside of the reports to the funding authorities. For example, the transnational spread of the network was constantly minimized in order to stay within the scope of the military mandate. The British and Norwegian nodes of the network were not represented in one of the most reproduced maps of the ARPANET published in 1985, and a footnote explained that experimental satellite connections were not shown on the map. Back in 1972, the Defense Communications Agency (DCA) established another packet switching network—WIN—used for operational command and control purposes. It was around that time that the idea of transferring control of ARPANET to a private organization consolidated (Abbate 1999).

The work environment remained open all throughout the ARPANET experiment, with scientists taking the lead for developments and funding streams. Part of it had to do with the research tradition and the technical challenges, meaning that there were frequent exchanges about what worked, what had to be fixed, and what could be improved. The developments that would come on top of this were not envisioned at that point, therefore the scientists working on it preferred an open format (Crocker 2012). However, political sensitivities existed; some were carefully mediated by those in charge, as an endeavour to create a community of practice that gave no attention to what was happening outside the technical space. As Elizabeth Feinler explains:

In the early days we put out the directory, which was sort of a phone book of the internet. And there were a lot of military people, there were a lot of graduate students, so there was a spectrum of users and developers. In the 1970s, there were [...] lots of strong feelings about the Vietnam war and what not. So I took it upon myself not to put anybody's title in the directory, so that meant that everyone was talking to everybody and they didn't know whom they were talking to. (Feinler 2012)

While the concept of *internetworking* was developed at ARPA (Leiner et al. 2009), linking computers in a network was an experiment tried in several other parts of the world, most importantly in France and the United Kingdom, where packet switching technologies were tested in the early 1970s. In 1971, plans for a European Informatics Network for research and scientific purposes under the direction of Derek Barber from NPL were announced by the European Common Market. That same year, at the French Research Laboratory IRIA, Louis Pouzin launched the Cyclades packet switched system based on datagrams. Despite concrete advancements in Pouzin's project, the funding from the French government was discontinued at the end of 1978.

The ARPANET project provided inspiration for a number of similar projects in other parts of the world. While physical connections were only established directly with Europe (first with Norway and the United Kingdom), academic networks were set up in Australia and later in Japan. By 1980, six main networking experiments were underway[6] and by 1988 their number more than doubled.

While the overwhelming majority had an academic purpose, the networks were generally subsidised by states. A few internetworking experiments, such as USENET, EUNET, BITNET, FIDONET, and EARN received direct user contributions.

In October 1972, scientists working on packet switching networks on both sides of the Atlantic convened at the first International Conference on Computer Communication held in Washington. ARPANET was successfully tested publicly, connecting twenty-nine sites in a demonstration organized by Robert E. Kahn of BBN (Townes 2012, 49). A group of network designers volunteered to explore how these networks could be interconnected in the framework of a newly established International Packet Network Working Group (INWG), similar to the ARPANET NWG, using the request for comments format for distributing the INWG notes. DARPA's Larry Roberts proposed to share the notes via the ARPANET NIC, and Vint Cerf, a graduate student working on one of the first ARPANET nodes at UCLA, volunteered to be temporary chairman. The group divided into two subgroups to consider 'Communication System Requirements' and 'HOST-HOST Protocol Requirements'. In June 1973, the first international node to the ARPANET was established, via satellite link, at Kjeller in Norway, in turn providing a cable link to University College London in the United Kingdom shortly after (Bing 2009).[7]

---

[6] This included NPLNET in the United Kingdom, ARPANET, SATNET, and USENET in the United States, CYCLADES in France, CERNet as a joint research initiative of European governments at CERN in Geneva.

[7] For a discussion about the spread of TCP/IP along Cold War lines, see Townes (2012).

In 1972, Robert Kahn joined the ARPA team to develop network technologies and to initiate the billion-dollar Strategic Computing Program, the largest computer research and development program funded by the US government. Kahn played a key role in the development of the ARPANET and is credited for the open-architecture networking and for coining the phrase 'National Information Infrastructure'. In 1973, together with Cerf, by then an assistant professor at Stanford, Kahn developed the Transmission Control Protocol (TCP), which encapsulated and decapsulated messages sent over the network, with gateways able to read the capsules, but not the content, decrypted only on end-computers. This protocol, meant to replace the ARPANET's original NCP, was presented in the paper published in April 1974 and entitled 'A Protocol for Packet Networks Intercommunication'. Working on the datagram network and a connectionless packet switching protocol, the French scientist Louis Pouzin joined Vint Cerf and his colleagues at INWG to propose a transport protocol across different networks. In 1975, they submitted their proposal to the standard-setting body in charge of telecommunications, the International Telegraph and Telephone Consultative Committee (CCITT).

Private Initiative and Competing Protocols

In parallel with the work conducted at ARPA, major computer companies in the United States proposed their own proprietary products, such as IBM's Systems Network Architecture, Xerox's Network Services, or Digital Equipment Corporation's DECNET, which were all in operation in the mid-1970s. It is around that time that IBM, Xerox, and several national European post, telephone, and telegraph organizations (PTT)—functioning as monopolies at the national level—proposed their own packet-switched common-user data networks, for example in the United Kingdom, France, and Norway. These were based on 'virtual circuits', able to make use of the routines of circuit switching employed by telephone exchanges. The virtual circuits solution and TCP/IP had a different architecture and were proposed by distinct groups of specialists: on the one hand, there were the engineers and scientists that worked on voice telecommunications; on the other, computer scientists explored data traffic via the transmission control protocol. Their references and terminology were different, they attended different conferences and they read other journals. There was scepticism in both camps regarding the technological upgrades needed to make packets communicate effectively.

In 1977, representatives of the British computer industry, supported by the US and French representatives, called for the establishment of a committee for packet switching standards within the International Organization for Standardization (ISO), an independent nongovernmental association whose work did not focus exclusively on telecommunications. The Open Systems Interconnection (OSI) committee was set in place and led by Charles Bachman, the American developer of a database management system called Integrated Data Store. After long negotiations, two camps consolidated within the OSI committee: on one side, Bachman and former members of the INWG pushed for the Pouzin-inspired connectionless protocols, whereas the IBM representatives and some of the industry delegates favoured the 'virtual circuits' option. Their proposed interconnection solution, designed as a universal standard, was published by the CCITT in its Recommendation X.25 and became the international standard. This standard required a reliable network, unlike what Cerf and Pouzin proposed. Their solution did not place any substantial function on the network and ensured that processing was performed directly at the edges, on end-computers (McCarthy 2015). The work on the TCP continued amidst international negotiations for the adopted standards.

At the outset, the developments at ARPA and those originating in private computer labs remained completely separate. A few years passed before the important advances in different camps would converge, in particular to bridge the private–public gap. The email system was developed by Raymond Tomlinson from BBN in 1972, while the Ethernet system was the outcome of the work of Robert Metcalfe[8] and his team at Xerox's Palo Alto Research Center in 1977. That year, the Apple II personal computer (PC) was launched at the West Coast Computer Fair, offering, for the first time, a ready-made unit,[9] easy to access and operate. The Apple II PC was accompanied by a reference manual detailing its source code and providing machine specifications. This trend for publishing the source code was also followed by IBM, when their first PC was released in 1981 (Ryan 2010). A number of other services were made available to go along with developments in PCs, including network mailing lists and multiplayer games (e.g. Adventure). The first mobile phones were also developed in the 1970s. Moreover, the UNIX operating system, with its kernel in C programming, was publicly released outside the AT&T's Bell Labs in October 1973 and became widely adopted by programmers as a portable, multitasking, and multi-user configuration.

By the mid-1970s, a number of technical breakthroughs from private labs started to be integrated into ARPANET through its contractor

---

[8] Metcalfe was the graduate student who connected the MIT site to ARPANET.

[9] Prior to the Apple II computer, PC manufacturers were selling parts to be assembled, meaning that access was also restricted to the technical savvy.

network. Among these, the case of the UNIX operating system is poignant. UNIX was developed at Bell Labs in the early 1970s and quickly became widespread in universities as its source code was made available, allowing computer scientists to experiment with different features. In 1975, Ken Thompson from Bell Labs took a sabbatical as visiting professor at Berkeley, where he contributed to installing Version 6 Unix and began a Pascal implementation project on computers bought with money from the Ingres database project. Version 6 UNIX was further developed by two graduate students, Chuck Haley and Bill Joy, and publicly released as part of the Berkeley Software Distribution (BSD) in 1978. By 1981, (D)ARPA was funding the Computer Systems Research Group at UC-Berkeley to produce a version of BSD that would integrate TCP/IP, to be released publicly in August 1983.

Similarly, the Data Encryption Standard developed at IBM for businesses received the endorsement of the National Bureau of Standards in 1977, making available to a wider public what was formerly proprietary information. Local area networks such as Ethernet and dial-up connections at a maximum speed of 64 Kbps became more widely spread in the 1980s. In 1981, IBM started selling their first PC with the following specifications: 4.77 MHz Intel 8088 microprocessor, 16 kb of memory (expandable to 256 k), two 160 k floppy disk drives, and an optional colour monitor. Its price started at US$1,565 and it was the 'first to be built from off-the-shelf parts and marketed by outside distributors' (Bing 2009, 34).

As access to computers grew, the OSI work got rapid traction among computer vendors like IBM and garnered political support from national governments, including from the European Economic Community. By 1985, CERN opened a 'TCP/IP Coordinator' position as part of a formal agreement, which restricted the use of TCP/IP to the CERN site and mandated the ISO protocol for external connections (until 1989). According to Ben Segal, who occupied the position until 1988, the Internet protocol was introduced at CERN a few years before via the Berkeley UNIX system. Around that time, CERN became the Swiss backbone for USENET, the UNIX users' network that carried most of the email and news between the US side and the European side, *EUnet*.

Notably, the US government was also among the first adopters of the OSI standard. In 1985, two years after the publication of the ISO 7498 international standard, the US National Research Council recommended that the ARPANET move from TCP/IP to OSI; by the same token, in 1988, the Department of Commerce requested that the OSI standard be implemented on all US government computers after August 1990.

TCP/IP and the Birth of the Internet

As of 1977, the TCP was used for cross-network connections at ARPA. The Internet Protocol (IP) was added a year later to facilitate the routing of messages. The IP solved the problem of locating computers in a network, by designating them concomitantly as both 'hosts' and 'receivers'. Each connected device was assigned a unique 32-bit number (represented in dotted decimal form: 92.123.44.92) that a user could employ to send a message to his or her desired destination. In the early days, each computer was also given a name, in addition to a corresponding IP address. Each computer received a copy of a database (hosts.txt) file, so a user would be able to copy the numeric address into the designated header of the message before sending it. The 'hosts.txt', performing a similar function to that of a phone book, together with a list of technical parameters, was maintained at the NIC based at the Stanford Research Institute and was managed by Jon Postel at the Information Sciences Institute at the University of Southern California. This set of functions later evolved into the so-called Internet Assigned Numbers Authority (IANA) functions, playing a key role in future political disputes, as detailed in Chapter 4.

Despite increased complexity as the network grew bigger and bigger, the tasks continued to be performed by individuals. Between 1977 and 1982, a set of technical documents entitled 'Internet Experiment Notes' (IENs) were released in order to discuss the implementation of Kahn–Cerf protocols, modelled on the RFC series that Crocker initiated at ARPANET. Jon Postel helped to revise the TCP/IP version in 1978 and again in 1979. The specifications of the protocol were open to everyone. In 1979, ARPA founded the Internet Configuration Control Board (ICCB) to assist with TCP/IP software creation. The editor of IENs was Jon Postel, and about 206 documents were published in the series before it was discontinued.

ARPA's TCP/IP network became known as the 'Internet'. In 1981, the TCP/IP was integrated into the Berkeley version of UNIX developed by Bill Joy, thus expanding the reach of the ARPA-born communication protocol. Looking back at the early days, Vint Cerf located the birth of the Internet on 1 January 1983, when the transition plan to migrate the 400 hosts of the ARPANET to TCP/IP was completed. That year, the domain name system (DNS) was invented by Paul Mockapetris, together with Jon Postel and Craig Partridge and was announced in RFC 882. The DNS converted IP addresses consisting of numbers only into letters and words that could be easily remembered by Internet users. The DNS represented a hierarchical system allowing for instant database queries and information retrieval for turning names into numbers and replicating the structure at each level: the 2nd-level domain maintains a name server containing the zone file with the IP Addresses for all 3rd-level domains. In the early days, SRI was one of three hosts of the root zone file.[10] According to RFC 920 from 1984, the initial set of generic top level domains (gTLDs) included .com, .edu, .gov, .mil, .org, with .net being added later. In 1988, .int was introduced for international organizations, following a request from NATO.

The expansion and growth of the ARPANET was no longer easy to contain. By 1983 it had over 100 nodes and was further divided into two parts: an operational component, the military network (MILNET), to serve the operational needs of the DoD, and a research component that retained the ARPANET name. After the network split, the MILNET expanded, and it reached over 250 nodes within a year. In 1985, two important decisions were made: first, two-letter country-code top level domains (cc-TLDs) specific to each jurisdiction were incorporated in the DNS, based on a pre-defined ISO 3166-1 list;[11] second, the adoption of the DNS was made mandatory by ARPA. A year later the general adoption of the DNS was ensured at a major congress held on the West Coast in the presence of all major network representatives (Hafner and Lyon 1999). At that point, the running cost of ARPANET was around $14 million per year (McCarthy 2015) and its decommissioning was in sight. By 1989, the early packet switching network was dismantled into smaller networks (detailed in Table 1), most of which were moved under the local administration of universities.

Similar to ARPANET, DARPA also funded other computer-related projects of high impact. Between the 1960s and 1990s, it sponsored studies on artificial intelligence (AI)—in particular at MIT and Carnegie Tech—at first for research purposes only and, later, for military applications. With the MILNET split on the ARPANET, all unclassified military communication underwent increased protection. A number of gateways made possible email exchange via ARPANET, but disconnection was facilitated for security reasons.

A large part of the work on ARPANET was entrusted to graduate students engaged in ground-breaking projects from the beginning and able to develop

---

[10] Until 1987, only four root name servers were in operation, but their number increased to thirteen, of which ten are located in the United States and three in Sweden, the Netherlands, and Japan. The root zone file was maintained and updated on a master root server called, as of 1995, 'authoritative root server' or 'A' root server.

[11] According to Jon Postel (1994), 'the IANA is not in the business of deciding what is and what is not a country. The selection of the ISO 3166 list as a basis for country code top-level domain names was made with the knowledge that ISO has a procedure for determining which entities should be and should not be on that list'.

Table 1 ARPANET and its successors

Start	Name	Protocol used	Purpose	End of operations	Department in charge/ funding
1972	ARPANET	TCP/IP	research	1990	DARPA, under DoD
1981	BITNET	IBM RSCS	university network	merged into CREN in 1991	users
1982	CSNET	PhoneNET MMDF, TCP/IP	research		NSF, member organizations funding
1985	NSFNET	TCP/IP	research	1995	NSF
1983	MILNET (military network)— split from ARPANET	TCP/IP	unclassified DoD traffic	became the Defense Data Network	DoD
1990s	NIPRNET (Non-classified Internet Protocol Router Network)— building on MILNET	TCP/IP	sensitive, unclassified data between internal DoD users	still active	DoD
1994	SIPRNET (Secret [for- merly Secure] Internet Protocol Router Network)	TCP/IP	classified data (up to and including information classified SECRET)	still active; replaced the Defense Data Network	DoD and Department of State

and grow a community of practice, subsequently involved in running the successor networks. The co-existence of policy practitioners and scientists, rotating in leading positions, unified the vision for how ARPANET could develop. This mutual influence, while not resulting in equal power, created a hierarchy of preferred solutions and policy directions. As soon as the net-work developed, special measures were introduced for military communica-tion and that was clearly distinguished from ARPANET's academic research and public use.

From ARPANET to NSFNET

Alongside the DoD investment in ARPANET, the US NSF began funding the establishment of the Computer Science Network (CSNET) in the early 1980s. The project—awarded $5 million for its first five years—aimed to link computer science departments at academic and research institutions that could not be directly connected to ARPANET. The proposal for the grant was prepared by Lawrence Landweber from the University of Wisconsin-Madison on behalf of a consortium of universities,[12] after receiving seed funding of $136,000 from the NSF. As the concern for sustainability became more apparent, the NSF tied to the CSNET funding a clause that the network would be self-sufficient after five years.

By 1984, CSNET included eighty-three sites in the United States and one in Israel, expanding to computer science departments internationally in Korea, Australia, Canada, France, Germany, and Japan. At its peak, the network had 180 institutions with independently operated networks. Starting in 1985, CSNET charged universities an annual fee of $2,000 to $5,000 and industrial sites (e.g. DEC, IBM) a fee of $30,000 to participate. By 1989, CSNET merged with BITNET and created a larger network managed by the new Corporation for Research and Educational Networking (CREN).

Moreover, the NSF also supported research that no other agency agreed to fund, such as cryptography. Work on public-key cryptography—in particular by Martin Hellman and Whitfield Diffie at Stanford University—started in the early 1970s. Partnering with the Office of Naval Research, the NSF continued to support this stream of research by funding the work of Ronald Rivest, Adi Shamir, and Leonard Adleman at MIT on public-key method using number theory. Openly shared, these advances in cryptography became fundamental for computer security textbooks, despite the National Security Agency pressure to keep this research secret (National Research Council 1999).

The NSF also provided funding for the creation and interconnection of five supercomputer centres across the United States at top universities.[13] To

---

[12] The consortium comprised: Georgia Tech, University of Minnesota, University of New Mexico, University of Oklahoma, Purdue University, University of California-Berkeley, University of Utah, University of Virginia, University of Washington, University of Wisconsin, and Yale University.

[13] The five supercomputer centres established in the mid-1980s were: the John von Neumann Center at Princeton University, the San Diego Supercomputer Center on the campus of the University of California at San Diego, the National Center for Supercomputing Applications at the University of Illinois, the Cornell Theory Center, a production and experimental supercomputer center, and the Pittsburgh Supercomputing Center, jointly operated by Westinghouse, Carnegie-Mellon University, and the University of Pittsburgh.

connect these centres, the CSNET technology and framework were upgraded to a higher speed and the extended network evolved into the National Science Foundation Network (NSFNET), eventually the backbone of the modern Internet. NSFNET was developed by three private firms: IBM, MCI, and MERIT. The total funding allocated to NSFNET from 1986 to 1995 was $200 million (Leiner et al. 1997).

On its network, the NSF implemented the 'Acceptable Use Policy', specifying that the use of the network must be consistent with the purposes of NSFNET: research, instruction, and support activities (for academia and not-for-profit institutions of research[14]). Importantly, this provided access to research facilities, universities, academic networks, and centres beyond computer science departments, linking different areas of work and expanding resource sharing. In this context, non-military domains would no longer be funded by the DoD and a number of responsibilities were transferred from the DoD to the NSF. The latter established, through a competitive bidding process in 1992, to entrust domain name registration (at no charge until 1995), directory management, information services to three companies (Network Solutions, AT&T, and General Atomic, respectively), which formed InterNIC in 1993. These responsibilities were partly taken over by the Internet Corporation for Assigned Names and Numbers (ICANN) in 1998.[15]

The distinction between 'Internet' and 'internet' dates back to the 1980s, when attempts were made to distinguish between the federally sponsored network and any other network using TCP/IP (Bing 2009). Concepts like 'cyberspace' or 'the knowledge society' also became popular in that decade. The term 'cyberspace' was first used by Gibson (1984) in his sci-fi novel *Neuromancer*, where he described it as 'a consensual hallucination ... A graphic representation of data abstracted from the bank of every computer in the human system. Unthinkable complexity' (1984, 51). The French social critic Jean-François Lyotard is credited for coining 'the knowledge society' (1979) and highlighting the central role of information and computerization in its consolidation. Yet, by the time the decision to commercialize the Internet was taken, the US administration gave currency to the 'information superhighway' discourse, promoted by Al Gore (Broad 1992).

---

[14] The exact formulation was: 'use for research or instruction at for-profit institutions may or may not be consistent with the purposes of NSFNET, and will be reviewed by the NSF Project Office on a case-by-case basis'.

[15] Chapter 4 discusses in detail the formation of the organization and the transfer of responsibilities from Jon Postel to the new entity.

Mechanisms of Governance

It is difficult to disentangle the early mechanisms of governance from the informal network that set them into motion and the key individuals taking the lead in the creation of standards and institutional structures. The first two decades of networking experiments, resulting in the development of the Internet as we know it today, share a number of characteristics that structured—constrained and favoured—the future evolution of the field. Most important among these are the transversal links between academia, government, and, eventually, the computer industry. Equally significant for the evolution of the Internet in the first decades was the highly permissive regulatory milieu in the United States, discussed in detail later. These two dynamics enabled the development of a strong culture of volunteerism and innovation that crossed the US border when the Internet globalized in the early 1990s.

Research Funding: Basis for the Emergence of Multidisciplinary Cooperation

The strong involvement of scientists from elite universities in both technical and leadership positions at ARPA created an environment of sharing and collaboration, further enabling the open exchange with and among graduate students. While access to the network remained restricted to contractors, ARPANET benefited from the movement of leading figures from research and teaching to implementation teams and finally to decision-making posts. Among the key strategists at ARPA were pioneers Kleinrock from UCLA and Licklider from MIT and Lincoln Lab, who envisioned a network of networks that would later be opened up to a larger community through the work of Lawrence Landweber from the University of Wisconsin-Madison. Landweber proposed the creation of CSNET to link computer science departments in the United States and abroad. Formerly working for the Irish Higher Education Authority (HEAnet) and for the Trinity College Dublin, Dennis Jennings started acting as Program Director for Networking to lead the establishment of the NSFNET in 1985, enabling general purpose access to a wide network. With very few exceptions (such as 'Jake' Feinler), women were mostly absent from this early community.

Earlier on, experimentation with internetworking at ARPANET was supported by the DoD, which awarded research contracts to academic teams (rather than individuals) for developing projects that would then be carried out by industrial groups. A key element in the success of the Information

Processing Techniques Office was its leadership style: programme managers brought in from academia for two-year-long positions were given broad latitude in deciding strategic directions and funding. They were carefully selected for their expertise and were able to work closely with the researchers they contracted, providing intellectual leadership. This management style also eliminated the need for a separate monitoring and evaluation track of activities, giving enough flexibility to managers to adjust financial support according to the progress made and to respond quickly to developments (National Research Council 1999). Unlike the DARPA practices of restricted access (generally limited to the military and to contractors from selected universities), the NSF operated on an open, accessible research basis. Complementing this approach, the NSF also supported the public dissemination of results and funded participation in conferences, thus investing in building a robust research community, just like ARPA did in the early years, in particular by organizing student conferences on internetworking.

The success of the CSNET—which was open to all computer science researchers—also influenced the decision to fund NSFNET, further expanding access to other research facilities. On NSFNET, the regional academic networks initially connected were also encouraged to seek commercial customers and open their facilities to them (Leiner et al. 2009). Yet, the NSF budget dedicated to computer-related activities as part of its Computer and Information Sciences and Engineering Directorate continued to grow between 1987 and 1995 (National Research Council 1999).

Domestic Regulation: New Rules for Computing Services

In addition to sustained funding from DoD and NSF, the development of the Internet in the American context was facilitated by the minimal state ideology, dominant at the time. In 1988, the Federal Communications Commission (FCC) created the special category of 'value-added' services, which left computer-mediated information virtually unregulated by the government. This created a permissive environment for the creation and development of *sui generis* institutions for its technical management (Mueller 2004), in charge of protocols and standards of operability. As the chairman of the FCC said in his speech before the World Economic Development Forum in September 1999:

Our hands-off approach wasn't entirely a choice. The reality is that the Internet grew so fast that policy-makers could not have written a code to govern it even if they wanted to. (Kennard 1999)

This regulatory direction was prefaced by a set of developments aimed at addressing the technological evolution and convergence challenges, in a context of national telecommunications monopoly.[16] In 1966, the FCC commenced its Computer Inquiries, an investigation trio into data transfers and the conditions for a related competitive market, thus providing rules and regulations for computing services. Adjusting an earlier categorization, the 1976 Computer Inquiries II distinguished between basic and enhanced services. Basic services referred to processing the movement of information and computer processing, which included protocol conversion, security, and memory storage. Enhanced services, on the other hand, altered a subscriber's information or electronic signals (any service transmitted over common carrier facilities employing computer processing applications acting on the format, content, code, protocol, or similar aspects of the subscriber's transmitted information, that restructured information or involved interaction with stored information). Services developed around that time, such as protocol processing, email, or newsgroup fell in the 'enhanced services' category.

In 1985, the third FCC Computer Inquiry aimed to structure the conditions of the market before the deployment of the Internet to a broader audience. Accordingly, the FCC established two safeguards: the Comparatively Efficient Interconnection and Open Network Architecture, which removed the structural remedies previously imposed on incumbent players from the telephone industry, in particular AT&T and its Bell System, which functioned as a legally sanctioned monopoly.[17] In Europe, a similar constraint was imposed via the principle of interoperability plus physical interconnection between networks (Coates 2011).

Up to the late 1970s, the developments at ARPANET and those in the industry remained separate, each conducting research according to different priorities. By the 1980s, the trend changed, and developments from different sectors started to build on one another, sometimes as a result of joint teams. While NSFNET, operating on TCP/IP, implemented restrictions against the commercial use of the newly established public infrastructure, it granted, in 1988, limited access to MCI Communications Corp. to experiment with commercial email services (Shah and Kesan 2007).[18] Moreover, starting in

---

[16] For an extensive discussion of this transformation, see Rioux (2014).

[17] A noteworthy development prior to Computer Inquiry III was the 1982 finalization of the eight-year-long antitrust suit by the US government against AT&T, resulting in the separation of the local exchanges component of AT&T (where the natural monopoly continued to apply) and the Bell System long distance, manufacturing, and research and development open to competition from that point on. This led to the divestiture of the company in 1984 and the creation of a reformed AT&T and seven regional Bell operating companies.

[18] The person facilitating this was Vint Cerf. As vice-president of MCI Digital Information Services from 1982 to 1986, he led the engineering of MCI Mail, the first commercial email service

1988, NSF initiated a series of conferences at Harvard's Kennedy School of Government on 'The Commercialization and Privatization of the Internet', as well as on the 'com-priv' list on the net itself, meant to enable dialogue on privately funded networks (Leiner et al. 1997). In 1992, the NSF started a bidding process for the organization and maintenance of the DNS registry and related services resulting in the creation of the Internet Network Information Center (InterNIC) in 1993.

The transition from ARPANET to NSFNET was important not only in terms of expanding access, but also for the perpetuation of particular organizational forms. Just like during the ARPANET era, collaboration between academic networks involved a mix of informal governance alongside formalized arrangements and emulation of a set of practices. NSF took on the organizational infrastructure developed at DARPA under the Internet Activities Board (IAB). The joint authorship by the IAB's Internet Engineering and Architecture Task Forces and by NSF's Network Technical Advisory Group of RFC 985 (Requirements for Internet Gateways) ensured that DARPA and the NSF segments remained interoperable. When the Internet was privatized, these institutional forms endured.

International Governance

The history of the Internet explored so far indicates that international legal constraints were near-absent in the early days of the Internet. But that does not mean there was no governance. While the practice of standard-setting goes back to 1865,[19] Internet-specific organizations tasked with it emerged in the 1980s to respond to functional needs for coordination. To ensure the stability and development of the network, the architecture set in place was the primary vehicle of regulation, and it was mostly the business of technologists. Yet this became a hot topic of debate a decade later, when certain features of the architecture were understood to have far-reaching policy implications, for aspects such as anonymity or innovation at the edges. Lessig (2006) referred to this as 'regulation by code' or the '<built environment> of social life in cyberspace' (2006, 121) with long-ranging effects on what could

to be connected to the Internet. Prior to re-joining MCI in 1994, Cerf was vice president of the Corporation for National Research Initiatives.

[19] This practice stood at the basis of cooperation for the creation of the first international organization: International Telegraph Union (later renamed the International Telecommunication Union, ITU).

and could not be done online. In that sense, Lessig perceived code writers as 'lawmakers'.[20]

Globally, until the 1990s, the governance of global telecommunications was carried out mainly through interaction among governments, who owned and controlled national incumbent operators, and the ITU, which was in charge of regulating issues related to interconnection. UNESCO's New World Information and Communication Order (NWICO) placed on the global agenda a set of issues of relevance to the spread of new technologies. Building on the 1980 MacBride Report—which documented the emergence of global communications governance dominated by industrialized nations-led commercial and military infrastructure—the NWICO agenda raised the first serious controversies at the international level (Zehle 2012) between the US principle of 'free flow of information' and the demands of the Soviet Union and of the Non-Alignment Movement of independent states. In particular, the unequal distribution of radio spectrum and the restricted spread of satellite and computer technologies to developing countries were perceived as key imbalances in global information flows. The Soviet Union, China, India, Cuba, and Tunisia were key players in the NWICO movement, covering the period spanning from the heights of decolonization to the collapse of communism. The pursuit of this agenda by the UNESCO leadership in the first part of the 1980s led to a few countries withdrawing from the organization: United States (1984–2003), United Kingdom (1985–97), and Singapore (1986–2007).

De facto, the landscape change resulting from technological development and convergence, hinted at in the NWICO agenda, would continue to affect the balance between developed and developing countries over the years to come. The analysis of governance mechanisms at the outset reveals that treaties, conventions, and agreements constituted the preferred form of regulation (36 per cent prevalence), followed by operative international and regional guidelines (20 per cent), and the formation of specialized bodies. Table 2 provides an overview of the governance landscape between 1970 and 1993, with examples on the hard–soft law continuum using the tripartite framework introduced in Chapter 2, consisting of legal enshrinement, institutional solidification, and modelling instruments. Notably, with institutional consolidation in its infancy, monitoring mechanisms were not given priority at the outset. General rules for telecommunications were designed to remain broad and applied to the Internet in a non-specific manner, be it as part of

---

[20] In Lessig's words: 'code writers are increasingly lawmakers. They determine what the defaults of the Internet will be; whether privacy will be protected; the degree to which anonymity will be allowed; the extent to which access will be guaranteed' (2006, 79).

Table 2 Governance mechanisms (global and regional) from 1970s to 1993 (based on a total of twenty-five instruments recorded in the database)

Mechanisms	Instruments	%	Examples
Legal en-shrinement	*Treaties, conventions, agreements*	36%	1981 CoE Convention for the Protection of Individuals with regard to Automatic Processing of Personal Data
			1988 ITU International Telecommunication Regulations
	Court judgments	12%	1984 ECtHR *Malone v United Kingdom*
Institutional solidification	*Specialized bodies*	16%	1986 High Technology Crime Investigation Association
			1988 TMFORUM Industry Association
			1990 APEC Telecommunications and Information Working Group
			1993 UN Commission for Science and Technology Development
	Strategic framework/ agenda	12%	1980 UNESCO NWICO
			1993 UNDP Sustainable Development Networking Program
	Monitoring and benchmarking	0%	
Modelling	*Discursive*	4%	1985 OECD Declaration on Transborder Data Flows
	Operative	20%	1990 UN Model Treaty on Mutual Assistance in Criminal Matters
			1990 UN Guidelines for the regulation of computerized personal data files
			1992 OECD Guidelines for the Security of Information Systems

transborder data flows, privacy and personal data protection, or information systems security.

In 1988, ITU's member states adopted, at the World Administrative Telegraph and Telephone Conference in Melbourne, a treaty to 'establish general principles which relate to the provision and operation of international telecommunication services offered to the public as well as to the underlying international telecommunication transport means used to provide such services' (ITU 1988). The treaty, entitled 'International Telecommunication Regulations' (ITRs), came into force in 1990 and facilitated the liberalization of pricing and services, encouraging a more innovative use of basic services, such as international leased lines. The ITRs established an international regime for the exchange of telecommunications traffic across borders, promoting interoperability and interconnection. Their revision would come under discussion again in 2012 in light of the accelerated digital transformation (see Chapter 5).

A number of international organizations started to establish committees whose work covered Internet-related aspects, such as the Directorate for Science, Technology and Industry within the OECD, the Telecommunications and Information Working Group in APEC (dating back to 1990), or policy commissions within ICC, whose activities remained ascribed to a broader mandate. In the UN system, in 1993, the Commission for Science and Technology for Development was formed under the UN Conference on Trade and Development (UNCTAD), and the United Nations Development Programme (UNDP) received funding for their Sustainable Development Networking Program. These developments set the stage for the quick expansion of the Internet as a social and political medium in the subsequent decade, enabling the involvement of developing countries to various degrees.

Actors

A number of technical bodies exclusively concerned with the Internet—equipped with their own *modus operandi*—emerged during the first decades of internetworking. The most important of them grew into global entities and continued to function largely unchanged. Some of the practices established back then continue to shape the way in which decisions are taken with regard to protocols and standards. Informality and open communication remain key features of the community, modelled extensively on the interactions during the ARPANET period.

The small community which formed around the (D)ARPA project revealed a high degree of informality manifested through cherry-picked collaborators and informal agreements. Personal relationships—primarily formed in the university environment—and limited access to the network gave ARPANET contractors a strong sense of ownership and commitment. The cross-sectoral work conducted through early networks and, later, through NSFNET for both advanced research and education networking put forward complementary strengths, a high degree of flexibility, and space for open-ended experimentation. It is around these values that an early community began to form.

This progress was also backed by the development of a new discipline, computer science, and related departments in the United States and abroad. Between 1968 and 1994, the number of PhD dissertations submitted annually in computer science in the United States grew from one to almost 3,000 (National Research Council 1999, 221). As part of the efforts to lower the technical barrier of entry through knowledge creation and sharing, common language and expertise were codified in textbooks for computer science programs. A key test which revealed the extent of this consolidation was the TCP/IP versus OSI dispute, in which it became clear that the community of computer scientists on the one hand and engineers and telecommunications experts on the other proposed different solutions informed by their specialized jargon and references.

Trust and cooperation appeared as the underlying values of the emerging community, alongside the idea that anyone could initiate work on any project that would add to the common network. The latter, closely rooted in the American distinctive culture of volunteerism, shaped the collective action outcomes. Open standards and architecture, sharing and collaboration allowed for user-developed functionalities to be added to the network. This is the case with the development of the first email program that Raymond Tomlinson, who was working for BBN to develop ARPANET, coded in his free time. Another example of volunteerism was the original distribution of cc-TLDs to whomever in a national jurisdiction offered to administer the delegation. In Australia, .au was given to Robert Elz of the University of Melbourne (Malcolm 2008).

The number of individual players who were at the forefront of innovations with long-lasting impact grew in time, in both academia and the private sector. The development that steered this further came in 1991, when Tim Berners-Lee announced the public release of the World Wide Web (WWW), an application he developed[21] together with his colleagues while working at the European Organization for Nuclear Research (CERN) on the Swiss-French border. The Hypertext Transfer Protocol (HTTP) they proposed made the Internet easier to navigate with point-and-click programs, based on the CERN code library. The WWW was a game-changer as of 1993, when CERN made it available in the public domain. To further improve the WWW, Berners-Lee created, in 1994, the World Wide Web Consortium (W3C), where he continues to act as director.

---

[21] This was funded by European governments participating in the programme.

Other institutional forms dating back to the first two decades of the Internet persisted over time, building on the legacy of personal involvement and dedication of some of the key figures. The IANA was informally established in the early 1980s. Prior to it, the central numbering authority of the network, in charge of keeping records and assigning host names (the famous HOSTS.TXT-file) was the NIC, based at the Stanford Research Institute and managed by Jon Postel at the Information Sciences Institute, University of Southern California, under a contract with (D)ARPA. IANA functions evolved to include the allocation of unique names and numbers in the global network, including the cc-TLDs and gTLDs, but continued to be managed by Postel until 1998.[22] IANA represents a textbook example of informal governance, generally understood to 'prevail when informal influence overrides legal procedures, or when important rules are unwritten' (Stone 2013). For the latter, the DNS is a case-in-point. It was innovative for its time as it made use of datagrams, but was not perceived as a major development, and important work around it was left in the hands of graduate students. As Paul Mockapetris recalled:

People got the job to do something and it was so much fun doing it because nobody at the time thought it was important. And it was clear, because I was a recent graduate and this was a nice little project while all the important people were off doing other things. Now, it turned out to be a very important thing, but nobody at the time thought it was. (Mockapetris 2009)

Another technical body, the Internet Architecture Board was created in 1984 as the Internet Activities Board to coordinate the work on the development of the Internet suite of protocols (changed to its current name in 1992). It currently oversees and advises the IETF, which was formed after the 1986 meeting of fifteen researchers sponsored by the US government. The IETF developed as a voluntary open standards network for promoting Internet usability and currently functions as a consensus-based organization comprising technical experts, network operators, hardware and software implementers, and researchers. Entirely private, not-for-profit oriented from the outset, both the IAB and the IETF continue to involve members in their personal capacity rather than based on their affiliation. This is a legacy of the early days in which a limited community of computer scientists and academics interacted on a daily basis for the purpose of operating the Internet seamlessly. During the early 1990s, the IETF became an independent international body

---

[22] IANA is currently incorporated in ICANN, whose first Chief Technology Officer was supposed to be Jon Postel, but he died unexpectedly in October 1998, just a month after ICANN was founded.

under the umbrella of the Internet Society (ISOC), which continues to provide its legal framework and coordinate sponsorship to this day. As of 1991, it holds three annual meetings on different continents that are open to everyone contributing to the standard development process, conducted through the RFC—the only documents issued by the IETF.

It is in the CSNET context that the Landweber seminars developed as a venue for people to meet annually and, starting in 1984, CSNET-related discussions took place in Paris, Stockholm, Dublin, Princeton, Jerusalem, and Sydney. In 1990, in Sydney, it was decided that the seminar should become a conference, and the next year INET 91 was held in Copenhagen. At INET 92, in Kobe, Japan, the conference also marked the first annual meeting of ISOC. Together with Robert Kahn, Vint Cerf established ISOC in 1992, to provide an institutional home and a legal framework to the various task forces, including the IAB and the IETF. Cerf was the founding president of ISOC from 1992 to 1995 and in 1999 served a term as chairman of the Board.

In a short time-span, the roles of scientists and of the limited number of network users grew, including by formal representation in coordination committees. In 1990, selected members of such communities were invited to join an advisory committee for the newly created Federal Networking Council (FNC), a body established by the NSF for consolidating the coordination of oversight for Internet administration and funding. The FNC brought together representatives from federal agencies that participated in the development of the Internet, including NASA and the Department of Energy. The FNC mission was to 'provide a forum for networking collaborations among Federal agencies to meet their research, education, and operational mission goals and to bridge the gap between the advanced networking technologies being developed by FNC research agencies and the ultimate acquisition of mature versions of these technologies from the commercial sector' (FNC 1990), signalling the privatization trends in the 1990s.

Underlying this multidisciplinary collaboration was a strong emphasis on common values, standards, and protocols, perpetuated from the outset of internetworking by all key players, from funders to developers. The early Internet standards stemmed from a sheer need for coordination: to send information from one computer to another, multiple ways could be employed, but choosing to perform the task in the same manner had obvious benefits. Standardization was of practical value to the early NWG. Based on early decisions and practices in the ARPANET group, standards continue to be open, free of cost, and available in a simple format. The next section explores how we got there through the 'request for comments' enduring routine.

Anchoring Practice: RFCs

The process of establishing standards and protocols was—and continues to be—an exercise in reaching consensus among a community of Internet enthusiasts who volunteer their time to the process. Standards are generally discussed in a layered approach, allowing work in one layer while abstracting the other, and thus respecting the end-to-end principle. While not all specifications of protocols or services for the Internet 'should or will' become Internet standards (according to RFC 1310 from 1992), RFCs may be initiated from early discussions of new research concepts or from status memos about the Internet and they would be marked as 'experimental' or 'informational'. The standards are summarized periodically in the 'IAB Official Protocol Standards'. To reach the final stage, they need to match the following criteria: high quality, prior implementation and testing, openness and fairness, and timeliness. When they are published, they offer specifications that manufacturers of equipment and software can integrate into their production processes.

The RFC process to design standards was born out of sheer need and contingency. Steve Crocker, who coined the term, summarized this clearly in 2012:

As our ideas started to permeate, we knew we had to write them down and we also knew that the mere act of writing them down was going to trigger some reaction, and possibly, even a negative reaction. We were just graduate students, nobody put us in charge, we had no authority. And it came to me to organize these notes that we were going to write and I found myself extremely nervous ... so I hit upon this ... silly trick ... saying we're just going to call every one of them, no matter what they are, they might be super formal or they might be completely informal, but we're just going to call every one of them a Request for Comments. I thought that this was a temporary device that would last a few months until the network was built and we had organized manuals and documentation and so forth. So here we are, more than 40 years later, requests for comments are still the lingua franca for the standards process, RFC is in the Oxford English Dictionary.

To minimize any claim of authority, Crocker, who graduated from UCLA a year before, drafted the first RFC on behalf of the NWG. It was 1969, and internetworking was in its inception phase, consisting of a network established between four research centres: UCLA, SRI, the University of California, Santa Barbara; and the University of Utah in Salt Lake City. Dedicated to the IMP host software, RFC 1 had open questions and diagrams. The idea of an unfinished product on which the others could comment meant cooperation and collective input were welcome. The culture of the rather small community of computer scientists (less than 100) clashed directly with that of the engineers in the telephone networks, where special approvals to introduce new features were needed from hierarchy.

The drafting of RFCs started before email was invented, and in order to reach the members of the group, a copy was sent by post to each research group lead, who would then photocopy more for the rest of the group. As a shared practice, the RFCs became influential across dispersed memberships, at first only in the United States and subsequently across the world. Deciding to avoid patents, restrictions, or financial incentives on the side of the proposers of RFCs meant that agreement could be reached much more easily. As the community became larger, more formal meetings had to be organized. A legitimating purpose was intrinsic to this functional exercise. Until today, the RFCs invite comments from everyone in their first phase as proposed standards, then they become draft standards and finally Internet standards.

The main characteristics of the dominant practice embedded in the RFCs are telling of the in-built values: agreement around the appropriateness of this method, a need for replication and wider adoption. Yet the implementation of standards, just like their creation, is voluntary; they become operational if they are functional and deliver what is needed. The IETF standards are authoritative, being widely adopted despite lacking legal or enforcement powers. Apart from functionality, they are influential because they mobilize the expertise and the support of a larger group beyond the proposers. The decision-making process around RFCs is based on 'rough consensus and running code' (as explained in RFC 7282), in practice designating a majority agreement and a proof of reliable and replicable work. Sometimes rough consensus is determined by participants 'humming' when prompted by the chair of a working group; used as a means to get a 'sense of the room', having either everyone present at the discussion or the separate sides in a discussion humming in favour or keeping silent on a certain proposal.

RFCs are thus also used as a consensus-building ritual. In the vocabulary of technical bodies that have adopted similar consensus-oriented practices, this is equivalent to substantial support for a position or proposal and indicates the absence of substantial hostility. In the wording of RFC 1603 formalizing the process in 1994, a separation is needed between procedural disagreement (for which a review and appeal system was designed) and disagreement on technical decisions:

Technical disagreements may be about specific details or about basic approach. When an issue pertains to preference, it should be resolved within the working group. When a matter pertains to the technical adequacy of a decision, review is encouraged whenever the perceived deficiency is noted. For matters having to do with preference, working group rough consensus will dominate. (Huizer and Crocker 1994)

When the IETF community expanded, the practice of reaching rough consensus needed not only formalization, but also further specification. The creators' imprint was apparent in the way opinions based on preference or interest could be overridden by rough consensus to achieve a functional, user-oriented solution inside an organization with no formal membership. The status of the RFC has consolidated over time into a publication mechanism (RFC series) comprising the totality of drafts discussed, independent of whether they turn into standards or not. As a communal reference point, it re-enacts a specific way of building a community around a shared purpose.

More than documenting developments and enabling dialogue, RFCs also represented a mechanism to include individuals outside established relationships (the small group of people in ARPA-related projects), as they could follow the progress at ARPANET and keep abreast of the technical advances from the sidelines. The NIC, based at the Stanford Research Institute, played a key role as a dissemination node, and its example was followed by successor organizations. Through the work of the NIC, more and more decisions, from ad-hoc groups to formalized procedures, started to be documented, in response to the need for 'getting things done' when a higher number of people became involved; it also created a domestic and an international audience, as attention was focused on successful experiments; and it increased transparency.

Yet the early Internet was overwhelmingly based on English-language content, limited access to outsiders, and was mostly dominated by male researchers and technologists. Most of the information transmitted was textual, making the environment relatively homogenous. The term 'open Internet'— though in many cases open standards were a necessity of the time—was not formally introduced until March 1992, when Lyman Chapin, the chairman of the IAB, published the RFC 1310 entitled 'Internet Standards Process' (Russell 2014). The document outlined procedures 'intended to provide a clear, open, and objective basis for developing, evaluating, and adopting Internet Standards for protocols and services' and identified openness and fairness as a key goal for Internet standardization.

Characteristic of Internet standard-setting organizations was a certain emulation of existing practices in the small community forming at the time: the NWG model was followed when establishing the INWG, and the IENs were modelled on the RFCs format. Moreover, the tradition of delegating decision-making to specialized committees for different purposes (providing information, legal, technical matters, etc.) continued to be observed by technical bodies. Among these, the IETF remains a relatively informal and loosely institutionalized standardization body, with no membership, no fees, and no board of directors, preserving the principles developed in the early days of the Internet.

As an anchoring routine shared more broadly by the technical community based on the IETF practice, the RFC series reveals the like-mindedness of the initial group of practitioners who could thus reaffirm the joint enterprise they took part in. Importantly, it shows how practice fostered learning among old and new members, transforming identities and institutionalizing the norm of open and inclusive participation in discussions. This pattern of engagement is central to the evolution of the field, inspiring wide adoption in the Internet governance community.

Synopsis

This chapter showed that in the early days, the Internet was a rather homogenous domain, closely linked to computer science and networking experiments. Different forms of governance, combining public and private initiatives, were profiling, and that initial interaction shaped the way in which the Internet evolved. Until the commercial Internet in the mid-1990s, the predominant governance route for Internet-related decisions was the creation of standards and protocols to make different networks interoperable. Such processes were regulated via informal interactions among a relatively small group of pioneers able to cross sectoral boundaries.

Around this, a set of institutions formed—at first completely informal, later formalized—performing different functions as part of governing the network. In that sense, governance activities—primarily coordination and standardization—were set in place without being referred to as such. Notably, hybrid arrangements between academia, governmental funding agencies, and large computer companies, such as NSFNET, expanded the reach of the network. The process of governance diversification and transformation was led by a number of scientists-cum-practitioners, such as Vint Cerf, Bob Kahn, and Tim Berners-Lee, who were at the forefront of ad-hoc groups formed to answer functional problems. At the international level, through their leadership work and the founding of institutions, a transnational policy network started to form. Prior to 1993, with the exception of the work conducted around the OSI standard, most governance mechanisms at the global level remained telecommunications-specific and included more instruments with binding character than soft law.[23]

Despite the sustained funding directed first to ARPANET and later to NSFNET, the divergent agendas of funding agencies and their prioritization of various interests allowed for supporting innovative, complementary areas of research, such as AI, database management, and cryptography. This fragmentation of resources opened up the space for collaboration. When the transfer of responsibilities towards NSF started, infrastructure costs continued to be shared. While ARPA funded research groups rather than individuals, involving the same scientists ensured that developments could build on each other and that an early community could be formed. The management style also reflected trust-based contracting and long-term relationships with private providers, at first with BBN and later with IBM, MERIT, and NSI, contracted to do the high-speed upgrade for NSFNET in 1987.

The majority of pioneers continued to play key roles in the development of the network and the institutional architecture evolving around it. Kahn and Cerf formed ISOC in 1992 as an institutional home for IAB and IETF, Postel continued to run IANA and prepared its transition to the ICANN. Academic networks and universities—in particular those that developed computer science departments such as MIT, Stanford, UC Berkeley, UCLA—remained strongly involved in Internet advancements. The ARPA computer network benefited from generous funding and a wide degree of autonomy for the researchers, mostly brought in through peer-selection, via personal networks and scientific conferences (Hafner 1998; Abbate 1999). The network expanded to include a number of university centres not connected with ARPANET initially. Later on, a set of functionalities developed in the private sector were added to what became a public use network. Yet, as early as the first decade of ARPANET, politicization trends emerged: the high stakes were indicated by a number of instances of contestation, such as the early protocol 'war' (TCP/IP vs. OSI), the efforts to create interconnected networks in the private sector, and the push towards commercialization.

---

[23] In addition to their Declaration on Transborder Data Flows (1985), OECD prepared its Guidelines for the security of information systems as early as 1992.

4

Privatization and Globalization of the Internet

The 'Internet governance' discussions formally started around 1995, with the commercialization of the network that spurred out of the National Science Foundation Network (NSFNET) (Sylvan 2014). Two key advancements dating back to this period stand at the basis of the current functioning of the Internet: the development of the infrastructure, on the one hand, and of web applications and *dotcoms* on the other. Multiple for-profit Internet backbone and access providers (e.g. dial-up systems of CompuServe, America Online, Prodigy) emerged when the Internet was privatized. At first, Internet Service Providers (ISPs) preferred connections to the backbone networks in the United States, where more services and content were available. In many cases, such connections also meant charges lower than what the telecommunication monopolies in many countries asked for. As the number of providers grew, options for connection diversified and a variety of services became available at the regional and local levels, though unevenly spread across continents. The large amount of user-generated content, which set the Internet apart from other communications media, also became a competitive advantage. This fostered the emergence of an online market for domain names, a highly contentious issue for global regulation.

Mirroring the exponential growth of the network, the scale of Internet operations expanded at an unprecedented pace during the mid-1990s; international connections became the norm, rather than the exception. The driver of innovation throughout this period was the so-called 'knowledge-creating company' (Nonaka and Takeuchi 1995), which used the production of knowledge, including user-generated content, for developing or improving products and services. Aided by a permissive regulatory approach, advancements in website development, and the e-commerce boom, the Internet became the engine of economic growth in the 1990s in most developed countries.

This chapter investigates the privatization trends, the creation of the Internet Corporation for Assigned Names and Numbers (ICANN) as a core institution for the technical management of the Internet, and the expansion of the global online market. It analyses the distinctive features of governance arrangements from the mid-1990s to the early 2000s, which epitomize 'the search for governance models coherent with the neoliberal globalisation process' (Chenou 2014, 338). Here, I analyse the emergence of what is sometimes referred to as the 'private governance of the Internet', growing from the national level to a global scale. Applying the theoretical framework presented in Chapter 2, the articulation of governance during this period is deconstructed empirically to reveal the tensions of regulation and institutionalization.

A Global Internet (Fairy) Tale: Market Emergence

Despite its importance, a critical history of the commercialization of the Internet is a rare occurrence in Internet governance (IG).[1] The expansion of the Internet and the subsequent crisis of the late 1990s left an imprint: beyond shaking the enthusiasm of the early investors, it also shaped the very basics of the market and the modern structures of online advertising. Amid regulatory disputes, business practices became a dominant modality of governance, consonant with the classical definition of private authority as the 'ability by non-state actors to cooperate across borders to establish rules and standards of behaviour accepted as legitimate by agents not involved in their definition' (Noelke and Graz 2008, 2). Profit-seeking entities became co-creators of standards and norms and, in certain cases, held discretionary power for law enforcement, be it for criminal investigations or for the protection of intellectual property rights. The transformation of private intermediaries into law-enforcement institutions emerged as a reality early on, showing that the Internet space was hybrid by definition. Three main developments marked this period: the expansion of the infrastructure, the *dotcom* market, and the advent of web applications.

Infrastructure

The transition from a national network (with a few external links) to a global network of networks happened in a rather short time-span: from 1993 to 1995. The formal involvement of the private sector in the functioning of the network started a few years before on the NSFNET. When the higher-speed upgrade was authorized in 1987, NSFNET delegated the task to a consortium

---

[1] A notable exception here is Crain (2014).

known as Advanced Network and Services, led by Merit Network, Inc., IBM, and MCI. A number of commercial experiments—such as the MCI email service, introduced by Vint Cerf[2]—were tested and allowed on the NSFNET before the 1990s. When the Border Gateway Protocol was introduced in 1994, the network architecture was improved with the facilitated external Internet routing (the move of IP packets from sender to recipient across numerous autonomous networks) and decentralization. In reality, the Internet reached millions of homes before being placed on international agendas or discussed as a global issue. And, unlike the early Internet experiments, the globalization of the Internet did not rely on state subsidies anymore.

When the NSFNET was decommissioned in April 1995, the funds recovered from its dismantling were redistributed to regional networks to buy connectivity from the private providers that started to mushroom. The transition to the commercial Internet was completed through the introduction of five NSF-designated and partially funded network access points. A few years later, the role of access points was minimized as the majority of ISPs started contracting directly with backbone and transit providers. Technical standardization, infrastructure, and interconnection remained concealed to the public eye for the largest part of the Internet evolution, yet their profile on the political agenda was raised when the Internet became global.

The shift from government-owned to privately owned infrastructure was overseen by Steve Wolff from the NSF, who retrospectively assessed that it was necessary to conduct the transition in a coordinated fashion to maintain the network as a single Internet, rather than multiple separate networks. He also reiterated the commitment of the NSF to ensuring that the academic community would not remain aloof. In the words of Wolff:

There had to be commercial activity to help support networking, to help build volume on the network. That would get the cost down for everybody, including the academic community, which is what NSF was supposed to be doing. (NSF n.d.)

In 1995, responding to a solicitation made in 1993, NSF awarded contracts for three network access points to serve as links to commercial networks and one routing arbiter for exchange of traffic. It also signed a cooperative agreement for a new-generation Backbone Network Service, decommissioning NSFNET. But a global Internet required much more.

---

[2] Cerf acted as vice-president of MCI Digital Information Services from 1982 to 1986, before joining Bob Kahn at the Corporation for National Research Initiatives (CNRI). In the beginning, CNRI hosted the secretariat of the Internet Engineering Task Force (IETF), before moving under the Internet Society (ISOC).

To begin with, the physical connection with other parts of the world needed to be improved; this expansion process was led by the private sector. The underlying infrastructure on which the Internet was growing rapidly relied on submarine cables, an interconnected network originally used for telegraphy. The first of the transatlantic cables, carrying telegraphic correspondence between the United States and the United Kingdom was laid in 1859 by the Atlantic Telegraph Company. Ever since, underwater cables evolved from electromagnetic copper cables to fibre optic to support the faster transmission of messages. Historically, the telegraph cables were owned by the operators. Later on, the consortium model dominated, consisting of splitting the cost of submarine cables among telecommunication operators, but also sharing the risks and reducing competition. In the early 1990s, a strong push for adopting a common approach to the global Internet infrastructure came from the Telecommunication Standardization Sector of the International Telecommunication Union (ITU). The body has played an important role in drafting recommendations and guidelines for undersea cable development and deployment ever since. In 1958, the International Cable Protection Committee (ICPC) was established to serve as the undersea cable operators association, providing representation and leadership in international policy processes. The ICPC also acted as a forum for information exchange, technical expertise, and legal and environmental advice for its members.

Submarine connections currently carry 99 per cent of transoceanic digital communication and represent a billion-dollar business (Chesnoy 2015; Starosielski 2015). The fastest growth of this industry was registered at the end of the 1990s during the *dotcom* bubble. Part of what made the latter possible was the expansion of the infrastructure to Europe, Asia, and Latin America. The cables circling the African continent were laid down later, the first three being placed between 2000 and 2004.

Over the years, three tiers of networks developed, differentiated[3] according to whether they provided bandwidth (tier 1 and 2) or Internet services (tier 3). Tier 1 networks, such as AT&T, Verizon, or NTT Communications, operate based on peer-to-peer agreements, generally covered by non-disclosure clauses. There are no overt settlements among tier 1 networks, meaning they do not charge among themselves for traffic sent over the networks. Tier 2 networks pay transit fees to tier 1 providers, while tier 3 ISPs pay to tier 2 networks. Speaking to the high degree of informality that persists in the infrastructure layer, the largest part of the agreements was not—and is not, to the present day—recorded in writing. A Packet Clearing House study from

---

[3] This differentiation, frequently used by the industry, is a functional one that has not been formalized.

2010 to 2011 brings evidence that of 142,210 interconnection and peering agreements (representing approximately 86 per cent of all Internet carriers at the time), only 0.49 per cent were written.

Domain Name Registrations

The most contentious issue in the 1990s was the creation of a market for domain names. The commercial impact of domain name system (DNS) registrations changed the outlook of the decade, with the emergence of companies whose activities and profits derived directly from the Internet, the so-called *dotcoms*. In the shaping of the nascent market, the NSF (under the leadership of Steve Wolff) continued to play a steering role. The Department of Defense (DoD) subsidies for domain registrations ended in the early 1990s, and responsibility for non-military domains was transferred to NSF, which continued to subsidize the civilian Internet and awarded, in 1993, a five-year contract for managing it to Network Solutions, Inc. (NSI), at the time supporting around 7,500 domains. It was the 'information superhighway' time, and the potential of the Internet was just beginning to be explored.

A 1994 National Research Council report, 'Realizing the information future: the Internet and beyond', commissioned by NSF and prepared by a team chaired by Kleinrock,[4] articulated the benefits of this evolution, but also pointed to a number of issues that became heatedly debated throughout the decade: intellectual property rights, regulation for the Internet, pricing, education, and ethics. Evaluating the performance of the InterNIC contractors through an expert panel, NSF followed the expert recommendation and authorized the NSI to begin charging for *.com* domain name registrations. In 1995, the NSF 'acceptable use policy' was ended, and NSI was authorized to charge annual fees for generic Top-Level Domain names (such as *.com* and *.net*) until 1998. In this period, the NSI profits increased from $5 million to approximately $94 million.

Initial registration would cost $100 for the first two years (minimum amount of time for registration), with a subsequent annual renewal of $50. The informal allocation of domains—based on the interactions in the small technical and academic network at the time of the DNS expansion—was perpetuated by NSI, their allocation of domains also being performed on a first come, first served basis.

The NSF continued to subsidise the *.edu* registrations as well as, for a limited time, the *.gov* domains. The high increase in registrations compelled

---

[4] Among the members were also Kahn and Clark.

InterNIC to adopt automatic processing and to no longer distinguish between different types of registrants for *.com*, *.net*, and *.org*[5] (Mueller 2004, 112). Unlike manual processing, no reviews were performed under the new model, making the InterNIC domain registrations more popular than country-code domains, which were generally more restrictively allocated. Notably, by July 1996, the number of registrations under InterNIC was 3.96 million, compared to only 1.52 million for the seven largest country domains combined: the United Kingdom, Japan, Germany, Australia, Canada, the Netherlands, and France (Mueller 2004, 114). The interest in *.com* second level domain names skyrocketed from 200 applications per month in January 1993 to more than 30,000 by late 1995, and to more than 200,000 by January 1998. For total registrations, that meant an increase from less than 15,000 *.com* second level domains in 1992 to approximately one million in January 1995 and over 8 million by 1998 (Post and Kehl 2015). This high number of registrations drove the Internet browser developers to make *.com* the default (Mueller 2004) and, in turn, increased the value of the domain.[6]

This gave way to the formation of the so-called '*dotcom* bubble',[7] with a burst around 2001. What became widespread during the 1990s was the practice of cybersquatting: the registration, trafficking in, or use of an Internet domain name with bad faith intent to profit from a trademark belonging to someone else. Intellectual property disputes became a concern, bringing into sharper focus the DNS and the authority over it. In reaction to trademark lawsuits, NSI issued a Domain Dispute Resolution Policy Statement in July 1995 for InterNIC-operated domains, serving two purposes. The first was to make public the fact that it 'had neither the legal resources nor the legal obligation to screen requested Domain Names to determine if the use of a Domain Name by an Applicant may infringe upon the right(s) of a third party' (NSI 1995, § 1). The second purpose was to impose an obligation on the registrants to certify that there was no infringement or interference with trademarks or intellectual property for the proposed registration and that there was bona fide intention in the use of the name. NSI reserved the right to withdraw or transfer a domain name if a court or an arbitration panel so decided. Under this policy, there was a massive increase in dispute resolutions cases, going from around 200 in 1995 to over 907 in 1997. In mid-1998,

---

[5] In the process, the practice of assigning one domain name per person was also renounced.

[6] In the beginning, no differentiation was made in the fees perceived for domain names, all of them being charged the same amount.

[7] In academic parlance, the '*dotcom* bubble' is generally seen as an economic cycle, between the late-1990s and early-2000s, whereas the Internet boom refers to the constant growth of the Internet following the introduction of the World Wide Web (WWW) and search engines.

the number of cases exceeded 750. The creation of ICANN later that year—which solved this problem—is discussed further in this chapter.

Throughout this period, the NSI had physical possession of the 'A' root, while Jon Postel (under contract with DoD, still physically based at the University of Southern California) continued to have policy authority over top-level domain names approval and allocation (Weinberg 2011). In 1995, the control of the main research backbone was entrusted to MCI Communications, operating alongside other commercial, academic, and non-profit networks.

Web Applications, Information Intermediaries, and E-commerce

Following the US administration's decision to allow commercial Internet activities, the network became the largest global market; the development of web applications facilitated the e-commerce boom and raised the political profile of the Internet. It was the time of the 'information superhighway', as the Clinton-Gore electoral campaign highlighted. In 1993, the WWW, publicly released two years before, was popularized through the broad adoption of the Mosaic browser, co-programmed by Marc Andreessen. Email and file sharing, video and audio streaming, web pages, and voice telephony, or interactive multi-player games all became profitable areas of investment. To a large extent, this market boom tapped into the potential of the Internet architecture itself, with its separation of transport and application layers, as the Internet protocol remained indifferent to the packets it carried.

Yahoo.com, eBay.com, and msn.com were all launched in 1995. Amazon, created one year earlier, started as an online bookstore, but soon diversified its offer to software, video, and music downloading, as well as commerce in tangible goods. Alongside the giants of the day, many businesses opening up online promised overnight success and attracted investors effortlessly. Cassidy (2002) revealed that the myth of 'companies started in a garage' was so strong at the time that Jeff Bezos, the founder of Amazon, rented a house with a garage in Seattle to preserve it. In 1995, Netscape Navigator was launched featuring the secure sockets layer, a protocol for encrypting information, used primarily for transactions. Microsoft introduced Internet Explorer at the end of that year.

Online advertisements also contributed to shaping this virtual market. The first online ad, dating back to 1994, was an art museum 'banner ad' sponsored by AT&T which appeared on HotWired.com. This gave way to one of the most successful business models of the Internet era—also known as 'third-party advertising'—based on indexing content and increasingly more targeted marketing.

Information intermediation, closely linked to operations such as profiling, transactions, or advertising, offered more than what the infrastructure providers could promise, namely carrying information from point A to point B. The selection, ranking, aggregation, and sharing of content created by others (generally users) proved to be extremely profitable. Google—currently operating the most successful search engine worldwide—was formally registered in 1998, with the mission to 'index the world's information'. This fast-expanding company originally used Stanford University's website with the domain *google.stanford.edu* for the development of the search engine, to be later incorporated as a company in a garage in Menlo Park, California. In 2000, Google launched AdWords, a system for selling search advertising with real-time auctions for keywords.

Online social networks began developing in 1997, when Six Degrees facilitated contact with former school mates. They were inspired by the user-created Usenet discussion and bulletin boards of the 1980s. In 2002, MySpace and Friendster were among the first to target primarily young people and became more widely used as Internet penetration rates increased. Facebook was released in 2004, and it was built on the original Facemash platform that Mark Zuckerberg designed in 2003 for his fellow Harvard students. The development of social networking sites remained largely outside regulatory purview during their first years of operation, encouraged to self-regulate.

The *dotcom* bubble was built on enthusiastic confidence and stock speculation for extra profits sought by an increasing number of Internet-based companies (known as *dotcoms*)[8] and venture capital investment firms. California's Silicon Valley and New York's financial district were at the centre of it. In the crash, many companies went bankrupt, while others suffered huge recessions: the case of Amazon.com is emblematic, with shares dropping from 107 to 7 before starting to recover steadily. Relying on a 'first mover advantage' into a new market, company managers predominantly pursued fast business development strategies that required substantial financial backing. This mostly came via risk investment, as nearly 80 per cent of all venture capital resources went to Internet companies in 1999 and 2000. Investment growth went from about $7 billion in 1995 to nearly $100 billion in 2000, dropping to less than $40 billion per year for the next decade (Zook 2008).

What remained unchanged before and after the *dotcom* bubble was the relatively strong position of information intermediaries. With data as their

---

[8] This included ISPs such as Netscape, Amazon, Yahoo, etc., but also online advertising companies such as DoubleClick.

main asset, they started to set the technical constraints and guidelines for social behaviour online, defining the codes of conduct for activities ranging from defamation to cyberbullying and obscenity. The terms of service, the equivalent of the Acceptable Use policy in the early days of the NSFNET, were commonly used to define the conduct of the users. The permissive regulatory environment in the United States led to a concentration of key players in the Silicon Valley, a region of California that became a leading innovation hub following the invention of the microprocessor and microcomputer in the 1970s.

Regulatory Framework

The globalization of the commercial Internet around the mid-1990s coincided with the spread of hybrid governance, involving both the public and the private sector, often with blurry delimitations of their functions and attributions. Replacing the 1934 Communications Act, the Telecommunications Act signed into law by President Clinton in 1996 defined the regulatory regime for services using the same underlying infrastructure. It separated voice telephone services and cable television from information services, which remained added-value services (comprising services offering a capability for generating, acquiring, storing, transforming, processing, retrieving, utilizing, or making available information via telecommunications). The law separated 'telecommunications carriers' from Internet services carriers, placing broadcasting and spectrum allotment for the Internet under a different regime. The first broadband service, starting at 256 Kbps, was introduced in the United States shortly after by @Home.

The Telecommunications Act of 1996 also included a controversial section: the Communications Decency Act (CDA) criminalized the knowing transmission of 'obscene or indecent' messages to any recipient under 18; and also knowingly sending to a person under 18 anything 'that, in context, depicts or describes, in terms patently offensive as measured by contemporary community standards, sexual or excretory activities or organs'. That section of the CDA was declared unconstitutional on freedom of expression and medical grounds in the first major Supreme Court ruling on the regulation of materials distributed online, *Reno v. American Civil Liberties Union* (1997), but that did not reduce the plea to regulate online indecency.

Importantly, the CDA also introduced, in section 230, one of the most important provisions for information intermediaries in the history of the Internet, namely protection from liability for the online actions of their users.

Accordingly, section 230, still valid today, states that 'no provider or user of an interactive computer service shall be treated as the publisher or speaker of any information provided by another information content provider'. With few limitations in place for criminal and intellectual property-based claims, this regime for the protection of intermediaries represented a cornerstone for private governing, endowing the intermediaries with rule-setting power after a long legal dispute.[9]

Being the first country to introduce protections against liability for online platforms, the United States established itself as a safe haven for Internet services, attracting the majority of providers. An outcome of this favourable legal environment was the growth of Silicon Valley into a prominent hub for high-tech innovation. Moreover, at the international level, the CDA triggered John Perry Barlow's famous declaration on the Independence of Cyberspace written in Davos, Switzerland, hailing a space in which governments would have no role to play:

> Governments derive their just powers from the consent of the governed. You have neither solicited nor received ours. We did not invite you. You do not know us, nor do you know our world. Cyberspace does not lie within your borders. Do not think that you can build it, as though it were a public construction project. You cannot. It is an act of nature and it grows itself through our collective actions. (Barlow 1996)

The decade starting around the time Barlow wrote his declaration was marked by strong privatization tendencies, with governmental intervention providing the space for industry self-regulation in the 'shadow of hierarchy'.[10] The deregulatory agenda of the Clinton administration was enhanced with the introduction of the 'Framework for global electronic commerce' in 1997, which proposed a strategy for promoting global commerce via the Internet and empowering the Department of Commerce to be the lead agency on this initiative. According to the document, 'governments must adopt a non-regulatory, market-oriented approach to electronic commerce' based on a

---

[9] The CDA resulted out of a longer legal battle, fought around two court cases decided in New York in the early 1990s, with conflicting outcomes. In the first of these, the 1991 case *Cubby, Inc. v. CompuServe, Inc.*, the court concluded that CompuServe could not be held responsible for the defamatory comments posted by a special-interest forum columnist against a competitor as it did not review forum content before publication. In the second case, the 1995 case *Stratton Oakmont, Inc. v. Prodigy Servs. Co.*, the court found that Prodigy, a web service company with more than 2 million subscribers and over 60,000 postings a day, did not act as a blind host. It had, in the past, moderated some of its online message boards and deleted posts for 'offensiveness and bad taste', which, for the court, meant that it acted as a publisher and was thus liable for defamatory postings.

[10] According to Héritier and Eckert (2008), industry self-regulation is more likely to appear when positive incentives are provided or when the threat of legislation is present.

decentralized, contractual model of law in order for the Internet to deliver its full economic potential (White House 1997). The first principle of that roadmap, that 'the private sector should lead', set the standard for the globalization of the Internet. It envisioned governmental oversight applicable only to nine areas of regulation, including customs and taxation, electronic payments, intellectual property protection, privacy, security, and technical standards.

Not only did the US government delegate a number of functions to businesses, it also actively shaped the future global market. The value and potential of the Internet were widely recognized when the Fourth Protocol to the General Agreement on Trade in Services entered into force in 1998. This Protocol stirred the liberalization of telecom markets, through the privatization of national monopolies, the promotion of competitive services, and the establishment of national regulators.

New Rules under Construction

The framework for global electronic commerce was accompanied by a Presidential directive calling on the Department of Commerce to 'support efforts to make the governance of the domain name system private and competitive and to create a contractually based self-regulatory regime that deals with potential conflicts between domain name usage and trademark laws on a global basis' (Smith 2002). In response to this, the Department issued a Request for Comment on domain name administration to which it received more than 650 comments.

What prefaced this move by the US administration was a heated debate around the creation of new top-level domains (TLDs). This matter was approached by the technical community on a dedicated mailing-list, *newdom,* created in September 1995. Following discussions on this list, an Internet draft was issued, 'New Registries and the Delegation of International Top-Level Domains' widely known as 'draft-postel', which proposed the introduction of 150 new top-level domain names, multiple registries for *.com* and other domains and the chartering of Internet Assigned Numbers Authority (IANA) by ISOC. Proposals for alternative TLDs were also popular at the time, backed by entities like AlterNIC, Iperdrome, or pgmedia, which intended to create and sell new TLDs such as *.web*, *.arts*, or *.xxx*. While technically feasible, these domain names were not authorized by IANA to be added to the root, and NSI refused to make them visible, meaning that they had a minimal perceived value for potential buyers.

Most importantly, the draft-postel grouping faced the coalition led by the incumbent, the NSI, gathering support around a competing proposal, the International Forum for the White Paper (IFWP). NSI had been in charge of administering additions and deletions to the authoritative root server database since 1993, in accordance with the cooperative agreement it had signed first with the NSF, and later with the Department of Commerce (DoC). In 1998, the IFWP held public meetings in Reston (Virginia), Geneva, Singapore, and Buenos Aires.[11] A smaller successor group to the IFWP, referred to as the Boston Working Group, put forward a proposal for the National Telecommunications and Information Administration (NTIA).

At the time, private sector consensus was also shaped in the framework of a different platform, the Global Internet Project (GIP) formed in 1996. The GIP was less vocal, but brought together a highly influential group of senior executives of sixteen Internet and e-commerce companies (including MCI-Worldcom, IBM, etc.). It served as an advisory committee to the World Information and Telecommunication Association (WITSA), a consortium of ICT industry associations worldwide. In 1998, the GIP was led by IBM's vice-president for Internet technology, John Patrick and started working on IG by providing strategic direction for corporate interests, which would be subsequently implemented by the Information Technology Association of America, a Washington-based business lobby group hosting the secretariat of WITSA. The primary goal of the GIP was, in their phrasing, 'not to shape government regulation, but instead promote industry actions that will minimize the need for such regulation'. Alongside the GIP, the International Chamber of Commerce also contributed to the White Paper debates presenting an Internet economy perspective.

In response to the harsh critiques to the Postel plan, ISOC announced, in mid-November 1996, the formation of the International Ad Hoc Committee (IAHC). The IAHC was chaired by ISOC's Don Health and comprised representatives of standard-setting organizations such as the IETF, intellectual property organizations such as the World Intellectual Property Organization (WIPO), as well as the International Trademark Association (INTA) and civil society and business representatives. Joining them was also a delegate from the NSF. The proposal they came up with differed from the Postel plan in three regards. First, it projected the addition of seven new generic TLDs[12] to the DNS, as opposed to the 150 suggested before. Second, it introduced the functional differentiation of the registry and registrar functions, which did

---

[11] Harvard's Berkman Center was originally involved in facilitating the meetings, and withdrew subsequently.
[12] The new gTLDs proposed were: *.web*, *.rec*, *.info*, *.firm*, *.store*, *.nom*, *.arts*.

not exist in the NSI model. The registry function referred to the collection, storage, and maintenance of data, alongside the operation of name servers that provided updated authoritative lists of domains. The registrar performed the retail function, managing the reservation of the domain names (if not already taken).

To manage the new governance system, the IAHC plan envisioned a global monopoly registry co-owned by multiple, competing registrars, sharing access to the same TLDs. The total number of registrars was limited to twenty-eight companies selected by lottery, four for each of the seven geographical regions. Registrars would be incorporated in a not-for-profit Council of Registrars (CORE) headquartered in Geneva, Switzerland, upon an entry fee of $20,000 and a monthly payment of $2,000. For the stewardship of the domain-name space, a Policy Oversight Committee would be formed, grouping represen-tatives of ISOC, IANA, Internet Activities Board (IAB), CORE, but also the ITU, WIPO, and INTA (similar to the composition of the IAHC), sup-ported by the Policy Advisory Board that could be joined by any signatory of this governance framework. The third key difference was the introduc-tion of a complex mandatory arbitration system centred on domain name challenge panels placed under WIPO's Arbitration and Mediation Center. The IAHC later drafted the Generic Top-Level Domain Memorandum of Understanding (gTLD-MoU).

Glaringly, the issue of trademarks in Internet domain names was neglected by the technical community despite its increasing commercial and political salience at the time. In contrast, the IAHC attempt to design a system that took into account the varied interests garnered more support, just like the NSI initiative bringing together private stakeholders under the IFWP. Both had a multi-stakeholder composition: the IAHC gathered representatives from various intergovernmental organizations such as the ITU, WIPO, the US NSF, trademark interest representatives, and intellectual property owners, whereas the IFWP, steered by NSI, had the private sector and members of academia involved.

The most significant attempt to internationalize the debates and to include civil society actors, the IFWP, was by-passed in the final stages of the creation of ICANN. In March 1997, the gTLD-MoU was signed by Heath and Postel in an official ceremony in Geneva at the ITU. It was drafted by the IAHC, building on support from trademark owners. In spite of the controversies it stirred, the document garnered the support of over 223 public and private or-ganizations several months after its announcement, in particular from entities outside the United States. The ITU Secretary-General presented the MoU as a form of 'voluntary multilateralism' (Tarjanne 1997) and his institution offered to serve as the official repository of the MoU. Opposing the MoU were US multinationals such as IBM and AT&T, the incumbent NSI, but also European companies such as British Telecom, trademark holders, and those concerned with a more prominent role of the ITU in Internet matters, including the US government.

At the time, more than half of Internet users were based in the United States.[13] A proposal for creating a new governance system outside the United States prompted the formation of the Interagency Working Group in the US government. As the MoU was gaining momentum, Secretary of State Madeline Albright confirmed, in a cable sent to the US mission in Geneva on 1 May 1997, that the US government 'has not yet developed a position on any of the proposals to reform the Internet domain name system, including the gTLD-MoU, nor on the appropriate role, if any, of the ITU, WIPO, or other international organisations in the administration of the Internet' (cited in Mueller 2004, 157). The day after, the Interagency Working Group announced that it opposed the plan. On 2 July 1997, the DoC issued a Request for Comments on DNS administration, soliciting public comments on four specific aspects: overall framework, the creation of new TLDs, policies for domain name registrars, and trademark issues. More than 430 comments—totalling over 1,500 pages—were received during the comment period. This astonishing interest in the direction the DNS privatization would take is indicative of the high stakes in the process and the growing awareness around it.

Before the issue was settled, Jon Postel demonstrated his authority over the root though a redirection of the root server from NSI to IANA at the beginning of 1998. This was done by eight of the twelve operators of the Internet's regional root nameservers. The remaining four were under the direct control of the US government. Although the transfer did not affect the experience of the users, Postel was forced by senior US officials to restore the management of the DNS and complied with the request. His action also prompted a formal response from the NTIA, which issued 'A proposal to improve technical management of Internet names and addresses' the week after, on 30 January 1998. The proposed rulemaking, or 'Green Paper', was published in the Federal Register on 20 February, and invited comments on the outline of the process by which the US government planned to privatize the DNS. Among the rationales listed were the need to move away from ad-hoc decision-making by individuals and entities not formally accountable to the Internet community and the inadequacy of continuous funding from US research agencies (NSF and the Defense Advanced Research Projects Agency

---

[13] According to the US Census Bureau data, there were more than 40 million Internet users in the United States in 1997.

(DARPA)) for an increasingly more commercial Internet. In the process, the DoC would coordinate the US government policy role.

On 10 June 1998, the DoC announced in a 'White Paper' its readiness to sign an agreement with a new non-profit corporation formed by private sector Internet stakeholders. The policy statement mentioned that 'overall policy guidance and control of the [TLDs] and the Internet root server system should be vested in a single organization that is representative of Internet users around the globe' (NTIA 1998). The organization would be constituted based on the four principles put forward in the public consultation: Internet stability, competition, private bottom-up coordination, and global representation.

Postel continued to play a key role in the process. He appointed the IAHC members and, together with IBM's Brian Carpenter, active in the GIP under the IBM leadership and chair of the IAB, also appointed an IANA Transition Advisory Group (ITAG) in 1998. With five out of its six members with for-profit affiliations,[14] the ITAG reflected the strong position of the private sector at the time and throughout the negotiations. The Postel-led group subsequently established ICANN in September 1998 as a private, California-based, not-for-profit corporation. In September 1998, the DoC signed an MoU with NSF for transferring the responsibilities performed by NSI to the DoC, which then amended the agreement to continue to have Network Solutions as the operator of the Authoritative root server, this time under the direction of the DoC (GAO 2000).

That month, ICANN was legally incorporated and indicated to the DoC that it would submit a bid in response to the policy statement. In October, the DoC signed three agreements with ICANN: (a) an MoU for a joint DNS project, (b) a cooperative research and development agreement, and (c) a sole source contract for technical function relating to the coordination of the DNS (GAO 2000). The four months that passed between the White Paper and the allocation of the decision to ICANN were marked by intense debates. The innovative approach adopted by the US administration[15] was explicit in the DoC NTIA prioritization of 'private sector leadership' and

[14] The ITAG had six members: Brian Carpenter (IBM and IAB), Randy Bush (Verio, Inc.), David Farber (University of Pennsylvania), Geoff Huston (Telstra), John Klensin (MCI), and Steve Wolff (Cisco). Wolff formerly acted as director of NSF's Computer and Information Sciences and Engineering Division, supervising the transition to the commercial Internet. He joined Cisco in 1994.

[15] This approach also faced harsh critiques, such as the one from the Harvard professor Lawrence Lessig: 'we are creating the most significant jurisdiction since the Louisiana purchase ... and we are building it outside the review of the Constitution' (2006, 318).

'industry self-regulation'.[16] According to Stuart Lynn, president and CEO of the Corporation between 2001 and 2003, ICANN was to serve as an alternative to the traditional multilateral treaty model pre-dating the Internet:

> I have come to the conclusion that the original concept of a purely private sector body, based on consensus and consent, had been shown to be impractical ... But I am also convinced that, for a resource as changeable and dynamic as the Internet, a traditional governmental approach as an alternative to ICANN remains a bad idea. (Lynn 2002)

At the end of 1998, ICANN was granted the authority to set policy for and manage the DNS, as well as the allocation and assignment of Internet Protocol (IP) addresses. It operated on a contractual basis, primarily with registries (in charge of operating and administering the master database of each TLD name registered) and accredited registrars (the companies or organizations from which consumers buy domain names). The delegation of authority from the US government was, however, not complete. The DoC retained 'residual authority' (Mueller 2004) over the DNS root via the IANA functions for longer than the two-year period originally envisioned, which continued to be the focus of debates for the next two decades. The voice of developing countries was little heard in these initial negotiations establishing the governance framework for the technical ruling of domain names and related market formation.

The Creation of ICANN

Both the White Paper and the initial Board of ICANN presented the new organization as a 'technical coordinator'. The narrow mandate thus delimited would serve a legitimation purpose for the subsequent conflicts around the functions to be performed in the new context. The policymaking process within ICANN and the extensive influence of the US government remained a Gordian knot over the years. In ICANN's phrasing, 'policy' refers to guidelines for making technical decisions, for instance the way in which parameters for protocols are assigned, or the conditions under which the IP address blocks are allocated or country-code top-level domains (cc-TLDs) are redelegated. Similarly, policies could regard the creation of new TLDs and

---

[16] For Mueller (1999, 504), industry self-regulation was 'an appealing label for a process that could be more accurately described as the US government brokering a behind-the-scenes deal among what it perceived as the major players—both private and governmental' (in relation to the creation of ICANN).

related specifications as discussed in the key proposals preceding the establishment of ICANN.

The 1998 White Paper made reference to bottom-up governance as a characteristic of Internet development and specified that 'the US government policy applies only to management of Internet names and addresses and does not set out a system of Internet "governance"'. In a written exchange with consumer advocates back in 1999, Esther Dyson, Chair of the ICANN Board of Directors, made the following statement:

> The White Paper articulates no Internet governance role for ICANN, and the Initial Board shares that (negative) view. Therefore, ICANN does not 'aspire to address' any Internet governance issues; in effect, it governs the plumbing, not the people. It has a very limited mandate to administer certain (largely technical) aspects of the Internet infrastructure in general and the Domain Name System in particular. (Dyson 1999)

However, for almost a decade after, Internet governance was synonymous with the management of technical resources and the work of ICANN (Mueller 2004; Chenou and Radu 2015). The attention it raised was mostly due to the legitimacy and accountability concerns around its new role. To overcome the tensions of a UN- versus a US-solution and to respond to the increasing number of cybersquatting cases, WIPO was invited to initiate a process for resolving domain name trademark disputes. Deeply involved in the consultations around the best institutional design for ICANN, WIPO also played a formal role in the creation of the organization, as envisioned in the NTIA 1998 White Paper. This involvement at the early stage was seen as a compromise for the Europeans and Australians, who sought to counterbalance the American oversight of ICANN (Mueller 1999, 505–6).

From the start, WIPO was represented in the Governmental Advisory Committee of ICANN, together with the ITU, Organisation for Economic Co-operation and Development (OECD), the European Union (EU), and fifty-nine national governments. Back in 1998 and 1999, the close relationship between WIPO and ICANN was built around creating new rights or expanding rights to names (Mueller 2010, 232). Early cooperation between the two organizations revealed fears regarding the use of pre-emptive regulation, for example through name exclusions (blocking the use of particular names or words).[17] In this debate, WIPO originally asked for the exclusion

---

[17] The cooperation between ICANN and WIPO was strengthened in the new gTLD programme launched in 2012, as the latter was deemed the exclusive provider of dispute resolution services for Legal Rights Objections (LRO) through its Arbitration and Mediation Center. The LRO allows trademark owners and intergovernmental organizations to file a formal objection to a third party's application for a new TLD for infringement of an existing trademark, IGO name, or acronym in the pre-delegation phase.

of major trademark holders from the first domain name process, but the proposal was turned down. Nonetheless, the other WIPO recommendation—the implementation of an alternative dispute resolution method for Internet cases—was accepted. This initiative, known as Universal Domain Name Dispute Resolution Policy (UDRP), became the 'overwhelmingly preferred mechanism for domain name dispute resolution'[18] as early as 2001 (Sharrock 2001, 819).

The UDRP was stipulated in advance as a dispute resolution mechanism in all contracts involving the registration of gTLDs and some cc-TLDs. Uniquely, its arbitration awards were applied directly through changes in the DNS without resorting to enforcement via national courts. Domain name disputes treated under this policy rarely reached the litigation phase. Binding all registrars, the UDRP stipulated that most types of trademark-based domain name disputes must be resolved through agreement, arbitration, or court action before a registrar would take action (cancelling, suspending, or transferring a domain name). In practice, the complainants must prove that the disputed domain name is identical or confusingly similar to a trademark or a service mark in which the complainant has rights; the registrant does not have any rights or legitimate interest in the domain name; and the domain has been registered and is being used in bad faith. All disputes launched under UDRP are submitted to independent panellists, primarily trademark lawyers selected from an expert list.[19]

The creation of ICANN gave birth to multiple compromises, also visible in the initial structure of the organization. The IANA functions, previously performed by Jon Postel, remained separate in the ICANN structure. ICANN administered IANA under a contractual relationship with the NTIA, which continued to have an oversight role until 2016. The IANA functions have historically included: (1) the coordination of the assignment of technical IP parameters; (2) the administration of certain responsibilities associated with Internet DNS root zone management; (3) the allocation of Internet numbering resources; and (4) other services related to the management of *.arpa* and *.int* TLDs. For the IP addresses, as of 2003, IANA delegated the distribution of blocks of addresses to the Number Resource Organization (NRO).[20]

---

[18] The number of domain names in WIPO cases in 2013 peaked at 6,191, a 22 per cent increase compared with the previous year. For the same year, 2,585 cybersquatting cases were filed with the WIPO Arbitration and Mediation Center, a 10.4 per cent decrease compared to 2012 (Chenou and Radu 2015).

[19] WIPO is one of the five UDRP service providers curating one such list of potential panellists.

[20] In turn, NRO assigned the blocks of addresses via its five member organizations, the Regional Internet Registries (RIRs), covering Europe, Africa, America and Canada, Asia-Pacific, and Latin America and the Caribbean.

Governments started being involved in ICANN in an advisory capacity via the Governmental Advisory Committee (GAC) as early as March 1999. The first GAC was chaired by Australia's Paul Twomey and comprised representatives of fifty-nine national governments and of the EU, OECD, ITU, and WIPO. Upon their first meeting in 1999, GAC members affirmed the status of the DNS as a 'public resource'. Some governments subsequently started being involved via the country code supporting organizations, responsible for policies exclusively concerning national domains, whose ownership diversified over the years. The initial delegations made by Postel relied on personal relations established in the technical community; the growth of the Internet and its increasing salience compelled a number of governments to ask for increased and oftentimes formalized control at the national level.

At the outset, ICANN comprised two constituencies, namely the Domain Name Supporting Organisation (DNSO) and the membership structure set to elect the nine At-Large board members. A ground-breaking attempt to enhance community participation was the 2000 global election for five At-Large Directors, one from each geographical region. It was the first time ICANN designed a process that would involve the global public by giving them a direct online vote in determining the governing structure. The At-large Directors election was an attempt to implement broad inclusiveness, but only 30,000 out of 176,837 registered electors (anyone in the world could register with an email and postal address) casted a vote. The practice of global elections has since been dropped.

Recurrent questions of legitimacy and accountability undermined the work of ICANN over the years. In 2000, ICANN introduced the set of seven TLDs,[21] including specialized TLDs[22] with a sponsor, which would generally be delegated a number of responsibilities over policy-formulation for that defined group of interest. The newly introduced sponsored domains constituted a proof of concept for a larger expansion phase, started at the end of 2003 and completed in 2004, which brought eight new TLDs.[23] As the DNS was expanding, the need for an appropriate repartition of roles among stakeholders and a better inclusion of national governments seemed necessary. A report by ICANN president Stuart Lynn entitled 'ICANN—The case for change' (Lynn 2002) paved the way for a deep reform of the organization in order to strike a new balance between public and private governance and to gain more legitimacy at the global level. One of the main changes in the ICANN structure

[21] Among the seven new TLDs were: *.biz*, *.info*, *.name*, and *.pro*.

[22] The three sponsored TLDs were: *.aero*, *.coop*, and *.museum*.

[23] The following gTLDs were successfully introduced in 2004: *.asia*, *.cat*, *.jobs*, *.mobi*, *.post*, *.tel*, *.xxx*, and *.travel*.

was the strengthening of the role of the GAC. Developing countries saw the GAC as the policy forum of IG, while the other bodies of the organization were to take charge of technical matters. The result of the reform process was embodied by the new by-laws of the corporation that entered into force on 15 December 2002. The resulting structure has been described as 'ICANN 2.0' and as a 'public-private partnership' (Kleinwaechter 2003). The reform also triggered the creation of an At-Large Advisory Committee designed to include the 'community of individual Internet users' and to strengthen the participation of civil society in the daily operations of the organization.

The reform was oriented towards enhancing the legitimacy of ICANN through a structured participation of affected parties in the policymaking process. To achieve that, ICANN divided participants based on the constituency they belonged to (ISPs, intellectual property owners, and commercial business users; non-commercial users, not-for-profits, registrars, and registries), the nature of their interests (commercial or non-commercial) and the function they intended to perform: supporting organizations for the recommendation of specific policies, or advisory groups to the Board of Directors on any ICANN-related issue. As these changes indicated, the ICANN stakes were not strictly market-related. In the construction of a new system of rules, the management of key Internet resources was a source of tension for the power positions it allocated. The historical control of the Internet's name and address space was important not only for the technical community seeking to preserve its independence, but also for trademark owners looking to enforce claims about exclusive rights. Similarly, governments, computer industry, and civil society groups expressed strong interest in ICANN policymaking processes and demanded a seat at the table.

Following the restructuring mentioned above, the business community and civil society organizations were offered two ways to participate in the ICANN policy development process: either through the Generic Names Supporting Organisation (GNSO), which made policy recommendations specifically related to gTLDs, or through the At-Large community, which advised the Board. Non-commercial interests subsequently found a home in the Non-Commercial Stakeholder Group (NCSG) of the GNSO, to advance policy objectives such as human rights, education, access to knowledge, freedom of expression, privacy rights, etc. End-users were invited to participate in ICANN in an individual capacity via the At-Large structures.

ICANN Negotiations: Political Stakes

The proposals for governing domain names prior to the creation of ICANN embedded the tenets of the time: the free-market, open competition ideology

(Postel-plan) faced the public resource discourse, be it under a form of public-private oversight (IAHC) or under industry self-regulation (MoU). In the plan designed by Postel, the governance of the Internet was strictly understood as the technical allocation of unique domain names and IP addresses. Other aspects, mentioned in the 1996 draft-postel abstract, were bound to be 'determined, and coordinated, by contractual agreements between private interests'. Tough reactions from intellectual property owners, intergovernmental organizations, and some states confirmed that a broader support base was needed in order to obtain legitimacy and acceptance for the new governance system, since a number of stakeholders were marginalized throughout the process.

The debates that led to the establishment of ICANN involved only a small number of individuals and organizations, mostly from the United States. National governments from developing countries did not take part in the negotiations. Historically, civil society groups played a limited role in the founding of the institution and its early years (Gross 2011), gradually increasing its presence in different committees over time. Given the structure envisioned at the outset, civil society did not exert the same influence as the other three stakeholder groups (Commercial Stakeholder Group, the Registrars Stakeholder Group, and the Registries Stakeholder Group) in the development of policies. Even after several reforms, ICANN's governance structure continued to be a unique hybrid power structure involving the technical community, businesses, governments, and different groupings of civil society. The restructuring of the organization happening in the early 2000s did not put an end to the debates around the core questions of legitimacy and the specific role of governments and, in particular, that of the United States in global processes of IG. While greater autonomy was given to ICANN by the US DoC, the successive Memoranda of Understanding and the Affirmation of Commitment have come under heavy critique as illegitimate supervision by a single government (e.g. Singh 2009, Weber and Gunnarson 2012). The extensive scholarly literature that was critical of ICANN also played a role in raising awareness of this issue (Mueller 1999).

The creation of a private sector-led governance system outside traditional organizations for regulating a global network raised important transparency and accountability issues. If ICANN was to manage some of the critical resources of the Internet, who was it accountable to? And how could its operations be supervised? The ICANN structure gave way to asking broader questions about the legitimacy of the entire governance system. Transparency was seen as an important aspect of the organization's legitimacy. One of the most discussed aspects of the ICANN by-laws before their adoption was the inclusion of transparency procedures and participation mechanisms. A suit was successfully filed against ICANN for the lack of transparency provisions in its original procedures (ICANN 2002). Broader concerns about democratic procedures within ICANN were also in focus (Koppell 2005).

As a result, participation in ICANN processes remained contested. Among the key questions were the following: Who were the stakeholders? How were they represented? And in what proportion compared to other stakeholders? Marginalized actors such as civil society organizations, individual users, and developing countries' governments were part of peripheral bodies whereas the representatives of the Postel-led 'dominant coalition' controlled the core of the organization. A global membership was foreseen in the by-laws but was never implemented. The failure of the ICANN global elections in 2000 illustrated the difficulty of implementing meaningful participation mechanisms.

Finally, in retrospect, the tension stemming from the evolving role of the GAC did not diminish. The GAC—comprising representatives of national governments and intergovernmental organizations—was originally designed as an advisory body that would act only upon the request of the Board, in accordance with the US DoC vision (articulated in 1998) of a limited role of national governments in the management of the network. The US NTIA retained the oversight power over the IANA function, while other governments struggled to become more influential in the organization, gradually drawing attention to the political nexus in IG. Divergent views regarding the role of the state consolidated and ICANN became the symbolic *locus* of central IG struggles.

After the 2003 reform, the organization resembled a public–private partnership and continued to clash with the traditional 'one state, one vote' principle of intergovernmental organizations. The Board remained the central body of the California-based corporation and, in the view of many, ICANN largely escaped the control of national governments (Mathiason 2009). Thus, the institutional development of ICANN did not completely solve the issues of participation and legitimacy that had emerged at the time of its creation. The changing international context of the early 2000s accelerated the debate on the role of national governments in IG, making it apparent that the conflict of governance modes would enduringly shape the nascent issue domain. The *dotcom* crisis had undermined confidence in the self-governance of the private sector and the organization that merged private initiative with public interest functions, but remained under US government oversight, only inspired more controversy.

Mechanisms of Governance

The decade leading up to 2005 marked a new turn in the interaction between the public and the private domain. Innovative forms of private governance, brought into place by governmental action, revealed a strong dimension of hybridity. The expansion of the Internet worldwide embedded the neoliberal ideology and the deregulation trend, which in turn gave rise to power and legitimacy concerns relative to the new institutional creations. While the state did not disappear completely after defining the market conditions, rule-making processes for the Internet had to be positioned against property rights regimes, existing governance structures and rules of exchange.

The incomplete privatization of the DNS was the exception, rather than the norm, in the dominant private ordering that solidified during the 'Internet boom' decade. Corporate strategies and policies, coupled with market-driven approaches to regulation fostered the salient role of corporate actors, bringing about new online business models. Peer-to-peer agreements, exchange contracts, content development and management, and end-user contracts became the main instruments for the functioning of the newly created market. But there was more to it. The privatization trends also touched the technical standardization work of groups that presented themselves as independent and autonomous.

The policy development process in technical organizations such as ICANN or the World Wide Web Consortium (W3C), generally bottom-up, consensus-based, and open to anyone,[24] suffered transformations. The focus shifted from protocols and standards for the smooth functioning of the Internet to a business-driven agenda. The IETF was not exempt from it, as remarked by one long-term contributor to its processes, Avri Doria:

It was quite blatant. At some point we needed to bring forward at least two companies willing to develop something before we could put a new tech project on the table. It has since softened a bit, but for a while it was quite absolute. (McCarthy 2016)

The strong self-regulation trend fomented by the US DoC brought to the fore competing logics, meanings, and practices associated with the Internet. They all converged in the negotiations for establishing a new organization for the management of the 'phone book' of the Internet, presently known as ICANN. The focus on trademarks and the litigation in domain names illustrate the concerns of the late 1990s that intensified over the years. The pre-emptive regulation via name exclusions and the sunrise procedures for trademark owners were rooted in the regulatory logic dominating at the beginning of the *dotcom* boom. The privileged position of the intellectual property industry—not least in the ICANN–WIPO dispute resolution system—expanded as the Internet spread worldwide.

---

[24] Exceptions include some closed meetings of the W3C, and the membership limited to RIRs in the NRO.

The de facto institutionalization of IG happened with the participation of private actors. A similar evolution can be noted for the merging of technical, legal, and economic logics in establishing the priorities of IG. Based on the analysis of the governance instruments in the dataset—presented in Table 3—the focus on operative modelling dominated the decade (23 per cent of the instances recorded). E-commerce, cybercrime, and intellectual property rights were explicitly targeted in efforts to create new rules.

The majority of authoritative governance instruments deployed during this period fall in the modelling category. Legal enshrinement follows suit, representing the preferred solution in almost a third of instances. Absent the consensus needed for a cyberspace treaty—regularly called for in the 1990s— conventions and agreements established regionally defined a set of rules for state–state and state–private sector interactions. Illustrative of this were two important developments. The first was the fact that the Convention on Cybercrime adopted by the Council of Europe (CoE) in November 2002 was open to non-CoE members to sign and ratify. The political process behind this revealed the need to act in a unified way for tackling challenges that could no longer be isolated to a national or regional context.

The second key development was the landmark decision of the *Tribunal de grande instance* in Paris in the case *Ligue contre le racisme et l'antisémitisme et Union des étudiants juifs de France v. Yahoo! Inc. et Société Yahoo! France* (*LICRA v. Yahoo!*), reaffirming the anchoring of the Internet in geography and in existing law. LICRA complained that Yahoo! allowed their online auction service to be used for the sale of memorabilia from the Nazi period, contrary to Article R645-1 of the French Criminal Code. After establishing its competence to hear the case, the high court concluded that the auctions for Nazi memorabilia were open to French residents, despite their prohibition under French criminal law, and that Yahoo! was aware of the location of users accessing these pages, as proved by targeted advertising in the national language for computers connecting from France. It subsequently ruled against Yahoo!, thus imposing a geo-location obligation. Yahoo! contested the decision through a declaratory relief action in a Californian court, which found that geo-location filtering software violated Yahoo!'s First Amendment rights and was therefore unenforceable. This case set a precedent and fomented important discussions about the links between freedom of expression, regulation of online content, and technical means for selective display of items.

Such tensions, testing the exceptionalism of the Internet against existing laws, also articulated an important legal debate extending into the mid-2000s. Was the Internet to be bound by new, cyber-sensitive laws? Or could it be integrated under rules already in place, since those remained applicable nonetheless? Data communication introduced a set of policies that were inherently

Table 3 Governance mechanisms (global and regional) for the period 1994–2004 (based on a total of seventy-four instruments recorded in the database)

Mechanisms	Instruments	%	Examples
Legal enshrinement	*Treaties, conventions, agreements*	**16%**	1996 WIPO Performances and Phonograms Treaty
			2000 Safe Harbour Agreement (USA–EU)
			2001 CoE Convention on Cybercrime
			2001 CIS Agreement on Cooperation in Combating Offences related to Computer Information
	Court judgments, directives, policies	**11%**	1999 WIPO–ICANN Uniform Domain Name Dispute Resolution Policy
			2000 E-commerce Directive
			2000 ECtHR *Rotaru v. Romania*
			2001 *US v. Microsoft Corporation*
			2002 Directive on Privacy and Electronic Communications
			2004 IPR Enforcement Directive
Institutional solidification	*Specialized bodies*	**15%**	1995 Article 29 Working Party on Data Protection
			1995 Global Information Infrastructure Commission
			1997 APEC Intellectual Property Rights Expert Group
			1998 OAS Special Rapporteur for Freedom of Expression
	Strategic framework/ agenda	**12%**	1998 WTO Work Programme for Electronic Commerce
			2000 UN Millennium Development Goals
			2002 APEC Shanghai Program of Action
			2004 London Action Plan
	Monitoring and benchmarking	**3%**	1998 Spamhause—abuse tracking and notification
			1999 World Bank/UNESCO ICT Statistics in Education (WISE)

(*continued*)

Table 3 Continued

Mechanisms	Instruments	%	Examples
Modelling	*Discursive*	**20%**	1998 OECD Ministerial Declaration on Authentication for Electronic Commerce
			1999 CoE Recommendation for the Protection of Privacy on the Internet
			2002 UNGA Combating the Criminal Misuse of Information Technologies (56/121)
			2003 UNESCO Charter on the Preservation of Digital Heritage
	Operative	**23%**	1996 UNCITRAL Model Law on Electronic Commerce
			1997 G8 24/7 Network of Contacts for High-Tech Crime
			2002 Guidelines for the Security of Information Systems and Networks
			2004 Arab League Model Law on Combating Information Technology Offences

global, as the identifier space was not bound by a territorial dimension. At the same time, the issues emerging in the cyberspace were not entirely different from those regulated offline, although their salient features might have transformed in the process of moving online. Infringements of intellectual property rights and online fraud, in particular, expanded in scale and speed favoured by the low costs associated with their enactment.

The period leading up to 2003 marked the emergence of Internet-specific regulation at the global and regional levels. Unlike in the previous decade, more than half of the instruments negotiated during this period focused directly on the Internet, as opposed to covering it tangentially. Representing a key moment for the institutionalization of IG in the late 1990s, this attention to further specialization also represented an act of politicization. The delicate balance between formal and informal governance constantly evolving, formal mechanisms were no less the result of interactions with informal networks or with lobbying. In the case of ICANN, that was obvious in the concerted attempts towards establishing a more accountable governance system, while preserving a fragmented nature of supervision and narrow enforcement power.

As the domain continued to mature, the links between the private sector and the public authorities started to be formalized via regulation, gradually reducing the dependence on individuals and interpersonal networks. The common use of binding legislation stands proof to that. The lack of attention to sanctions and the limited efforts invested in monitoring exposed the fact that the new ordering was in-the-making. The political stakes exposed in the negotiations indicated strong ideological and diplomatic tensions that materialised in threats of sanction.

As Figure 1 shows, throughout this period, the focus revolved around security concerns (in particular cybercrime and spam), and legal issues, targeting particularly jurisdiction, arbitration, and intellectual property rights (IPRs). For authors like Castells (2001, 177–8), it was the threat posed by cybercrime that restored state power during the early 2000s: 'it became necessary for the most important governments to act together, creating a new global space of policing … a network of regulatory and policing agencies'. He linked that to the focus on surveillance, a tool which allowed for regulation and policing by traditional forms of state power. In connection with the focus on trade and e-commerce, another preoccupation arose: what risked jeopardizing the new market was the increase in cybercrime and the expansion of the 'deep web'. Michael Bergman (2001) coined this terminology using the metaphor of dragging a net across the surface of the ocean, missing the information hidden in the underwater depths (outside the reach of search engines, and thus more difficult to find). In 2001, the deep web consisted of 7.5 petabytes.

The success and the collapse of the indexed web and the online market it created brought into sharper focus the two main preoccupations of regulators at the end of the 1990s: ensuring security online and promoting trade. In its fight against cyberterrorism following the 9/11 attacks on the World Trade Center and the Pentagon, the US government introduced the Patriot Act of

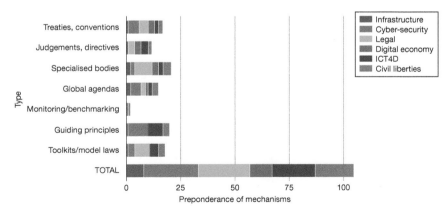

Figure 1 Variation of governance mechanisms across subfields (1994–2004)

Note: total does not add up due to multiple cases in which an instrument covers several subfields

2001, which made it illegal to advise or assist terrorists, including via online means. Many private initiatives emerged to curb the availability of terrorism-related materials online in partnership with Internet service providers, with varying degrees of success. Four years later, in the aftermath of the London attacks, stricter content controls were also introduced by European countries, in particular in the area of hate speech. Together with child online sexual abuse, these were the two focus areas for the illegal content monitored by the European network of hotlines, INHOPE, established in 1999.

As early as 1998, discussions started in the UN General Assembly with a draft resolution proposed by Russia on 'information security' with yearly iterations, followed by the 2002 'culture of cybersecurity' resolution sponsored by the United States (Radu 2013). Another significant 1998 development at the international level was the successful negotiation by the US delegation of an amendment to the World Trade Organization (WTO) agreements to treat the Internet as a duty-free trade zone. Accordingly, exchanges through the Internet were exempted from tariffs and duties on the basis of a temporary moratorium on taxes on cross-border data flows, which has been continuously renewed. This represented a competitive advantage for the American companies providing Internet-related goods and services. The United States thus became the first country to apply trade policies to govern cross-border information flows (Aaronson 2015).

Concomitantly, the developmental aspects grew in salience in Internet governance discussions. The intensification of debates around information and communication technologies for development (ICT4D) deserves a separate discussion here. Driven by UN agencies, OECD,[25] the G8, or the World Economic Forum, the plethora of transnational efforts to reduce the global digital divide stemmed from the recognition of this problem as a multidimensional gap and economic limitation with long-term consequences. The meaning of the 'digital divide'—a term coined by Lloyd Morrisett, president of the Markle Foundation—came to incorporate more elements than the original divide between information haves and have-nots (Gunkel 2003). It was initially linked to the ownership of personal computers, but evolved into encompassing more than just patterns of Internet access. Popularized with the 1998 publication of the report of the NTIA having the term 'digital divide' in the title, the concept acquired media attention in the United States and worldwide (Parker 2000). 'Falling through the Net II: New Data on the Digital Divide', a continuation of the 'Falling through the Net' project from

---

[25] The OECD (2001) defined the digital divide as: 'the gap between individuals, households, businesses and geographic areas at different socio-economic levels with regard both to their opportunities to access ICT and to their use of the Internet for wide variety of activities'.

1995, found that variation in the penetration levels was linked to income, education level, and race. The instruments capturing development aspects remained predominantly linked to modelling, rather than direct institutional involvement and resource allocation. ICT4D remained the focus of attention on a discursive level and a key dimension in subsequent UN negotiations.

Actors

With the creation of ICANN, the grouping of 'technical bodies' crystallized in IG. They represented stable arrangements in a shifting policy milieu and fostered recursive interactive relationships in a space of volatile institutional arrangements. The main activities they engaged in had no territorial binding: the development of IP standards; the administration, coordination, and allocation of IP addresses; the delegation of domain names; the coordination of the root server system; the coordination of procedures related to the technical coordination of the Internet, were all global. Mueller (2010, 4) argued that organically developed institutions provided 'a new locus of authority for key decisions about standards and critical resources'. Yet their authority also derived from and consolidated via transversal links with other organizations, including those that were in competition in the early days.

From the beginning of the 1990s, the IETF and the ITU Telecommunication Standardization Sector (ITU-T) were already cooperating informally. In the context of the emergence of a specific institutional framework for the Internet in the second half of the 1990s, the cooperation between the IETF and other organizations was clarified and in some cases formalized. A Request for Comments (RFC 2436) on the 'Collaboration between ISOC/IETF and ITU-T' was published in October 1998. It introduced, among others, a liaison position to foster exchange between the two bodies. The rationale behind this creation was the explosion in the growth of IP-based networks. It also foresaw the cross-referencing and the use of IETF documents in ITU-T processes and vice versa. This type of procedure was designed to integrate the two standardization processes and enable cross-organizational work, in particular as the operating logics of the two differed substantially.

The work of *sui generis* non-profit standard-setting organizations (such as ICANN, IETF, W3C) was authoritative because they were internationally accepted as rule-makers from the early days. All these bodies continued to function alongside inter-governmental and private-sector initiatives. Yet, unlike the ITU-T, for whom governments represent full members and non-governmental organizations need to obtain 'sector' or 'associate' status, 'native institutions' (Mueller 2004) operated on an open membership model and did not generally limit participation to organizations or official structures.[26] In their governing bodies, they all represented their primary constituencies—remaining, by definition, transnational. Table 4 offers an overview of the key bodies during that decade analysed in this chapter, including the governance structure in place for each, together with their status and function. As the comparative analysis shows, these organizations share a number of characteristics, such as their mission and a board to report to. NRO represents an exception, as its 'core community' was made up of RIRs, whose representatives constituted the Executive Council, annually rotating officers. The NRO did not develop policy directly, but served as ICANN's Address Supporting Organization and reviewed and developed recommendations on global IP address policy for ratification by ICANN's Board of Directors.

Alongside the consolidated role of technical organizations, new private and state-led bodies started profiling their work throughout the deregulatory decade, in particular on the developmental aspects of IG. In 2000, the World Economic Forum initiated the Global Digital Divide Initiative (GDDI) for increasing opportunities for private–public partnerships in diminishing the digital gap. It set in place three steering committees dedicated to Entrepreneurship, Policies, and Strategies, and Education. Similarly, the G8's Digital Opportunities Task Force (DOT Force) was developed as an initiative to 'bridge the global digital divide' (Hart 2004, 2) in the aftermath of the 2000 Okinawa Summit, where the Charter on Global Information Society was signed. In paragraph 7, the Charter reaffirmed the strong lead of the private sector, relegating to governments the responsibility to 'create a predictable, transparent and non-discriminatory policy and regulatory environment necessary for the information society', placing on them the onus of avoiding 'undue regulatory interventions'.

With the recognition of the basic right of access to knowledge and information as 'a prerequisite for modern human development' (DOT Force 2002), the high-level task force aimed to facilitate discussions with developing countries, international organizations, and other stakeholders to promote international cooperation with a view to fostering policy, regulatory, and network readiness; improving connectivity, increasing access, and lowering cost; building human capacity; and encouraging participation in global e-commerce networks. The advancement monitoring

---

[26] With the exception of W3C, which accepts both individual and institutional members (business and governmental).

Table 4 Overview of technical private bodies specific to the Internet and related decision-making procedures

Body	Creation	Location	Function	Status	Sub-bodies/ membership	Governing bodies
ICANN	1998 NTIA/DoC White Paper Jon Postel	Los Angeles (US)	Coordinate the Domain Name System ($169.9m general budget in 2015)	Non-profit corporation registered under California Nonprofit Public Benefit Corporation Law	Internet Assigned Numbers Authority (IANA) Constituent entities: Supporting Organizations (ASO, GNSO, ccNSO) Advisory Committees (Root Server, GAC, SSAC, ALAC)[a]	Board of Directors selected by Supporting Organizations and Nominating Committee (representatives of ICANN constituent entities)
Internet Society (ISOC)	1992 Vint Cerf, Bob Kahn, Lyman Chapin	Reston, Virginia (US); Geneva (CH)	Support the Internet standards development process; public policy leadership; ($39m general budget in 2015)	Non-profit international membership association, organized globally and through national 'chapters'	IAB (comprising IETF and IRTF), organizational and individual members; national chapters	Board of Trustees (elected by ISOC organizational members, by chapters and by the IAB)

(continued)

Table 4 Continued

Body	Creation	Location	Function	Status	Sub-bodies/membership	Governing bodies
Number resource organization (NRO)	2003 4 RIRs existing in 2003 (oldest created in 1992); AFRINIC added in 2005	Five headquarters for each Regional Internet Registries (RIRs)	Providing and promoting a coordinated Internet number registry system Coordination and representation of the activities of RIRs	Association of the RIRs, which manage IP addresses in different regions	Five RIRs for Europe, Africa, America and Canada, Asia-Pacific, and Latin America and Caribbean; some include National Internet Registries[b]	Executive Council (annually rotating offices held by representatives of RIRs)
World Wide Web Consortium (W3C)	1994	Host institutions: MIT/CSAIL (US), ERCIM (FR), Keio University (JP)	Develop protocols and guidelines that ensure long-term growth for the Web. (Public-private funding, membership fees, individual donations)	International industry consortium and standard-setting organization	Advisory Committee (with representatives from each member organization) Technical Architecture Group The team (appointed staff)	Advisory Board (elected by the Advisory Committee)

a. The acronyms stand for: Address Supporting Organization, Generic Names Supporting Organization, Country Code Names Supporting Organization, Government Advisory Committee, Security and Stability Advisory Committee, At-Large Advisory Committee

b. The total membership of the RIRs (including NIRs) as of 29 February 2016 is 35,519 (NRO 2016).

and fostering was delegated to four implementation teams: National e-Strategies, Human Capacities, Global Policy Participation, and Local Content and Application.

Notwithstanding its specialized fields of action, the DOT Force lifespan was short. The entity formally concluded its work after the meeting in Canada in June 2002. By 2002, the African continent benefited the most from the programme by the development of more than five transnationally funded projects and the renewal of the New Partnership for Africa's Development (NEPAD), with a focus on the activities of the e-Africa Commission. For the latter, ambitious objectives were envisioned. Among these, the increased tele-density to two lines per 100 persons by 2005, the achievement of e-readiness for all African countries, and the development of local content software were hardly realized by the set time frame. When the World Bank (WB) led the creation of InfoDev in June 2005, the interest had moved from developing an action force to shaping and sustaining a global development financial pro-gramme, led by a Donor's Committee and a Programme Manager, as well as organizing an InfoDev Symposium. Alongside the WB and the EU, ten governments contributed to its projects at the time. The focus was on three main directions: (1) enabling access for all, (2) mainstreaming ICT as tools for development and poverty reduction, and (3) innovation, entrepreneur-ship, and growth.

Among the most interesting bodies created at the time within the UN was the ICT Task Force (UNICT), that UN Secretary-General Kofi Annan established in November 2001 in response to a UN Economic and Social Council (ECOSOC) request from July 2000. This followed the recommendation of the high-level panel of experts convened from 17 to 20 April 2000. The UNICT had a three-year long mandate, subsequently extended until 31 December 2005 to allow for its active participation in the World Summit on Information Society (WSIS) process. The task force had a hybrid composition, with fifty-five members appointed by different sectors in representative capacity, which would elect the chair. IBM, Cisco, Hewlett-Packard, Siemens, Nokia, and Sun Microsystems were represented among the members of the industry, alongside civil so-ciety organizations, governments, and international organizations. It had a panel of thirty technical advisers and a secretariat of six at the UN head-quarters in New York.

The UNICT acted as a platform for dialogue open to multiple stakeholders (Flyverbom 2011) and served a purpose similar to the World Economic Forum (WEF) and G8 initiatives. Unlike the latter, it enjoyed a broader le-gitimation, in particular from developing countries. Its main activity was the organization of global forums, which enabled discussions around a wide set of concerns ranging from education to IG. Between 2001 and 2005, it held ten global forums: four in New York, three in Geneva, and one in Berlin, Dublin, and Tunis, respectively. Epitomizing the drive for deregulation, UNICT proposed in its 'Business plan' that governments facilitate competition by opening markets, encouraging investments in infrastructure, and removing barriers to competition.

The rise of organizations dedicated to Internet-specific work, either technical or developmental, attests to the way in which the field was institutionalized via operational measures. Specialized authorities, from ICANN to InfoDev, become subject to a number of formal requirements, such as transparency and a continual base of legitimate support. As IG was gradually recognized as the shared responsibility of multiple organizations and diverse stakeholders, a dominant practice developed around it: multi-stakeholder participation.

Anchoring Practice: Multi-stakeholder Participation

The intense negotiations around the creation of ICANN shed light on the number of stakeholders interested in the global governance of the Internet. Beyond what NTIA identified as 'key' stakeholders (NTIA 1998), a broader group of enthusiasts and sceptics expressed opinion on the privatization of the DNS. Most of these engaged as part of a specific (interest) group and spoke on behalf of a constituency that they presented as global. In the design of the institution, several stakeholder splits became obvious: contracted and non-contracted parties, policymakers and implementers, or government and users. This multiplicity of entities helped to address some of the legitimacy concerns. Among these were the limitations stemming from the reality of a handful of people making decisions of worldwide relevance; it was seen as a disguise for agendas that benefit particular actors more than others, especially when their lobbying power was higher. The inclusion of a limited number of stakeholders—with powerful voices—in the structure of ICANN became contested and led to the first reform of ICANN in 2003.

The dominant practice of multi-stakeholder involvement—no matter what definition was adopted for it—became a pillar for community formation during that decade. The constitutive rules of the community were re-iterated in setting up the membership practices through the categorization of groups, officially institutionalized within ICANN. Defining how certain actors could participate, however, was not restrictive to newcomers, as long as they had the technical expertise, would take on board the volunteer culture, and could participate in the relevant processes. Although the involvement of actors belonging to different sectors was practised before the formation of ICANN, never before was the diversity of the community celebrated so visibly. The different subgroups forming the 'community' gave it a new identity, uniting rather than dividing it. The public assertion of diversity became a strong community-building goal.

By the same token, the WEF and G8 initiatives also included a multi-stakeholder approach with broad participation by stakeholders from industrialized and developing countries in public–private partnerships. Enjoying more legitimacy due to its origin in an intergovernmental agreement, the UNICT also operated on multi-stakeholder logic. Despite its lack of binding power, its work was influential in agenda-setting functions, as it was required to submit annual reports and recommendations to the UN Secretary-General. Starting in 2004, the general impetus for multi-stakeholder practices in the UN ambit was strengthened with the release of the Cardoso report endorsing the wider participation of civil society in UN activities.

In effect, unlike at ICANN, where the multi-stakeholder practice materialized in bottom-up policies, in the daily works of the UNICT or the DOT Force (which were not decision-making bodies) the practice remained primarily formative and mostly discursive. In their case, authority was vested in the organizations' UN-appointed Chairs or Secretariats. The power asymmetries and the concerns for legitimacy were recognized in the functioning of the UNICT: stakeholders involved in the ICT Task Force had competing or conflicting aims and there was as a contest of influence and power among multilateral, bilateral, and civil society groups (Malcolm 2008).

In addition to being seen as an instrumental governance mode which gave the United States dominance over the Internet and its development, multi-stakeholderism also meant, for numerous developing countries, a move away from intergovernmental decision-making and international law. Negotiating new rules for the increasingly more commercial Internet in the absence of an equal vote guaranteed via international processes dissatisfied many. As an anchoring practice for legitimacy, multi-stakeholder participation presented a strong normative dimension. It was based on the idea that those most affected by a policy change or measure should in some way be involved in its management, governance, and resolution (Gurstein 2013). In effect though, not all affected interests were represented. This came under scrutiny by the supporters of a governmental leadership model. In December 2003, China, backed by developing countries, proposed the adoption of an Internet treaty and the creation of a global Internet organization (Kleinwaechter 2009).

But the multi-stakeholder practice was also under scrutiny by its adopters. In the early days of this practice, the principles of representativeness and openness were not reified in the decision-making processes for IG, according to Palfrey, Chen, Hwang, and Eisenkraft (2003). Their study on public participation in ICANN revealed that an insufficient assessment of public involvement and a limited collection of substantive comments from Internet users accounted for the failure of the organization in attracting and incorporating 'representative' input (Palfrey et al. 2003). Gradually, the practice became an element of regulatory design (Drake and Wilson 2008; DeNardis 2009) and even an '-ism' (Doria 2014), with a two-fold significance: on the one hand, there was a claim for distinctiveness in 'multi-stakeholderism'; on the other hand, its habitual use pinpointed that the principles and tenets behind it were held to be intuitive to everyone.

In the ICANN context, supporters of multi-stakeholderism saw a legitimization of the ICANN model in the use of the principle within the UN context. Other IG bodies also labelled their practices as multi-stakeholder. Western governments saw in the multi-stakeholder model a way to promote the delegation of authority and a way to improve self-regulation and the limited state intervention that they had been implementing in various sectors, and especially in the telecommunication sector since the 1980s. Civil society organizations and some governments interpreted multi-stakeholderism as participatory democracy and hailed the effort to improve democratic processes in global governance. Only some non-Western governments and some critical factions within civil society castigated multi-stakeholderism as a pejoration of democratic practices compared with traditional intergovernmentalism.

Nonetheless, the multi-stakeholder practice continued to be implemented and applied on a global scale. It quickly opened the door for the participation of marginalized actors, even if not done in clearly defined terms. The enthusiasm for this practice gave rise to a 'vernacular moment' around multi-stakeholder involvement in IG, claiming a dominant position for it, beyond contestation. Over time, it resulted in the loss of the ability to look at this practice from the outside, to scrutinize it critically without being perceived as an 'enemy' of it. As an ideologically laden organizational principle (Mueller 2010), multi-stakeholderism had deep implications on community formation, further discussed in Chapter 6.

Synopsis

The evolution of the Internet has been profoundly shaped by the salient role of corporate actors, transforming the field into an economic and political contest. When digital markets began to prosper in the 1990s, the dominant US-driven 'hands-off' approach condemned any attempt to regulate the Internet and related markets. In 1997, the Clinton administration issued a 'Framework for global electronic commerce' ingraining this vision in the future development of the field. However, at the beginning of the 2000s, e-commerce and other Internet-related markets were far from meeting the optimistic expectations of the 1990s. The burst of the '*dotcom* bubble' further reaffirmed the crucial role of social institutions in the creation, reproduction, and expansion of markets.

Deeply influenced by neoliberal ideology, the regulation milieu that fostered the growth of the Internet left a global imprint. When the Internet became commercial, three major shifts occurred in governance arrangements: they grew in size, scale, and scope. First, the reach of the network extended, with connections being established all over the world. Second, the scope of governance arrangements diversified over time: from infrastructure and technical resources management, to an array of broader societal issues spurred by the '*dotcom*' boom; legal and security issues (in particular around cybersquatting), as well as e-commerce and digital economy more broadly. Overall, this meant that in addition to the technical community dealing with standards and protocols, a new set of actors entered the governance arena at the regional and global level. With it came a renewed interest in understanding the complex interaction of technology, society, and politics, played out in the digital divide debates.

The informal arrangements dominating the period prior to the commercialization of the Internet intensified and routinized over time. The decisions of standard-setting bodies were generally archived and publicly accessible, following open meetings or mailing list discussions (generally open for anyone to join). Importantly, the initiatives for policy processes and standards development could come from anyone. The standards were open, resulting from collaborative work and placed under the organization's name. This ethos, still present today, was slightly altered at the end of the 1990s with the rise of the for-profit ICT sector and its strong involvement in the policymaking of not-for-profit institutions.

The question of 'who governed the Internet'—asked more and more frequently in the period leading up to 2005—remained difficult to answer. Regional differentiation appears as a key governance trend during that decade: 43 per cent of all governance instruments reflect partial agreements and limited consensus, but they also reveal the emergence of localized approaches on issues of global concern such as cybercrime. Certain governance mechanisms resulted from (long-standing) political agendas, others were driven by the private sector, and some developed ad-hoc in reaction to these, presenting us with a fragmented picture. It is from this perspective that the articulation of governance in a heterogeneous, hybrid environment is explored in the next two chapters.

5

The WSIS Decade and the Public–Private Partnership Thirst

When the United Nations convened its first World Summit on the Information Society (WSIS) in Geneva in 2003, what surfaced was the merging of the ICT agenda with concerns regarding the uneven expansion of the Internet and imbalanced representation of states in its governance mechanisms. The Summit, split in two phases (Geneva 2003 and Tunis 2005), was the starting point for vocalizing the worries of developing countries, but also for collaborative institutional endeavours that would continue throughout the decade in what became known as the 'WSIS process'. The sheer breadth of topics covered by this process and the formal recognition of shared responsibility of different actors marked a turning point in the evolution of the Internet, setting the stage for an accelerated institutionalization of an emerging policy field.

Sprouting from the WSIS process, the tensions regarding the role of the United Nations and that of the United States in Internet-related decision-making were particularly significant for the evolution of Internet governance (IG). The WSIS Summit Outcome document contributed to the formation of IG as a public domain, providing a conceptual framework for understanding it and delimiting mandates and responsibilities. By sanctioning a broad definition for IG, WSIS provided a common vocabulary shaping the conversations for years to come. Mirroring the Geneva Declaration of Principles adopted two years before, the Tunis phase recognized the need to continue to involve a variety of stakeholders in relevant governance arrangements, without going much further in clarifying responsibilities for this hybrid order.

The period comprised between 2005 and 2015 also shed light on the regulatory efforts of various actors, primarily states and international organizations. The rise of smartphones and mobile Internet was unparalleled: the global mobile data traffic grew 4,000-fold between 2005 and 2015 (Cisco 2017) and facilitated the fastest expansion of connectivity worldwide. Accordingly, the governance arrangements of the time revealed a stronger involvement of corporations and civil society in IG processes, alongside a redesign of the

Negotiating Internet Governance. Roxana Radu © Roxana Radu 2019. Published 2019 by Oxford University Press.

public–private sector relationships, tested in watershed moments such as the 2012 World Conference on International Telecommunications or the 2013 Snowden leaks on mass surveillance. They also revealed stronger collaboration between governments and private actors on content controls in the context of the Arab Spring revolutions between 2010 and 2012, followed by the introduction of policing regimes for online activities. This chapter traces the evolution of the field throughout the WSIS decade, providing an analysis of the governance transformations that marked the field's coming of age.

Internet Governance @ WSIS

In both academic and policy discussions, WSIS is known to have given the first definition of IG endorsed in a globally negotiated outcome document. With its focus on a broadly understood 'information society', WSIS constituted a UN summit comparable in scope and purpose to the 1992 Earth Summit, the 1995 World Conference on Women, and the 2002 World Summit on Sustainable Development. The idea for a large-scale event that would tackle ICTs and development came from the International Telecommunication Union (ITU) in 1998 and was authorized through General Assembly Resolution 56/183 in 2001. The Summit was to link with the UN Millennium Declaration, starting a discussion around the use of ICTs to achieve the Millennium Development Goals (MDGs).[1] The Summit was held in two phases: the first took place in Geneva from 10 to 12 December 2003 and the second was held in Tunis from 16 to 18 November 2005; the preparations for and follow-up to WSIS-related activities are referred to as the 'WSIS process'.

The two Summit phases were preceded by PrepCom meetings, consultations, working group sessions, and roundtables which included a range of stakeholders, from UN member states to civil society actors. The process of designing the summit benefited from input gathered in three global preparatory meetings held in Geneva between July 2002 and September 2003, and four regional meetings in Africa, Asia-Pacific, Europe, and Latin America and the Caribbean. The process was open to non-state actors, who were allotted the status of observers. Hitherto, practices of inclusion in working groups varied throughout the preparations, from government delegates only to equal footing partaking by different sector representatives. In December

---

[1] MDG 8 called upon governments, 'in cooperation with the private sector, [to] make available benefits of new technologies, especially information and communications'.

2003, more than 11,000 participants attended WSIS-I in Geneva. Four preparatory global meetings (all in Geneva) and three regional gatherings took place before WSIS-II and over 19,000 representatives were present in Tunis in November 2005. The significant growth in attendance for WSIS-II was mainly due to a two-fold increase in the number of civil society representatives and a ten-fold increase in business sector participation. In total, the Summit attracted nearly fifty heads of state/government and vice-presidents and twice as many ministers and vice-ministers, the majority from developing countries.

Against the backdrop of state-negotiated telecommunication regimes, WSIS represented an unprecedented experiment, with 45 per cent of all participants in the Geneva phase and 60 per cent in the Tunis phase being non-state actors (Chenou 2014). Apart from the 'usual suspects' for large-scale UN summits, most of the attendees reflected the variety of entities that were directly affected by digital convergence. This phenomenon challenged the works of different sectors (telephony, radio, recorded music, film, video, books, magazines, and libraries), affecting the way in which they were governed by separate policies before. The governance of ICTs and media was traditionally placed under the control of states (Irion and Radu 2013) and the publishing, film, and music industries maintained strong positions on intellectual property rights. Their presence at the Summit meant that these issues would be addressed in the negotiations. Notably, technical Internet bodies such as the Internet Corporation for Assigned Names and Numbers (ICANN) or the Internet Engineering Task Force (IETF)/Internet Society (ISOC) were well-represented in the consultations. Last but not least, the business sector secured a double representation,[2] first as corporate entities speaking on their own behalf and second via the Coordinating Committee of Business Interlocutors (CCBI) organised by the International Chamber of Commerce (Raboy et al. 2010).

The WSIS process placed a strong emphasis on the developmental dimension of the information society, with a view to addressing the perceived inequalities. On the one hand, it discussed the terms of access to ICTs, in particular stressing the availability, quality, cost, and capability to connect to the Internet in developing countries. In this regard, WSIS called into question the commercial arrangements for traffic services established in the 1990s, resulting in a net flow of revenues into developed countries and higher costs for access in the global South. Moreover, capacity building was deemed necessary

---

[2] The WSIS process also received input from the United Nations Information and Communication Technologies Task Force (UNICTTF) and the G8-created Digital Opportunities Task Force (DOT Force), where business interests were strongly represented.

for developing the skills required to thrive in the information society. On the other hand, in addressing governance mechanisms, the focus was on the representation of developing countries in global ICT-related arrangements. Salient in the WSIS negotiations were two issues: first, gaining access to processes by which the Internet was managed; second, ensuring an equal say in debates that have been transformed by the Internet, such as intellectual property, trade, or consumer protection.

Without mentioning IG, the January 2002 UNGA resolution 56/183 announcing the Summit set in motion a process that would redefine the understanding of the terms, but also the rules of engagement. Participants (Drake 2005; Kummer 2007) recall that IG was not among the topics originally discussed and was added to the WSIS agenda gradually. Among the factors that increased the visibility of this topic were the intense IG discussions held throughout the ITU plenipotentiary conference of Marrakesh in September to October 2002 (marking a divide between the United States and developing countries on the management of the domain name system (DNS)) and the development of internationalized and multilingual domain names. IG was thus closely related to unresolved technical issues plus institutional turf battles and resurfaced as a subset of ICT for development (ICT4D) concerns.

In Search of a Definition

While the ITU assumed the leading managerial role, the Summit was facilitated by an open-ended intergovernmental Preparatory Committee (PrepCom) defining the agenda and the means of participation, as well as drafting the outcome documents of the Summit. Fewer than 1,000 people participated in the Geneva preparations for WSIS-I, which constituted an important arena for negotiation. The first PrepCom meeting on 1 to 5 July 2002 in Geneva was dominated by representatives of states and civil society.[3] The elected President of the PrepCom was Adama Samassekou (Mali), with elected Vice-Presidents from five geographic groups: Africa, Asia, Eastern Europe, Western Europe, and Latin America and the Caribbean, in addition to the two co-hosts (Switzerland and Tunisia) added *ex officio*.

---

[3] Attending the first PrepCom meeting were: 607 participants from 139 member states of the United Nations and of any specialized agencies; and observers. The latter category included: fifty-four participants from UN secretariat and organs, twenty-one participants from ten UN specialized agencies, thirty-five participants representing thirteen invited intergovernmental organizations, 223 participants from NGOs and civil society organizations, and thirty-four participants from business sector entities.

The themes put forward at the first PrepCom for initial discussions included access to ICTs, development of a policy and regulatory framework, ICT applications, infrastructure and network security, capacity building, as well as the role of different stakeholders in the promotion of ICTs for development. Calls to discuss IG were made by the European Union,[4] Brazil,[5] and a coalition of twenty-two NGOs, the latter calling, among other, for the democratization of ICANN. Notably, adding IG to the agenda meant the Internet was understood as a subcategory of the governance of the information society, with a particular set of concerns, the most poignant of these being its private nature. Integrating IG into the global governance approach shifted the focus away from the Internet exceptionalism discourse dominant in the 1990s (Chenou 2014).

Input from regional preparatory meetings and thematic multi-stakeholder roundtables on the discussion themes was presented at the second PrepCom meeting on 17 to 28 February 2003, where drafts for the Action Plan and WSIS declaration were also introduced. They were the product of a working group originally opened to all states and subsequently also open to all observers, chaired by Lyndall Shope-Mafole from South Africa. By the time the PrepCom for WSIS met for the third time in Geneva (PrepCom-3) on 15 to 26 September 2003, the draft text of the Declaration of Principles had already stirred controversy in the intersessional meeting on 18 July in Paris, where an Internet Governance Ad Hoc Working Group was created to discuss the issue. It was composed of state representatives and remained closed to non-state actors (with the exception of the first meeting). The proposed text reported at PrepCom-3 evidenced dissent around the formulation of roles and responsibilities outlined in paragraph 44 of the Declaration of Principles draft.

While they all agreed on the democratic, multilateral, and transparent management of the Internet, the opinions consolidated during the negotiations diverged in terms of participation entitlements, coverage, and role of states. I include below four alternative formulations that illustrate the divergent

---

[4] The EU statement: 'new mechanisms for governance at global and national levels encompassing a) issues related to the sector like electronic communications regulatory frameworks, data protection, network security and cyber-security, legal aspects of e-commerce and Internet governance as well as b) more general issues related to the new citizenship in the information age'.

[5] The Brazilian statement: 'democratic and representative Governments should not be replaced by arbitrary groupings of private business and non-governmental institutions in decisions regarding the economic space brewing within powerful digital networks, such as the Internet. Organizing this new environment to the satisfaction of all, and ensuring the beneficial participation of developing countries and their societies is central to our work'.

perspectives of key stakeholders in the WSIS preparations, as they appear in the final report presented by PrepCom-3 in September 2003.

Formulation 1 proposed by the drafting group on Internet management	*The international management of the Internet should be democratic, multilateral, transparent and participative with the full involvement of the governments, international organisations, private sector and civil society. This management should encompass both technical and policy issues. While recognizing that the private sector has an important role in the development of the Internet at the technical level, and will continue to take a lead role, the fast development of Internet as the basis of information society requires that governments take a lead role, in partnership with all other stakeholders, in developing and coordinating policies of the public interests related to stability, security, competition, freedom of use, protection of individual rights and privacy, sovereignty, and equal access for all, among all the other aspects, through appropriate [intergovernmental/international] organisations.*
Formulation 2 Original text from 21 March document, supported by Saudi Arabia	*Internet governance must be multilateral, democratic and transparent, taking into account the needs of the public and private sectors as well as those of the civil society, and respecting multilingualism. The coordination responsibility for root servers, domain names, and Internet Protocol (IP) address assignment should rest with a suitable international, inter-governmental organization. The policy authority for country code top-level-domain names (cc-TLDs) should be the sovereign right of countries.*
Formulation 3 proposed by the EU	*The international management of the Internet should be democratic, multilateral and transparent. It should secure a fair distribution of resources, facilitate access for all and ensure a stable and secure functioning of the Internet. It should respect geographical diversity and ensure representativeness through the participation of all interested States, including public authorities with competence in this field, of civil society and the private sector, with due respect to their legitimate interests.*
Final text, in paragraph 48 of the Geneva Declaration of Principles	*The Internet has evolved into a global facility available to the public and its governance should constitute a core issue of the Information Society agenda. The international management of the Internet should be multilateral, transparent and democratic, with the full involvement of governments, the private sector, civil society and international organizations. It should ensure an equitable distribution of resources, facilitate access for all and ensure a stable and secure functioning of the Internet, taking into account multilingualism.*

The two basic visions for IG—intergovernmental control or private sector leadership—remained the Gordian knot of debates throughout the WSIS process. The wording finally adopted at WSIS-II was strongly normative, yet remained ambiguous as to the specific responsibilities or lead roles. At the WSIS-I meeting in Geneva, a Declaration of Principles was adopted, as well as a Plan of Action aiming to provide guidance on the implementation of the first. As in previous negotiations, most contention emerged around the definition of IG, which would have elucidated the boundaries of participation and the extent to which the status quo was supported, as well as the roles of new actors in IG. The multi-stakeholder nature of the information society was not homogeneously understood by the delegations present at WSIS. What surfaced during the negotiations, before and after phase one in Geneva, was a split conceptualization of what multi-stakeholder governance meant: sometimes, the process was legitimized as a balanced representation of the state next to other stakeholders, via an equal number of members; other times, the state was understood as having a leading role in multi-stakeholder governance.

Moreover, strong contestation came from civil society groups which opposed the very notion of an 'information society' and, concordantly, opposed the organization and the Summit as capitalist endeavours (Raboy et al. 2010, 106–7). Hacker collectives refused to engage with the summit, while artists and activists designed alternative events, such as 'WE SEIZE!', which took place in front of the Palexpo complex where the Geneva Summit was held. The Geneva police intervened to disperse participants at other alternative events taking place throughout the city.

To overcome the lack of consensus discernible at the Geneva Summit, Kofi Annan, then Secretary-General of the United Nations, requested the establishment of a Working Group on Internet Governance (WGIG). The formation of this group was the only specific reference to IG in the Geneva Plan of Action. This WSIS outcome document translated the vision into eleven concrete action lines, with tasks mandated for governments including: facilitating the establishment of national and regional Internet Exchange Centres; managing or supervising, as appropriate, their respective country-code top-level domains (cc-TLDs); promoting, in cooperation with the relevant stakeholders, regional root servers and the use of internationalized domain names in order to overcome barriers to access, user education, and awareness about online privacy and the means of protecting privacy (2003a). An earlier reference to the contentious 'governments should work to internationalize the management of Internet resources in order to achieve a universally representative solution' (Draft Plan of Action, 21 September 2003, para. 19) was removed from the final Plan of Action. The private sector lead and the calls for an enabling environment had been toned down to:

Governments, in collaboration with stakeholders, are encouraged to formulate conducive ICT policies that foster entrepreneurship, innovation and investment, and with particular reference to the promotion of participation by women. (WSIS 2003a)

The role of governments in the international governance of ICTs, including, inter alia, the naming and addressing resources, continued to generate debate. Many discussions called into question, implicitly or explicitly, the special role of one government: the United States, whose approach was challenged in three respects. First, authorizing the publication of any modifications, deletions, or additions to the root zone file, via NTIA, was seen as an imminent threat. Some countries perceived this as a 'privilege' that would give the United States the power to remove specific cc-TLDs from the root and eventually restrict the communication of users under that cc-TLD. Second, the location on American soil of ten out of the thirteen root servers[6] was challenged. The third source of contestation was the informality of the arrangements among root server operators (Kleinwaechter 2005). The debate on IG at WSIS-I remained polarized, resulting in a compromise text focused on process rather than on substance. The proposal to establish a WGIG, mandated to develop a working definition of IG, was welcome. The expert group was also tasked to identify the public policy issues that were relevant to IG and develop a common understanding of the respective roles and responsibilities of governments, the private sector, and civil society.

Established in November 2004,[7] the WGIG was chaired by Nitin Desai, the Special Adviser to the UN Secretary-General for the WSIS, appointed directly by Kofi Annan. The group consisted of forty experts equally representing the tripartite classification of stakeholder groups (states–businesses–civil society),[8] but participating in an individual capacity. The majority of the selected members took part in WSIS-I and in the work of the UNICTTF or the G8 DOT Force. They had complementary skills and knowledge, ranging from technical specializations to development policy. A former Swiss diplomat, Markus Kummer was named executive coordinator of the working group after Switzerland announced that it would fund a secretariat for this new body.[9] The Secretariat was established in July 2004, and on 20 to 21 September that year it held a two-day open consultation on the composition of the WGIG and its agenda, to which multiple stakeholders were invited. For the selection

[6] For increased network reliability, the anycast system was introduced in the early 2000s; there are currently more than 100 anycast instances of root servers all over the world.

[7] As McLean (2005) notes, the group was formally announced on 11 November, but decisions about the membership were made in advance and the participants were notified informally by the WGIG Secretariat ahead of time.

[8] It has been argued, however, that the process leading to the formulation of the definition was 'not a multi-stakeholder effort' due to the overrepresentation of states (some with repressive Internet policies) in WGIG (Raymond and deNardis 2015, 16).

[9] This was announced at the UNICTTF Global Forum on Internet Governance in New York, 24–25 March 2004.

of the WGIG members, broad criteria were put forward by Desai: regional representation, stakeholders, gender, developed and developing countries, and differing schools of thought; yet the final selection of participants was made by the Secretariat using informal means of consultation (Mathiason 2009). The largest part of group members came from governments (44 per cent), with a significant representation of emerging economies (including Brazil, China, Cuba, Iran, Russia) alongside European states. About a quarter of the WGIG members were active in ICANN discussions (Chenou 2014).

The WGIG Process

The WGIG prompted a momentous political negotiation and represented an early example of a new anchoring practice in use throughout the WSIS decade: the reliance on expertise from senior members of the community to find a solution to a stalemate. The group was at the epicentre of a much larger IG argument, marked by failure to agree on a shared understanding of the field. At least six international meetings within and outside the UN system touched upon this issue earlier that year, either in preparation for the second phases of WSIS or in specialized conferences. All ICANN meetings from July 2004 onwards also held dedicated sessions. To advance the WSIS negotiations, the task of scoping IG was allocated to WGIG in 2004. This challenge was addressed procedurally by designing a process that consisted of four multi-stakeholder meetings, all including an open consultation part, deemed necessary to 'meet the concerns of those countries that did not want a small group process, but rather a full intergovernmental meeting' (Desai 2005, ix). Four open consultations with stakeholders took place at the UN headquarters in Geneva between November 2004 and June 2005; representatives of states, business, and civil society actors were heard during the consultations in plenary session. Beside these, the WGIG members also met in closed sessions.

The WGIG mandate was subject to repeated contest, in particular for clarifying whether a reform of the IG system was at stake. For some, the work of the group was about the narrow technical side of the Internet. At the first WGIG meeting, ITU Secretary General Utsumi recommended 'focus[ing] on the core activity of the management of Internet resources by ICANN, in particular top-level domains, which is where important issues remain unresolved'. For others, the WGIG task was inherently political.[10] Former WGIG member William Drake summarized this as follows:

[10] In the words of one of the WGIG members, Lyndall Shope-Mafole (South Africa): 'The focus and the main reason for the establishment of this group and for asking the Secretary-General of the UN to establish this group is because the issue is not technical. I think the issue is political' (statement made on 18 April 2005).

If I had a one US dollar for every time I was told—almost exclusively by my fellow Americans—that the WGIG was actually a UN plot to 'take over the Internet' and give it to the International Telecommunication Union (ITU), I could have a quite nice dinner—in Geneva no less. If in addition I had one US dollar for every time I was told that the WGIG was a plot against the ITU, I could have a nice dessert, and coffee too. (2005, 249)

The process that led to the final report of the WGIG was a collaborative exercise. A strong leadership role was taken by the Secretariat, led by Switzerland's Markus Kummer. Following four open consultations, the WGIG published its report in July 2005 in preparation for the November meeting in Tunis. The Final Report was drafted in seventy-two hours at the Château de Bossey retreat outside Geneva (McLean 2005). A decision was taken by the WGIG together with the WSIS Secretariat to have a short final report transmitted to the UN Secretary-General for WSIS-II and a longer version as a Background Report. In its report, the group gave more leverage to public policy[11] than to the technical standardization or technical resource allocation and assignment, thus enlarging the space for institutional engagement. In addition to Internet stability, security, and cybercrime, it covered intellectual property rights and trade-related issues, freedom of expression, data protection, and multilingualism. But it also included issues such as meaningful participation in global policy development, capacity building, or consumer rights, reflecting, to a large extent, the contribution of civil society participants.

The working definition it provided for IG sought to balance descriptive and normative dimensions and be as comprehensive as possible. Reflecting the academic influence in the group, WGIG equated IG with 'the development and application by Governments, the private sector and civil society, in their respective roles, of shared principles, norms, rules, decision-making procedures, and programmes that shape the evolution and use of the Internet' (WGIG 2005). Inspired by Krasner's 1983 international regimes definition, this wording garnered the support of the working group members and, subsequently, of the WSIS delegations, which agreed to insert it *verbatim* into paragraph 34 of the Tunis Agenda, the ultimate product of WSIS.

In the work of the WGIG, a large fraction of the time and energy was dedicated to investigating the position of ICANN, which was financially supporting the group. Not only was the *sui generis* organization discussed as a governance structure that did not give an equal standing to governments, but also as an embodiment of a privatized way of operating that needed to

---

[11] This was arrived at through the 'Inventory of Public Policy Issues and Priorities' put forward at the first open consultation. It was a list of forty-six issues prepared with inspiration from a similar list made by the then vice-chair of the UNICTTF (McLean 2005).

become more inclusive. As the Internet became widespread in other parts of the world, it could no longer have online content primarily in English and domain names could no longer be typed with Latin characters only. Support for multilingualism and local content was dominant. The final report released by the WGIG in July 2005 addressed the need for a restructuring of IG, but did not influence the status quo with regards to ICANN.

Drafted at Château de Bossey outside Geneva, with consideration for the opinions expressed during the open consultations, the report elaborated on an open forum function for all stakeholders and four proposals for public oversight arrangements. The members of the group did not reach agreement on whether one model would be preferable to the others, and Desai concluded that they all needed to be included as 'four equally beautiful brides' (Drake 2005). Three of these proposals envisioned an international body replacing ICANN or overseeing the Internet Assigned Numbers Authority (IANA) function (thus eliminating the control of the US Department of Commerce (DoC)), yet none was formally endorsed in the Tunis Agenda. One of the models discussed—an intergovernmental, UN-based 'Global Internet Council' (GIC)—replacing the DoC oversight and the ICANN Governmental Advisory Committee, garnered increasing attention in the following years, as discussed in the next sections of this book. In the various proposals put forward, the management of the root continued to be entrusted to ICANN or a globalized version of it ('World ICANN': linked to the United Nations with a host country agreement), yet the policymaking function would generally lie with a GIC, a Global Internet Governance Forum, or an International Internet Council. The non-state actors, both for-profit sector and civil society, were frequently side-lined in the models proposed, support being primarily shown for governments and for the United Nations (Raboy et al. 2010, 137).

In negotiating the oversight system, two main visions were consolidated (Kleinwaechter 2005). On the one hand, there were the supporters of the 'do not fix what is not broken' slogan—favouring the status quo and arguing for keeping ICANN unchanged. On the other hand, there were the proponents of a UN treaty, which would have allowed all governments to share responsibilities, oversight, and control. As the WGIG negotiations concluded in mid-June, the NTIA issued the US Principles on the Internet's Domain Name and Addressing System (on 30 June 2005), making three important statements: first, that the US government intended to 'maintain its historic role in authorizing changes or modifications to the authoritative root zone file'; second, that ICANN was the appropriate technical manager for the domain names system; and third, that IG should continue to be discussed in multiple fora, in which the United States 'will continue to support market-based approaches and private sector leadership in Internet development broadly' (NTIA 2005).

Without the endorsement of the United States and allies, nor that of the business sector, the negotiations on an alternative to ICANN did not advance in the following negotiation rounds for WSIS-II. What became obvious through the work of WGIG was the understanding that the Internet was, above all, a political issue with many more stakeholders asking for a seat at the table. The way in which the governance of the Internet was articulated up until that point came under heavy contestation and that was reflected in the interventions at the WGIG open consultations. The latter became, in the process, 'an "obligatory passage point" at a crucial stage in the ordering of the global politics of the digital revolution' (Flyverbom 2011, 117).

Moreover, the WGIG introduced a set of procedures that remained emblematic for IG processes: it introduced a multi-stakeholder extra-budgetary funding scheme (further pursued in the constitution of the Internet Governance Forum (IGF))[12] and it committed to a transparent process by holding open sessions and inviting open comments on draft documents (Mathiason 2009). One innovation that the WGIG adopted with inspiration from the ICANN meetings was the use of real-time captioning of the discussions in English. At the Château de Bossey, parts of the final report were drafted and fine-tuned collectively, using a projector so that all participants could work on the text at the same time (McLean 2005). The WGIG also validated the practice of setting up a working group to scope what was at stake, reconcile dissenting opinions and views, and propose ways forward. The practice of ad hoc groups in charge of finding a mediating position relied on legitimacy through expertise and, reiterated in multiple fora, became a defining routine in the IG field.

The WSIS Ordering

When the WSIS Summit came to an end in Tunisia in 2005 with the adoption of two outcome documents—the Tunis Commitment and the Tunis Agenda—the global ordering that was in flux during the negotiations authoritatively stabilized. The redefinition of the Internet as a sociopolitical field (in opposition to technical only) expanded the scope and exposure of what became a global public policy domain. A sustained public commons discourse surfaced in the contributions of the delegations from developing countries,

---

[12] The main donors supporting the WGIG—the Swiss, Norwegian, and Dutch governments, together with the Swiss Education and Research Network and ICANN—became significant contributors to the IGF.

countered by an understanding of the Internet as a 'global facility' in the eyes of the business sector and endorsed by some of the participants representing Western governments. Focusing attention on the overarching theme of digital divide, WSIS-II discussed themes such as spam (fraudulent and unsolicited harmful email), multilingual access to the Internet, and the international Internet interconnection charges.[13] These three points advanced throughout the PrepComs and as part of the WGIG consultations were arguably the most heated. A tripartite categorization of stakeholders (governments–businesses–civil society) hardened the positions of the key actors, each of which struggled with internal heterogeneity.

In the Tunis Agenda, governments agreed on the following distinction of roles and responsibilities of stakeholders, which continues to guide the current understanding of the shared competences in IG:

a. *Policy authority for Internet-related public policy issues is the sovereign right of States. They have rights and responsibilities for international Internet-related public policy issues.*

b. *The private sector has had, and should continue to have, an important role in the development of the Internet, both in the technical and economic fields.*

c. *Civil society has also played an important role on Internet matters, especially at community level, and should continue to play such a role.*

d. *Intergovernmental organizations have had, and should continue to have, a facilitating role in the coordination of Internet-related public policy issues.*

e. *International organizations have also had and should continue to have an important role in the development of Internet-related technical standards and relevant policies.* (WSIS 2005a, paragraph 35)

The Tunis Agenda also recognized, in paragraph 36, the 'valuable contribution by the academic and technical communities within those stakeholder groups mentioned in paragraph 35'. This further divided the core communities contributing to IG, 'unilaterally relegating all other stakeholders to subordinate roles' (Doria 2014, 124). Antagonizing these groups by relegating them to the side-lines, the Summit further called into question the extent to which technical standards and protocols were responsive to the needs of developing countries, in particular in promoting internationalized domain name and multilingual local content. The Tunis Agenda understanding— refining the wording of the Geneva Plan of Action from 2003—became a reference point in all subsequent discussions.

---

[13] To address this discontent, the Geneva Plan of Action encouraged 'the creation and development of regional ICT backbones and Internet exchange points' (2003, section C2).

In its IG section, the Tunis Agenda also reflected on the promotion, development, and implementation of a global culture of cybersecurity (in cooperation with all stakeholders and international expert bodies) in paragraph 39, reiterating what the United States proposed in related discussions in the General Assembly (Radu 2013). In the words of Kummer, the 'Tunis Agenda was a "diplomatic compromise", the beauty of which is that it is full of creative ambiguity that allows everybody to find something to satisfy their own wishes. As the Agenda was based on a decision-making Summit, the text on controversial topics such as IPR was carefully balanced in a way that avoided going into details that could be divisive and difficult to resolve' (cited in Dutton et al. 2007, 5). Using the common-denominator approach meant that no IG reform proposed by the WGIG was pursued, with the exception of the endorsement for the creation of an IGF[14] to address Internet-related questions in an open format, with non-binding recommendations.

The IGF was aimed at building consensus and shaping the development of Internet-related policies in a bottom-up manner, also fulfilling a socialization function by bringing stakeholders together for open discussions. Paragraph 72 of the Tunis Agenda established this forum for multi-stakeholder policy dialogue to discuss public policy issues, facilitate exchange among interested parties, identify emerging issues, and contribute to capacity building in developing countries. Organized by a small IGF Secretariat[15] based in Geneva and reporting to Department of Economic and Social Affairs (UN DESA), the forum has been convened annually in different locations around the world since 2006 under a UN mandate that was originally valid for five years, renewed for the first time in 2010. At the WSIS decennial review in December 2015, the IGF was renewed for another ten years.

The concession made on the thorny issue of government participation in IG processes is summarized in paragraph 69 of the Tunis Agenda:

We further recognize the need for enhanced cooperation in the future, to enable governments, on an equal footing, to carry out their roles and responsibilities, in international public policy issues pertaining to the Internet, but not in the day-to-day technical and operational matters, that do not impact on international public policy issues. (WSIS 2005a)

---

[14] For Mueller (2010, 78), the creation of the IGF 'was widely understood to be the kind of agreement that could get the WSIS out of its impasse; it allowed the critics to continue raising their issues in an official forum, but as a nonbinding discussion arena, could not do much harm to those interested in preserving the status quo'.

[15] It was originally funded through extra-budgetary contributions to a trust fund, with donations from governments, international organizations, and various stakeholders.

This wording led to a dialogue track perpetuated in what was known as the 'Enhanced Cooperation process'. Different reactions were triggered by this formulation: for some stakeholders, an active participation in the IGF met the conditions for an enhanced cooperation. This is why most of the stakeholders reporting to the UN Secretary-General mentioned their efforts in the IGF process as their contribution to an enhanced cooperation in IG. For others, the IGF and enhanced cooperation represented two different processes. It is the latter view that the UN Economic and Social Council (ECOSOC) endorsed when the issue was brought to the fore in 2012.

Once again, behind the separation or unification of the two processes stood a firmer decision on the role of the UN system in IG. The enhanced cooperation dialogue was mandated by the Secretary-General to his special adviser, Desai, tasked to report on progress annually. Subsequently, the process was assigned to the UN Commission on Science and Technology for Development (CSTD), which started conducting discussions in the framework of the CSTD Working Group on Enhanced Cooperation (WGEC) chaired by Peter Major of Hungary, active starting in 2013. The group comprised twenty UN member states and five representatives from each of the four identified stakeholder groups (business; civil society; intergovernmental organizations; technical and academic community). Discussion on the 'enhanced cooperation' track soon stalled over the definition of terms.

While the role of governments at the global level was not settled at the WSIS, a tacit agreement was reached that countries retained their rights to legislate nationally (Hill 2014). The Tunis Agenda did not debate the mechanisms already in place at the national level, be they legislative or executive. In terms of new mechanisms, the WSIS consensus was limited to encouraging the establishment of a national implementation instrument that would contribute to the achievement of the MDGs. Mainstreaming links between ICTs and development at various levels, the Tunis Agenda called on regional intergovernmental organizations to work with other stakeholders to implement activities, exchange information and share best practices.

Role of the United Nations

The WSIS permanently transformed the IG field by crystallizing the UN participation in its processes. First and foremost, it clarified the facilitator role to be played by a number of UN agencies. In the Tunis Agenda, responsibilities for action lines were entrusted to different UN agencies: UN DESA—development, e-government, international cooperation; ITU—cybersecurity, infrastructure, enabling environment, capacity building; WIPO—copyright;

UNESCO—access, science, e-learning, cultural and linguistic diversity, media, information ethics. Through WSIS, various UN organizations defined their interests more clearly with regard to the Internet. ITU, WIPO, and UNESCO linked their mission directly to the Internet, whereas bodies such as UN Institute for Disarmament Research (UNIDIR) or UN Office on Drugs and Crime (UNODC) saw the Internet policymaking debates as tangential to their mission.

Second, a formalized reporting system was set in place. Assigning responsibilities created a debate, with concerns being put forward regarding the very definition of the implementation and follow-up mechanisms for WSIS. Whether the process would result in new institutions or expanded mandates for certain international organizations and governments, and whether multistakeholder participation would be preserved were highly disputed. The need for a reporting and implementation system was stressed in the recommendations of the Ad Hoc Working Group of the GA, tasked to examine the integrated and coordinated implementation of and follow-up to the outcomes of the major UN conferences and summits on socio-economic topics. The work of the ad hoc group happened around the same time as WSIS-I and resulted in the UNGA 57/270B resolution adopted in July 2003, recognizing the responsibility of the UN system to assist governments to stay fully engaged in the stocktaking process.

The WSIS stocktaking process started in August 2004 following a decision taken at the first meeting of Phase II preparations for Tunis. Given the overlapping mandates of several UN bodies, the stocktaking exercise was seen as an opportunity to coordinate and harmonize efforts across the UN system. To arrive at a full picture of the different activities and responsibilities undertaken by various entities, the ITU Secretary-General, in coordination with the WSIS Executive Secretariat, sent a letter to WSIS participants to invite them to fill in a questionnaire regarding the field of activities and actions they contributed to in line with the eleven themes of the Geneva Plan of Action.

The negotiation of follow-up measures was as political as the definition of IG, going from the proposal of concrete implementation activities and the creation of a new organizational mandate to coordinate these to the vague text of 'a request to the Secretary-General of the UN to submit a report on implementation activities of the WSIS decisions' in a draft from August 2005. After a new round of negotiations, an agreement was reached to entrust ECOSOC with overseeing the system-wide follow-up. ECOSOC's subsidiary body, the CSTD was further mandated to evaluate progress on implementation and follow-up and to propose initiatives for improving their efficiency. In this process, the CSTD—with an agenda, mandate, and composition decided on by ECOSOC—was named focal point and given the ultimate responsibility over the follow-up process.

The ITU, on the other hand, remained in charge of the stocktaking process, following the organization of the first meeting on this topic in October 2004. In the understanding of the time, stocktaking consisted of compiling the information regarding the different activities and initiatives undertaken by various actors in connection with the themes of the Summit. Participation in this exercise was voluntary, and the ITU took the lead in publishing an annual report based on data related to the themes identified in the Geneva Plan of Action. The Tunis Agenda also introduced a quantification approach with strong reliance on data, indicators, and indexes for monitoring the evolution of the information society. It pointed to the periodical evaluation of problems identified at the WSIS, noting that different levels of development and national circumstances need to be taken into account. The Partnership on Measuring ICTs for Development was one of its outcomes, providing a measurement of the efficiency of the implementation measures through the ICT Opportunity Index and the Digital Opportunity Index. Building on paragraphs 109 to 110 of the Tunis Agenda, the ITU organized, together with UNESCO, UNCTAD, and UNDP, the annual WSIS Forum, the largest global meeting for ICT4D, annually held in Geneva.

On the question of coordination and harmonization of activities in the UN system, the Group on the Information Society (UNGIS) was established by Kofi Annan in April 2006 within the UN Chief Executives Board for Coordination (CEB). The UNGIS consisted of twenty-eight UN bodies and organizations facilitating the implementation of the WSIS outcomes and co-ordinating the mechanisms for national and international implementation established in the Tunis Agenda. They initiated a process of annual meetings to identify priorities and coordinate activities and joint initiatives, consolidating cross-sectoral cooperation and strengthening the role and visibility of the UN on information society matters.

At the end of the WSIS, it became clear that the institutionalization of an emerging and highly politicized field was well underway, with the involvement of the regional and international organizations. Not only was the Internet fully integrated in global governance processes, it also became a visible point of contention between developing and developed countries over participation in the creation of rules for the Internet, which progressively blurred the boundaries between traditional sectors of regulation. The process laid the foundations for a developmental angle to be added to the evolution of the Internet. The organization of the WSIS brought together different UN bodies working at the intersection of technology and development, it consolidated the role of the ITU, and mandated follow-up procedures though which a number of organizational mandates were extended. The Tunis outcome documents and UN General Assembly Resolution 60/252 further resolved to conduct an Overall Review of the Implementation of the WSIS Outcomes in 2015, a process discussed in the Post-Snowden Fault Lines section below.

WCIT-12

Soon after the conclusion of WSIS-II, the ITU met for its 2006 Plenipotentiary meeting in Antalya and decided, among others, to convene a World Conference on International Telecommunications in 2012 (WCIT-12) to discuss the revision of the 1988 International Telecommunication Regulations (ITRs) treaty in light of the changes in the international environment. The ITRs served as a global treaty binding signatories to comply with general principles for worldwide interconnection and interoperability of existing communication services and facilitate the availability of international telecommunication services and networks. It said little about the Internet, which was in its infancy at the time.

In the lead-up to the WCIT-12, core frictions emerged between stakeholders and interest groups on state involvement in Internet regulation. The United States[16] and many supporters of the multi-stakeholder practice voiced concerns that the revised ITRs posed threats to an open Internet and called for opposing the alleged UN intent to govern and regulate the Internet and related attempts by member states to impose governmental leadership via this treaty. On 22 September 2012, the US House of representatives unanimously approved a resolution urging the US government not to give the ITU control over the Internet. A broad coalition of non-state actors, including civil society organizations and large Internet companies, mobilized against the WCIT-12.

Amidst these tensions, the ITU Secretary General Hamadoun Touré (2012) repeatedly stated that the WCIT-12 would not address the Internet, yet a number of documents among the 1,275 revision proposals submitted by member states referred directly to the Internet. The Russian proposal was worrisome to many: 'member states shall have equal rights to manage the Internet, including in regard to the allotment, assignment and reclamation of Internet numbering, naming, addressing and identification resources and to support for the operation and development of the basic Internet infrastructure'. The talks around amending the ITRs were also prominently

---

[16] At the meeting in Dubai, the US delegation was one of the most numerous, consisting of 100 individuals, of which forty belonged to the private sector and ten to civil society organizations.

contested for increasing the jurisdiction and legal control of the ITU over the Internet (Blackman 2013). The WCIT-12 included, apart from the revision of the treaty, discussions around the adoption of a non-binding resolution for fostering an enabling environment for the greater growth of the Internet, which affirmed a strong and continuous role for the ITU in IG, stating that 'all governments should have an equal role and responsibility for international Internet governance'.

The concern that dominated the meeting—the potential intergovernmental control of the Internet—was by no means new. Since 2011, non-Western countries put forward various proposals to bring network governance into state-led global or regional frameworks: India, Brazil, and South Africa pushed for the creation of a UN Committee for Internet-related Policies (CIRP), while Russia, China, Tajikistan, and Uzbekistan called for an International Code of Conduct for Information Security, drawing on an older Russian proposal submitted to the UNGA on information security (Radu 2013). The latter included a call for the creation of 'a multilateral, transparent and democratic international management of the Internet', reiterating the WSIS wording from negotiation drafts. The ITRs conference revived this discussion around intergovernmentalism versus multi-stakeholderism in the governance of the field and divided participants over the extent to which the treaty covered the Internet (Radu et al. 2014).

When more than 1,600 delegates from 151 member states met in Dubai on 3 to 14 December 2012 for the UN-sponsored meeting to amend the ITRs, the talks epitomized ideological struggles and conflicts between different socio-economic and representation models. The text of the treaty was satisfactory to many developing countries, as it covered, among others, means to foster transparency and competition for international mobile roaming charges, to reduce electronic waste, increase accessibility to international telecommunication services for persons with disabilities, and ways to facilitate access to international optical fibre networks for landlocked and small island developing states. At the same time, the preamble made reference to the commitment of member states to uphold human rights obligations in the implementation of the new ITRs.[17] The stakeholders opposing the WCIT negotiations questioned not only the legitimacy of the ITU to oversee security-related issues, in particular in the context of the provisions regarding cybersecurity (Article 5A) and unsolicited bulk electronic communications (Article 5B), but also the fact that participation in the discussions was

---

[17] Paragraph 2 of the preamble reads: 'Member States affirm their commitment to implement these Regulations in a manner that respects and upholds their human rights obligations.'

relatively limited (observation and advisory role) and voting was restricted to states only.

In the revised ITRs, Article 5A bound states to 'endeavour to ensure the security and robustness of international telecommunication networks', which raised concerns about limitations on content that signatory countries might pursue, thus legitimizing potential infringements on human rights. In this case, the negotiations revealed older tensions between the approaches of Russia, China, and the United States on information security, which previously surfaced in the UN General Assembly. The revised Article 5B of the treaty, stating that 'Member States should endeavour to take necessary measures to prevent the propagation of unsolicited bulk electronic communications and minimize its impact on international telecommunication services', was seen as a possible avenue to interfere with content online, for example in order to limit freedom of expression. Similar concerns surrounded the wording of the preamble, which contained a provision upholding the right of access of member states to international telecommunication services.

Given these fault lines, consensus was impossible to reach at the WCIT-12 and majority voting was used instead. Out of the 144 delegations with voting rights, eighty-nine were in favour (including Russia, China, Arab states, Iran, Brazil, Argentina, Mexico, Indonesia, South Korea, Turkey, and many African states) and fifty-five were against (including the United States, the United Kingdom, Canada, EU member-states, Australia, Japan, India, Kenya). The possibility was left for other states to join the new treaty later. Figure 2 shows the block of countries opposing the treaty, revealing a split along the developed–developing country dimension in the vote of the national delegations.

The split in the votes was described as a 'digital Cold War' (*The Economist* 2012; Mueller 2013), with countries divided into two camps led by the United States and Russia. A similar grouping of states could also be observed five months after the WCIT, on 16 to 18 May 2013, when the ITU hosted the World Telecommunication/ICTs Policy Forum in Geneva, a non-binding meeting facilitating exchange and information sharing on emerging telecommunication regulatory matters for states and sector members. The revised 2012 ITRs entered into force on 1 January 2015, allowing for the new rules and the 1988 ones to operate alongside. Against this background, a number of IG processes (inter alia, the decennial review of the World Summit on Information Society) were perceived as potential battlefields for the definition of future IG mechanisms.

In the ICANN space, 2012 is remembered for the new expansion of the DNS. Applications for the new generic top-level domains (gTLDs) were invited in January that year. Unlike in previous rounds, new domains could

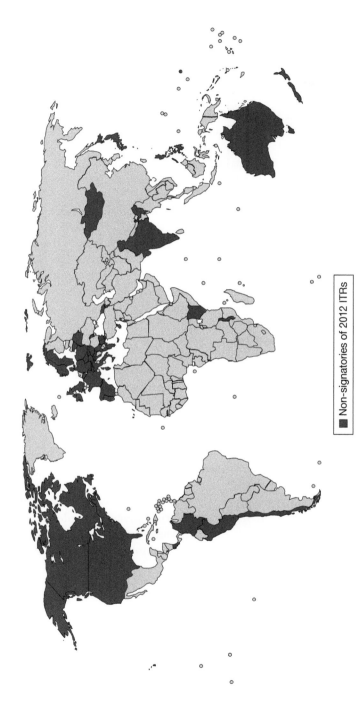

Figure 2 Non-signatories of the 2012 ITRs

be put forward in scripts other than Latin as Internationalized Domain Names, and be used for a variety of purposes, from business to community-oriented, including brand names or geographic strings. Policies to guide the application process had been in the making since 2005 in ICANN's Generic Names Supporting Organization, but the launch of the applications was met with a lot of criticism, this time by the private sector. In 2011, a coalition of seventy-nine corporations organized under the US Association of National Advertisers signed a petition against the new gTLD programme. Since 2014, their interests were channelled by the Coalition for Responsible Internet Domain Oversight, comprising seventy-nine companies and 102 associations.

Notwithstanding concerns regarding the protection of trademarks in domain name registrations and fears of confusing and predatory registrations, the new programme attracted a total of 1,930 applications at the end of the registration period and ICANN held a prioritization draw in December 2012 to move forward with independent third party expert processing. By October 2013, the first four new gTLDs were delegated,[18] followed by 475 more before January 2015. A string delegated in February 2015, *.sucks,*[19] brought the debate to a new level, opposing freedom of expression entitlements to suspicions of exploitation and coercion of brand holders.

Numerous underlying tensions in the IG space came to the surface between 2010 and 2012. States- or corporations-driven apprehensions over Internet ruling profiled more clearly the new interests at stake, whether it was agenda-setting power, policymaking, or direct influence over institutional processes. The Pandora's box was opened again in 2013, when confidential documents leaked by Edward Snowden showed the pervasiveness of the surveillance apparatus of the United States and its world-dominant national security agenda. The Snowden revelations brought to the forefront the cooperation between the US federal government agencies and Internet companies, overriding user privacy in pursuit of national interests. Beyond the specifics of the US intelligence-gathering practices under the PRISM mass surveillance programme, the disclosures marked a turning point in pushing for a more transparent and more accountable governance structure for the cyberspace.

---

[18] The strings delegated on 23 October 2013 were: 游戏(xn--unup4y)—Chinese for 'game(s)', сайт (xn--80aswg)—Russian for 'site', онлайн (xn--80asehdb)—Russian for 'online', شبكة (xn--ngbc5azd)—Arabic for 'web/network'.

[19] The domain *.sucks* belonged to Vox Populi, a Cayman Islands based registry which allegedly charged a premium for brands to defensively reserve anything related to their name.

Post-Snowden Fault Lines

A deep rift formed in IG in mid-2013. On 5 June, the British newspaper *The Guardian* started publishing a series of articles about the secret collection of data by the US National Security Agency (NSA) and subsequently disclosed the wide scope of the PRISM surveillance programme. The data came from classified government documents leaked by Edward Snowden, a computer security specialist and former NSA contractor, who left the United States to seek temporary asylum in Russia. Three international media outlets—the US-based *Washington Post*, the British *Guardian*, and the German *Der Spiegel*—analysed the documents released by Snowden and reported that thirty-five world leaders had their phone communications tapped (including Brazil's President Dilma Rousseff and German Chancellor Angela Merkel) and that the NSA surveillance capabilities had also been used in monitoring the communications of foreign companies like Huawei in China and Petrobras in Brazil (Globo 2013). According to the *Washington Post*, the NSA collected around 5 billion phone records every day (Gellman and Soltani 2013a) and 97 billion pieces of data in March 2013 alone. Part of the information was collected by tapping directly into the unsecured connections of Google, Yahoo!, and Microsoft data centres around the world (Gellman and Soltani 2013b).

It was not the first time confidential documents from the US administration were made public, generating reactions worldwide. Prior to the Snowden revelations, Wikileaks held the headlines for most of 2010 by publishing footage from the 2007 Baghdad airstrike, complemented, a couple of months later, by the Iraqi War Logs. In July, they released around 77,000 documents compiled in the 'Afghan War Diary' and in November the organization leaked diplomatic cables of the US State Department, generating a massive outcry from political leaders. The documents were disclosed by Chelsea Manning (born Bradley Edward Manning), who was soon after convicted on multiple charges and served time at a maximum-security facility in Kansas, United States.[20]

Manning's revelations showed the power of the Internet in disseminating information, yet Snowden's classified documents revealed the global ramifications of the US surveillance apparatus. Alongside the NSA, the British Government Communications Headquarters and Communications Security Establishment Canada also engaged in extensive spying on individuals and

---

[20] Manning was released in May 2017, after her sentence was commuted by President Obama in January 2017 to 7 years of confinement since her arrest.

on political organizations. The US-driven discourse on Internet freedom, promoted in particular by the US Secretary of State Hillary Clinton lost its credibility when the Snowden leaks went to press. There was a sharp contrast between the free flow of information discourse and the practices of the NSA. Back in 2010, Secretary Clinton argued that:

Information freedom supports the peace and security that provides a foundation for global progress. Historically, asymmetrical access to information is one of the leading causes of interstate conflict. When we face serious disputes or dangerous incidents, it's critical that people on both sides of the problem have access to the same set of facts and opinions. (Clinton 2010)

For the IG communities already divided over the roles attributed to each in the Tunis Agenda, the Snowden leaks provided an opportunity to call for reform, in particular to restore trust and increase collaboration towards transparency and accountability. The minimization of the role of the US government constituted one of the dividing lines, resulting in a transfer of the oversight role of the Department of Commerce over IANA. On 7 October 2013, the technical bodies in charge of managing global resources—ICANN, the IETF, the WWW Consortium, the Internet Architecture Board, ISOC, and all five of the regional Internet address registries—issued a common statement to call for 'accelerating the globalization of ICANN and IANA functions, towards an environment in which all stakeholders, including all governments, participate on an equal footing' (ISOC 2013). This was also echoed in an EU press release dated 12 February 2014, calling for the 'establishment of a clear timeline for the globalization of ICANN and the IANA functions', as well as 'strengthening the multi-stakeholder model to preserve the Internet as a fast engine for innovation'.

Following the revelations, Brazil and Germany drafted a UN General Assembly resolution on 'the right to privacy in the digital age' adopted unanimously on 18 December 2013. The resolution affirmed that 'the same rights that people have offline must also be protected online, including the right to privacy' and called upon member states to review their procedures, practices, and legislation on the surveillance of communications, their interception and collection of personal data, including mass surveillance, with a 'view to upholding the right to privacy by ensuring the full and effective implementation of all relevant obligations under international human rights law' (UNGA 2013). The initiative also stirred a related process within the Human Rights Council, which appointed, in July 2015, the first Special Rapporteur on the Right to Privacy.

Building on its efforts in the UN, Brazil hosted the April 2014 Global Multistakeholder Meeting on Internet Governance, known as NetMundial, announced after a tête-à-tête between the Brazilian President and ICANN's President and CEO Fadi Chehadé. Prior to the meeting, a proposal was made to hold online consultations drawing on the successful experience of the Brazilian Civil Rights Framework for the Internet (Marco Civil), a law that was drafted collaboratively over many years using an online platform to gather inputs from a wide range of stakeholders. Upholding the multi-stakeholder principle, NetMundial was innovative in its approach to assigning an equal number of slots for the four groups of interests identified: governmental, business, technical and academic, and civil society, offering a rowing microphone for interventions in the plenary discussions.

NetMundial concluded with a negotiated final statement outlining IG principles and a roadmap for further action. The anti-surveillance focus was toned down in the negotiations (Radu et al. 2015), yet the document became emblematic as it recognized the evolving roles and responsibilities of stakeholders, a heated debate post-WSIS. Part of the discussions focused on ICANN and the NTIA announcement from the month before of its intent to finalize the privatization of the IANA functions, started in 1998. Following the meeting in São Paulo, the NetMundial Initiative was launched in Geneva in August that year by the Brazilian Internet Steering Committee (CGI.br), ICANN, and the WEF, hosted by the latter. The initiative pursued very broad objectives that did not translate in concrete actions and came under criticism for its limited legitimacy and opaque procedures around the selection of its steering committee participants. It subsequently refocused on capacity development and lost visibility.

Around the same time, preparations for the decennial review of the World Summit on Information Society (referred to as WSIS + 10) intensified. The fears that the process would be less open than it had been in 2003 and 2005 were confirmed as the negotiations remained primarily intergovernmental. With the involvement of a number of UN bodies, and prominently the background work of the CSTD, the decennial review was completed with an evaluation of the progress made since 2005 and a GA High-Level Meeting, held at the UN headquarters in New York in December 2015. The merging of the WSIS priorities and the Sustainable Development Goals (SDGs) agenda were in focus, presenting many similarities to the Geneva Plan of Action and Tunis Agenda. While ICT-related goals were not listed among the SDGs (with the exception of Goal 9c regarding improved access), the Internet was discussed as an enabling platform for achieving the Agenda 2030 goals.

Importantly, throughout the WSIS + 10 negotiations and in the submissions of the different national delegations, consensus emerged around four key issues: digital divide—mentioned by all but three of the submitters (ISOC 2015a)—Internet access, child online protection, and support for multi-stakeholderism (broadly understood). While the first two issues represented areas in which significant progress was still needed, the latter were new items compared to the 2003 to 2005 WSIS discussions. The multiplicity of governance mechanisms acknowledged and evaluated ahead of the decennial review—stressing the multi-stakeholder component—revealed many instances of self-regulation and collaboration across sectors.

However, as in the past, the most heated discussion was around the 'roles and responsibilities' of actors, where no agreement could be reached. The final wording upheld the formulation included in the Tunis Agenda, recognizing that 'the management of the Internet as a global facility includes multilateral, transparent, democratic and multi-stakeholder processes, with the full involvement of Governments, the private sector, civil society, international organisations technical and academic communities, and all other relevant stakeholders in their respective roles and responsibilities' (paragraph 57). The long-negotiated outcome document, which received public input at different stages (with many contributions from civil society), made only one reference to surveillance in paragraph 46, as member states failed to agree on a more precise wording.

Mechanisms of Governance

The patchwork of international rules that emerged throughout the WSIS decade pointed to a clearer understanding of shared responsibility for Internet policymaking. More diverse and increasingly private sources of authoritative decisions were profiling, followed by regulatory responses at the national and international levels. Beside the hybrid configurations, a redefinition and scaling up of the public domain could be observed in the process. The much denser regulatory pressure during this period was driven by ideological, diplomatic, and technological developments. The governance arrangements thus formed—summarized in Table 5—relied much more on discursive and operative modelling than on hard law, making the voices of non-state actors better heard. Some of these were traditional players which acquired a significant responsibility for Internet regulation over the years; others were newcomers to the process and demanded self-regulation or an equal footing in the deliberations. As more international institutions introduced specialized mandates or expanded existing mandates to address the realm of IG, their political standing was called into question and status-quo maintenance drew supporters closer together.

Table 5 Governance arrangements (global and regional) for the period 2005–15 (based on a total of 212 instruments recorded in the dataset)

Mechanisms	Instruments	%	Examples
Legal enshrinement	*Treaties, conventions*	7%	2009 SCO Agreement on Cooperation in the Field of International Information Security
			2013 WIPO Marrakesh Treaty
			2014 African Union Convention on Cyber Security and Personal Data Protection
	Court judgments	9%	2012 ECHR judgment *Ahmet Yildirim v. Turkey*
			2014 CJEU judgment *Costeja v. Google*
			2015 CJEU judgment *Schems v. Facebook*
Institutional solidification	*Specialized bodies*	11%	2010 Broadband Commission for Digital Development
			2005, 2010, 2013, 2015 UN Group of Governmental Experts on Developments in the Field of Information and Telecommunication in the Context of International Security
			2014 Global Commission on Internet Governance
			2015 Global Forum on Cyber Expertise
	Strategic framework/ agenda	14%	2007 Global Cybersecurity Agenda
			2013 OSCE Confidence Building Measures (CBMs) Stemming from the Use of ICTs
			2014 Facebook's Free Basics
			2015 Europe's Digital Single Market
	Monitoring and benchmarking	6%	2011 Boston Consulting Group E-Intensity Index
			2014 ITU's Global Cybersecurity Index
			2014 Internet Traffic Monitoring Data Sharing (TSUBAME project)
Modelling	*Discursive*	33%	2009 CoE Prague Declarations on A New European Approach for Safer Internet for Children
			2011 Deauville G8 Declaration
			2013 UNESCO Sakhalin Declaration on Internet and Socio-Cultural Transformations
			2014 UN Resolution on Right to Privacy in the Digital Age (A/RES/69/166)

(continued)

Table 5   Continued

Mechanisms	Instruments	%	Examples
	Operative	**20%**	2005 WB ICT in Education Toolkit for Policymakers, Planners & Practitioners
			2008 GSMA Mobile Alliance Against Child Sexual Abuse Content
			2011 Consumers International A Guide to Developing Consumer Protection Law
			2013 CoE Model Framework on Net Neutrality

Globally, the WSIS decade can be seen as the 'golden era of regulation' (Levi-Faur and Jordana 2005) for the Internet. Governance instruments aimed at limiting and constraining—rather than merely shaping—the behaviour of other actors became the norm across all Internet subareas. The overall increase in the number of dedicated instruments for this period (212 recorded in the database, compared to seventy-four in the previous period) attested to the high salience of the field, which matured into an institutional domain open to political contestation. Modelling mechanisms employed during the WSIS decade—primarily discursive, but also operative—constituted 53 per cent of all formal instruments in use by relevant actors. In the wake of the 2013 revelations by Edward Snowden—evidencing the depth and extent of the NSA surveillance—the dominant position of the United States came under fire explicitly or implicitly in many statements. The operative measures that complemented the high-level speeches or declarations aimed at guiding the development of policies in developing countries or introducing soft law principles in the routines of various organizations.

In parallel, the rights agenda consolidated. Early references to it dated back to the 2003 WSIS Declaration of Principles which affirmed the importance of maintaining and strengthening rights—in particular in connection with development and freedom of expression. While that document remained vague about implementing this vision, later efforts to turn that into reality materialized first at the national level and subsequently at the regional and global levels. Access to broadband Internet was first declared a right in Finland in 2010. A year later, a report of the UN Special Rapporteur on the promotion and protection of the right to freedom of opinion and expression, Frank La Rue, concluded that disconnecting people from the Internet was against international law and constituted a human rights violation (La Rue 2011).

Time and again, fears of Internet fragmentation via data localization practices were also understood in terms of human rights: in response to the NTIA surveillance leaks, there were repeated calls by government leaders to keep their users' data on national territory. The human rights framing, used extensively both before and after the Snowden revelations, grounded a number of discussions that cut across subfields, such as net neutrality. Ambiguously defined, the human rights discourse remained open to a plurality of political articulations, opening certain positions up for change and reinterpretation. This stood in sharp contrast with the securitization discourse solidifying in the cybersecurity arena around the same time.

With no mentioning of human rights, China's prioritization of the 'cyber sovereignty' approach meant that everything happening on the networks inside its territory would be subject to national rule. By 2008, the decade-long development of the Great Firewall of China was completed and a new form of censorship was in place, limiting access to certain foreign websites and close control of cross-border Internet traffic. This was further enhanced via legislative action to stimulate the growth of the domestic Internet industry by limiting the presence of Western services[21] or by the introduction of explicit provisions for foreign companies to respect domestic regulations. The last step in the process of developing an own Internet was the implementation of the National Public Security Work Informational Project (or the Golden Shield Project) for online content monitoring via surveillance and filtering. Two policies implemented by Xi's government on anti-rumours and real name registration brought an ever-tighter control to the 560 million Chinese Internet users recorded in 2015. Harsh content controls were also introduced across the Middle East following the wave of Arab Spring protests in 2010 to 2012 and further expanded into authoritarian states in both Africa and Asia, in most cases implemented on Western technology (Deibert 2015).

Against this background, the strong emphasis on placing the Internet high up on global agendas and in strategic frameworks (14 per cent of all instruments recorded in the dataset) derived primarily from the creation of a global market based on the free flow of information. Improvements in connectivity speeds and mobile Internet made online transactions faster and more convenient. Be it for raising or disbursing resources, the Internet became a top global priority. Paradoxically though, financial mechanisms attached to Internet initiatives have varied in their success and the global Internet agenda has mostly been built discursively. The SDGs, part of the broad

---

[21] China developed its own version of popular services: Youku (YouTube), Weibo (Twitter), Renren (Facebook), WeChat (WhatsApp).

intergovernmental UN framework known as *Agenda 2030*, did not include the Internet[22] among its seventeen goals, but considered it a key enabling platform for achieving the targets.

At the end of 2005, half of the world's population—mostly in developing countries—was not yet connected to the Internet (ITU 2015). Programmes like Facebook's Internet.org (later renamed Free Basics), initiated in 2014 to connect hard-to-reach populations in developing countries at no cost for the user, saw a halt and a redesign amid protests for limiting access to only a few Facebook-sanctioned services online and violating net neutrality via its zero-rating agreement[23] with mobile operators in the target areas. Many activists accused the company of introducing a 'two-tiered Internet, on which new users could get stuck on a separate and unequal path to Internet connectivity, which will serve to widen—not narrow—the digital divide' (Hern 2015); Facebook's main competitors did not back the initiative. The programme was banned by the Indian regulator on net neutrality grounds in February 2016; however, it expanded and became operational in a number of African and Latin American countries (Zambia, Tanzania, Ghana, Kenya and South Africa, Colombia and Bolivia).

Like the Indian example shows, national regulation became overall more powerful vis-à-vis corporations towards the end of the WSIS decade, though wide differences persisted in terms of local regulatory capacity. The other route of Internet decision-making implementation was via the judiciary. In this period, 9 per cent of all authoritative decisions about the Internet came from courts. Gradually, the role of the judiciary in Internet policymaking strengthened, culminating with two key decisions of the Court of Justice of the European Union (CJEU) at the end of the WSIS decade: the introduction of the 'right to be forgotten' in 2014 and the 2015 invalidation of the Safe Harbour scheme for data transfers.

In the landmark case C-131/12 *Google Spain SL, Google Inc. v. Agencia Española de Protección de Datos (AEPD) and Mario Costeja González*, the CJEU established that, based on their right to erasure, individuals can ask for their personal information to be de-listed from search engines. Accordingly, it imposed an obligation on Google to act on the potential removal from search results of items that are 'inadequate, irrelevant or no longer relevant, or excessive in relation to the purposes for which they were processed and in the light of the time that has elapsed' (CJEU 2014), when the person concerned so requests.

---

[22] With the exception of Goal 9c, which refers to expanding Internet access.
[23] The zero-rating model consists of providing Internet access to certain websites free of charge as part of a user's data plan.

In practice, the CJEU judgment delegated to the company the case-by-case, human review of links for potential deletion, entrusting Google with a first decision on the matter; in case of dissatisfaction, the complaint could go to court, thus having the search engine's decision as a first step in a longer legal process. In the implementation of the 'right to be forgotten', Google acquired quasi-judicial powers, adjudicating on the display of personal information, which constituted the core of its business model (Chenou and Radu 2017). To comply with the court decision, Google opened an online delinking request form on 29 May 2014 and received 12,000 deindexing requests in the following 24 hours. From September to November 2014, it held consultations with the newly established Advisory Council (made up of invited experts) in seven European capitals. One year after the CJEU judgment, Google received 253,258 de-listing requests with a total of 918,699 links to be evaluated. Of these, 58.7 per cent were not removed.

In 2015, EU's highest court decided that the Safe Harbour agreement—which regulated data transfers to non-EU countries based on a guarantee of 'adequate protection'—was invalid, since it failed to ensure it in the case brought forward by the young Austrian lawyer and activist Maximilian Schrems against Facebook Ireland Ltd. His complaint, filed with the Irish Data Protection Commission, followed the suspected involvement of the company in the PRISM mass surveillance programme and requested the prohibition of further data transfers from Ireland to the United States. The CJEU decided on 6 October that government interference and lack of legal remedies for individuals who seek to access data about themselves on specific services meant the United States had lower privacy standards than the EU, thus triggering negotiations around a new transatlantic data transfer scheme.

The value-laden rules imposed in the two Court cases discussed showed the power of courts in reversing authoritative decisions from earlier periods of time, be they company practices or transatlantic agreements. With an embryonic Internet industry, the EU redirected its efforts towards carving out new spaces for regulation in data control and data protection (Radu and Chenou 2015). Europe's Digital Single Market, announced by the Juncker Commission in May 2015, aimed to create EU-wide regulation for e-commerce, telecommunications, and digital marketing, eliminating the national barriers and rendering the European market first in digital economy. With over 500 million Internet users with the highest purchasing power around the globe, the EU was, around the late 2000s, well-positioned to assume a strong digital regulator role by designing legislation and norms that were gradually adopted by many more countries outside its jurisdiction.

Governance throughout the WSIS decade was thus enacted though structural elements that directed, constrained, or defined action and partnership frameworks. Although not in focus in previous decades, efforts to closely monitor and sanction came to characterize the period in which the Internet became a truly global medium. Such developments revealed that the enforcement capabilities generally associated with international institutions did not vanish, but were in fact complemented by benchmarking initiatives and comparative rankings.

Variation of governance mechanisms across subfields was a constant in the data analysed here. A clear focus on two areas of regulatory action emerged throughout the WSIS decade. Figure 3 provides an illustration of the thematic grouping and distribution of instruments in the six areas of interest analysed throughout this study. One-third of the instruments recorded deal with security, primarily cybersecurity, child online protection, and cybercrime. Another third address civil liberties, in particular privacy, data protection, and freedom of expression. Often presented as a trade-off, cybersecurity and online personal freedoms remained top of the agenda following the 9/11 attacks in the United States and subsequent attacks in Europe. The frequency and high impact of online disruptions took centre stage in the work of many institutions. The ITU launched its Global Cybersecurity Agenda in 2007, at the same time as its cyberpeace discourse, which lost visibility shortly after.

Internationally, the first cyberattack to paralyse a country happened in 2007 in Estonia, when governmental and bank services were inaccessible for several days due to distributed denial of service attacks, allegedly coordinated from Russia. In 2010, during the Russian–Georgian war over the independence status of South Ossetia, online attacks blocked the Georgian channels

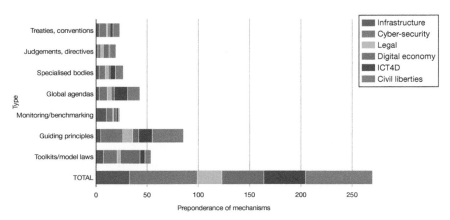

Figure 3 Variation of governance mechanisms across subfields (2005–15)

Note: total does not add up due to multiple cases in which an instrument covers several subfields

of communication at strategic points in time (Radu 2013). Pertinent cyber actions throughout the WSIS decade could range from probing the limits of cyber defence at the state level or in the private sector, to signalling power positions, and finally to inflicting damage. At the global level, responses came primarily under the form of ad hoc security governance networks and public–private cooperation. Existing transnational governmental networks—including the North Atlantic Treaty Organization (NATO), the Shanghai Cooperation Organization, and the G8—started developing dedicated programmes and units; new forums for discussion have also emerged: the 2011 London Process initiated the biennial series of Global Cyberspace Conferences and led to the creation of Global Forum on Cyber Expertise (GFCE);[24] the Munich Security Conference has included dedicated cyber activities since 2012.

Many other governmental initiatives focused on a broad understanding of cybersecurity and national capabilities, in particular as more and more Computer Emergency Response Teams (CERTs) and Computer Security Incident Response Teams (CSIRTs) were established for national-level coordination. Originally, the threats posed to Internet security were solved informally, without making appeals to other institutions, due to the localized nature of risks and their low impact. This changed with the rise of cross-border attacks and the limited expertise available, primarily concentrated within firms and closed communities of scientists (Schmidt 2014). While companies were often called in to work alongside state institutions in cyber crises, only governments could legally pursue perpetrators in the few cases in which attribution could be assigned. While intergovernmental cooperation on cybersecurity increased, other governmental initiatives, such as the Freedom Online Coalition, profiled themselves as fighting the downsides of securitizing and monitoring information flows. It is noteworthy that there was often overlapping membership in some of these divergent initiatives.

The civil liberties focus, captured in the human rights agenda and reinforced after the Snowden revelations, materialized in concrete efforts to design internet rights charters, such as those developed by the Association for Progressive Communication and the Internet Rights and Principles Coalition in 2013, which merged concerns for freedom of expression, access, and accessibility with privacy and security protections, as well as political participation and cultural and linguistic diversity. Soft regulation and self-regulatory tools also included significant references to rights, in particular at the level

---

[24] The GFCE acts as a global platform to share experiences, identify gaps, and strengthen cyber capacities worldwide. Its membership comprises fifty countries, international organizations, and companies.

of guiding principles. Going in the opposite direction, the CJEU decision against Google on the 'right to be forgotten' aimed at regulating dominant actors' behaviour in the market (Chenou and Radu 2017) by imposing an obligation on them to de-list information when requested to do so. This 're-versibility of authority' that Hall and Biersteker discussed back in 2002 was introduced via courts, but also via soft law.

In this shift to tackle the Internet economy, the discursive repertoires of various actors became unstable over time, resulting in institutional ambiguity and longer strategic negotiations in the framework of binding instruments. As in the case of cybersecurity, the concentration of efforts on digital economy showed that the new political tensions were no longer about infrastructure, but about the market value of the Internet. Admittedly, in the struggle be-tween states and the 'Internet giants', regulatory measures for information intermediaries have included a 'turn to infrastructure' (Musiani et al. 2015). Noteworthy cases include code remedies for interoperability.[25] The non-linearity of regulation, pushing certain priorities up and others down, made institutional ambiguity a permanent feature of the WSIS + 10 process. Global strategic agendas were reduced to the minimum common denominator to defer controversial choices.

The privileged role of the US administration continued to stir tensions. The legitimacy of the US government to set global rules via extraterritorial reach was questioned multiple times during the decade. In 2012, when the US Congress discussed two anti-piracy bills that triggered global protests, the Stop Online Piracy Act (SOPA) and the Protect IP Act (PIPA), the first global 'Internet strike' was organized on 18 January 2012. Over one billion Internet users worldwide (Sell 2013) were affected by the blackout of websites, con-sisting of temporarily making their content unavailable and redirecting users to a message opposing the proposed legislation. At stake were the regulatory over-reach powers granted by these laws and their wide-ranging consequences on Internet users worldwide.

In 2013, Microsoft challenged in court the request of the US government to turn over the emails stored in a data centre in Ireland of a target account linked to a drug investigation, opening a long-lasting inquiry into the extra-territoriality of law enforcement based on the 1986 Stored Communications Act. Meanwhile, Microsoft announced that it would open cloud servers in partnership with Deutsche Telekom in Germany, where the privacy laws are strict, to avoid warrants of a similar kind. The question of jurisdiction also

---

[25] This is what the European Commission mandated for Microsoft in the final settlement of its antitrust case in 2009 and what the Federal Trade Commission decided in the antitrust settlement of Intel in 2010.

continued to surround the IANA stewardship transition process, announced in 2014; at stake was the California-based incorporation of the body created in 1998, in a previous NTIA effort to privatize the domain name system.

Moreover, the alignment of the US government with the Silicon Valley industry interests resulted in a push for regulatory action in the EU. In 2014, the EU Parliament discussed a non-binding resolution to break up Google, while the European Commission opened an antitrust investigation into Google's search and advertising services. The role of private intermediaries was called into question as their financial and political power rose steeply. Their relation to governments was also probed, particularly from 2013 onwards. The digital business model based on the collection, storage, and third-party sharing of personal data, coupled with profiling for targeted advertising, was not the main target of regulation, but was subsequently affected by sectoral laws, such as those dealing with privacy and data protection.

As regulatory patterns evolved, the conceptualization of rule-making broadened. The use of modelling instruments became mainstreamed in the activities of organizations with tangential roles in IG. Importantly, during the WSIS decade and in particular post-Snowden, the authority of technical bodies expanded to public policies issues such as encryption and surveillance, whereas privacy and data protection became politically disputed. The continuous renegotiation of positions observed from 2012 to 2015 embodied a struggle over fundamental values and principles for global IG. In the absence of a central mechanism for coordinating Internet-related policies, hybrid configurations became the norm, building on the interconnectedness of actors.

Actors

The multiplication and decentralization of sources of authority during the WSIS decade brought about new challenges for legitimacy in IG, ranging from the protection of critical infrastructure to control over the domain name system. Not only did these challenges alter the position of bodies such as the ITU or ICANN, but they also defined fundamental choices for institutional trajectories. The WSIS decade activated a set of interests that solidified over the years and led to institutional mandate expansion, mission overlap, and alternative fora. Noteworthy, private intermediaries taking on authoritative stances, acting as defenders of human rights online, and calling on governments to protect individual freedoms were not uncommon in this space.

At the end of 2015, the United States was home to eleven out of the fifteen largest Internet businesses, ranked by market capitalization: Apple,

Google, Facebook, Amazon, eBay, Priceline, Salesforce, Yahoo!, Netflix, LinkedIn, and Twitter, followed by China, hosting Alibaba, Tencent, Baidu, and JD.com (Meeker 2015, 6). This dominance was closely mirrored at the IETF meetings, where the Americans and the Chinese became the best represented nationalities. This reconfiguration was closely linked to the growth of digital markets based on e-commerce and the development of new applications. The Chinese case is particularly interesting as it challenges the de-regulatory credo of innovation. Evolving in a tightly controlled space, the Chinese companies played a major role in reshaping the Chinese society, currently the largest Internet user base in the world.

Operating internationally, they also reshaped standardization procedures for the digital economy, along with other East Asian businesses like KT, Samsung, and LG in South Korea, or NTT, Panasonic, and Sony in Japan. The world's largest e-commerce platform Alibaba (founded by Jack Ma), the search engine Baidu or Tencent, which developed the mobile messaging app WeChat, have not only enhanced competition in the digital market, but have also exposed new ways of operating under the restrictions of the Chinese government, which blocked services like Twitter, Facebook, WhatsApp, Viber, or Line. Moreover, Chinese companies have also restructured the manufacturing and infrastructure market, providing lower-cost options via Huawei or Xiaomi. Rather than undermining state authority, market players such as the ones discussed above often joined forces with governments.

More than a proof of polycentricity, the diversification of venues and governance mechanisms indicated a weaker consensus and stronger contention over key issues in IG, particularly after the Wikileaks and Snowden revelations. Concerns about the long dominance of US actors—governmental or private—in IG were articulated by both developing countries and non-state actors. In addition to the efforts by emerging powers to situate themselves more prominently in the field, alternative venues were created for discussing what did not fit the 'mainstream' discourse. Noteworthy examples include the alignment of positions within G77 and the creation of the Internet Ungovernance Forum (IUF) and the Internet Social Forum (ISF). The IUF has been held annually alongside the UN-driven Internet Governance Forum (IGF) since 2014, and focuses on Internet censorship, freedom of speech, surveillance, and privacy. It was first convened in Istanbul with the support of a few international (Association for Progressive Communication, Article 19, AccessNow, Open Rights Group, Tactical Tech, WebWeWant, etc.) and local civil society groups (Alternative Informatics Association, Istanbul HackerSpace, etc.). The ISF was a thematic grouping of the World

Social Forum (WSF)[26] established in Tunis in 2015, proposing 'Another (People's) Internet' and aiming to serve as a global space for 'sharing information on endeavours and struggles for democracy, human rights and social justice in relation to the Internet, and developing collective action agendas'. Its founding document called for opposing surveillance, corporate dominance, and governmental abuse of power. Upon its creation, the ISF was endorsed by more than 100 civil society organizations.

While NGOs pushed for a more open environment and alternative opinion, some of the technical bodies remained confined to their traditional practices and were slow to respond to reforms. Within ICANN, in charge of the management of the Internet domain name and unique identifiers, the 'virtually unconstrained power' entrusted to its Board of Directors was first questioned at the beginning of the 2000s (Weber and Gunnarson 2012, 13), and subsequently in the work of CCWG-Accountability as part of the IANA Stewardship process. For the longest time, its decisions could not be reversed even in cases in which they contravened ICANN's by-laws or other written commitments and they could only limitedly be contested. The new process of reform started with the transition of the IANA functions, which also included an accountability reform, making it mandatory for the organization to undergo changes before the oversight from the DoC was completed (originally expected to happen in September 2015, prolonged for another year). Other technical bodies started to integrate policy experts in their boards and expert committees, but their membership did not reflect this diversity: American and Chinese male technologists with private sector affiliations constituted the large majority.

Watershed moments such as the WSIS, the WCIT-12, the 2013 Snowden revelations, and NetMundial re-affirmed the strong position of governments and the divisions within this nominal grouping. There was a lack of agreement over security-related matters stemming from basic contestation over locating authoritative decision-making, thus calling into question the status-quo relationships among stakeholders. Russia and China refused to sign the CoE Cybercrime Convention, but proposed and signed their own information security agreement in the framework of the Shanghai Cooperation Group. The two powers, along with India, Brazil, and South Africa—also referred to as

---

[26] The WSF was formed in opposition to the annual World Economic Forum (WEF) meeting in Davos, and its Charter calls for a different kind of globalization than that 'commanded by the large multinational corporations and by the governments and international institutions at the service of those corporations' interests' (WSF Charter). The first edition of WSF was held in Pôrto Alegre in 2001.

the 'BRICS' grouping—have been very vocal about creating an institutional environment in which formal equality among states was observed and power differentials were offset. Their demand for neutralizing power imbalances in decision-making amounted to a procedural fairness argument, albeit one possible only in an intergovernmental arrangement.

Yet seeing this period solely as state-dominated is misleading. Rather, it is an exemplary embodiment of hybrid arrangements, which transform, in their application, the very subjects and objects of governance concerned. Not only have there been cross-sector partnerships, but also influential technological developments resulting from the cooperation of institutions generally perceived to be in competition, especially over the intergovernmental or multi-stakeholder approach. For example, UNESCO collaborated with ICANN on the internationalization of Internet domain names. The IETF worked with the ISO for developing standards, for example codecs to manage audio and video content online, but also with the ITU-T for the development of basic protocols (Chenou and Radu 2015). Moreover, the Tunis Agenda mandated a set of UN specialized bodies to jointly conduct the follow-up and monitoring of the process, either by initiating actions or by convening annual meetings for self-reporting purposes.

The blanket cyber-surveillance plan known as PRISM revealed by Snowden encouraged many civil society organizations and activist groups, whether based in the United States or elsewhere, to take action to raise awareness regarding privacy protections and encryption systems. Challenging norms of inclusion and representation (Hintz and Milan 2009), grassroots tech groups such as *Anonymous* started profiling themselves more visibly around web-defacing operations to contest Internet-related negotiations conducted behind closed doors. Public protests around free trade agreements led to the rejection of the Anti-Counterfeiting Trade Agreement (ACTA) in 2012 and to the halting of comprehensive trade agreements in their drafting phase (e.g. Transatlantic Trade and Investment Partnership or the Trans-Pacific Partnership). Such instances of contestation revealed the centrality of the Internet in broader economic governance, including the request to uphold the established IG principles in new forms of decision-making.

The power of various actors was interest- and mission-driven, but their functional positioning had to do with the capacity to take on roles not available to others in a densely populated policy space. The Tunis Agenda perpetuated the artificial distinction between public policy and technical issues in IG, de facto endorsing the private sector-led management of the Internet via its emphasis on maintaining the stability and security of the Internet in an unchanged configuration. Yet, leaving international organizations out of the tripartite categorization of stakeholders did not accurately reflect the governance configurations emerging. By the end of the WSIS decade, we could distinguish among organizations with core, secondary, and tangential interests, be it in standard-setting processes or in regulating one or multiple areas pertaining to IG writ large. Technical bodies designed specifically for Internet standards and protocols or associated functions generally preserved that as their core mission.

Within these broad categories that place IG interests at the centre, there was variation over time as to where international organizations would position themselves. Bodies like the IGF Secretariat are designed with core IG interests in mind, whereas organizations traditionally involved in telecommunication regulation went through an expansion of mandates. It was the case for the ITU, but also for WIPO, which was among the first institutions to incorporate Internet-related matters in its daily work. Starting in the late 1990s, it was involved in negotiating different aspects of online intellectual property rights, as diverse as the 1998 Universal Domain Name Dispute Resolution Policy (UDRP) for domain names and the 2014 Marrakesh Treaty facilitating access to published works by persons who are blind, visually impaired, or otherwise print disabled.

For organizations with tangential interests, IG did not require a reconceptualization of the work they were involved in. For example, UNESCO presented itself as playing a threefold role in IG: (1) contributing to legal, societal, and ethical aspects of policymaking; (2) participating in discussions and assisting in reaching long-term solutions in IG; (3) advocating for safeguarding key values like freedom of expression, cultural diversity, and openness in current and future Internet policies (UNESCO 2004). With a less sizable involvement, UNIDIR was the convenor of policy debates around cybersecurity and use of online resources for terrorist activities—carving out an IG space after the stalemate of disarmament negotiations.

The decade in which the Internet knew its largest expansion was set against the background of state engagement in the articulation of governance, both as part of trans-governmental networks and as part of international organizations. This period also federated the participation of non-state actors in international negotiations, with growing legitimacy bestowed on them, thus giving birth to large cross-sector coalitions. The hybrid nature of such governance configurations also permeated national delegations to international congresses, which—more often than not—comprised members of industry and civil society. Moves across sectors, in particular from government to business and vice versa, a phenomenon referred to as the 'revolving door', facilitated the spread of ideas in support of the status quo. High officials in charge of US information policies either started or completed their careers in the private sector. The US DoC and the NTIA are telling examples in this sense, as they extensively consulted with the private sector in the development of policies on cybersecurity and innovation (McCarthy 2015).

Similar patterns of cross-sectoral moves could be seen with a number of early leaders involved in multiple IG fora, shifting from business gatherings to UN meetings. These patterns sometimes revealed an individual commitment to a particular issue; other times, engagement was circumstantial or position-dependent. In the civil society and technical and scientific community, the 'multiple hat' phenomenon was extremely common, as most influential individuals navigated between the public and the private sector in their careers and held several affiliations at a time (Chenou 2014).

Anchoring Practices: Ad Hoc Expert Groups

The increasing hybridization of governance processes during the WSIS decade played a pivotal role in laying the foundation for the habitual resort to ad hoc expert groups. They were supporting the institutionalization of initiatives specific to the Internet and signalling the key role of expertise in the construction of this issue domain. Formed on a case-by-case basis, ad hoc groups brought together, for a limited period of time, different stakeholders to develop and provide an expert opinion, generally summarized in a final report. The underlying tenet in the creation of ad hoc groups was the need to tackle problems as they emerged, in a piecemeal fashion, and legitimize courses of action and decisions in a technocratic manner. In some cases, establishing such a committee became a controversial process, but very few questioned the outcomes.

The practice emerged as a common solution in the work of the standardization bodies in the early days and its statute as a dominant practice post-WSIS in Internet-related policy issues at the end of the WSIS decade revealed the continuation of informal relations of authority. Out of functional necessity or in search for licensing one answer over many possible alternatives, ad hoc expert groups deployed expertise readily available. A key role continued to be played by individuals acting as authoritative community voices (Mathiason 2009). Influential members of the technical community (e.g. Vint Cerf) and academics-cum-practitioners who were active within and around the WGIG, such as Wolfgang Kleinwaechter, Bertrand de la Chapelle, Milton Mueller, William Drake, Jovan Kurbalija, or Jeanette Hoffman often received invitations to take part in high-level discussions and working groups reflecting on the future of the field (Chenou 2014).

Shaping processes such as the WGIG or the IGF, Nitin Desai and Markus Kummer continued to be at the forefront of UN-driven interactions with a plethora of stakeholders (Epstein 2012).

Despite the open nature in the operations of many of the groups formed at the time, concerns were raised from the outset regarding the authority entrusted in the newly formed committees and bodies. This was best illustrated by the heated discussions around the formation of the first Multistakeholder Advisory Group (MAG) for the IGF in 2006:

The MAG, an ad hoc creation of the UN Secretary General which is part of the WSIS decisions, was supposed to help the secretariat regarding IGF procedures, selection process to ensure pluralism and transparency, methodology—not predetermine content or agenda! This should be the task of the first IGF meeting itself—and the IGF should have final say on procedures as well. (Carlos Afonso cited in Raboy et al. 2010, 181)

As to the choice of establishing the MAG in the first place, Nitin Desai explained that the decision was influenced by discussions with donors. Answering a question from the floor during the February 2007 open consultations, Desai noted:

When you have a multistakeholder forum with everybody on an equal basis, the very process of constituting a bureau itself is problematic, but even more so when there's no membership. It's an open door. So then we clarified. We asked this question to the people that sponsored. And they said, 'This is what we had in mind'. Because I said, 'How do I constitute a bureau in an open forum?' And then they explained that this is how it was supposed [to be resolved]. (Epstein 2012, footnote 106)

Complementing the emergence of focal points and venues for IG-related discussions, the creation of ad hoc expert groups became a dominant practice for overcoming impasse in IG processes. It followed in the footsteps of WGIG and was emulated across a number of institutions, from private to intergovernmental. In the work of the UN Global Alliance for ICT and Development (UN GAID), ad hoc groups took the form of Communities of Expertise. These were networks convened by UN GAID to bring together motivated and capable actors to address specific, well-defined ICT4D problems in a results-oriented manner and to identify and disseminate good practices. Initiated by a group of at least three organizations, such networks needed to be multi-stakeholder, but could take a number of organizational forms, from the more exploratory 'green field' initiatives to being based at the UN. Serving a variety of purposes, this dominant routine was generally limited to a functional mandate, narrowly defined.

Within ICANN, the Country Code Names Supporting Organization (ccNSO) established an ad hoc Internet Governance Review group, whose mission was to provide an overview of the IG issues and discussions with relevance for the work of the cc-TLD community. The review group operated between 26 February 2014 and 12 October 2014. Similarly, the Council of Europe established an Ad Hoc Advisory Group on Cross-border Internet,[27] tasked to draft a Committee of Ministers Declaration on Internet Governance Principles in 2011. The practice was also adopted by the ITU. Following the WCIT-12, at its 2013 World Telecommunication/ICTs Policy Forum in Geneva, an Informal Experts Group (IEG) was convened to approve the text of the draft opinions to the ITU Secretary General report. Unlike the other groupings discussed above, the IEG had an exceptionally large membership, with 117 participants from member states, thirteen from regional and other IOs, twenty-nine from civil society and industry, alongside other members from scientific and industrial organizations. In their work, six draft opinions to the report of the Secretary General were discussed, including support for multi-stakeholderism and enhanced cooperation.

Beyond the intergovernmental space in which prolonged negotiations and time-demanding procedures represented the norm, rather than the exception, this dominant routine also gained currency in the industry, to mobilize support around a cause. This was the case of the WCIT Ad Hoc Working Group, an industry-led coalition with members such as AT&T, Cisco, Comcast, Google, Intel, Microsoft, News Corporation, Oracle, Telefonica, Time Warner, Verisign, and Verizon, active in 2012 around the ITU Plenipotentiary meeting in Dubai. On that occasion, particularly compelling was also the example of the Ad Hoc Group on Internet-related resolutions formed by a group of delegates during the WCIT negotiations. Not-for-profit actors embraced the practice as a means to involve political figures and bring important social capital to their initiatives. In January 2014, the Centre for International Governance Innovation and the Royal Institute of International Affairs (Chatham House) launched a Global Commission on Internet Governance made up of twenty-nine members and chaired by Carl Bildt, Sweden's Minister of Foreign Affairs, to work for two years on articulating a strategic vision of the future.

A characteristic of ad hoc expert groups is the autonomy in deciding how the work would be conducted. Some groups start with a narrowly defined

---

[27] Its members were: Bertrand de la Chapelle, Wolfgang Kleinwaechter, Christian Singer, Rolf H. Weber, and Michael V. Yakushev.

issue, while others call for a mapping exercise to understand what is covered and is not covered adequately by existing mechanisms or institutions. The modality of work usually includes face-to-face and online meetings. The ad hoc meetings are usually conducted under Chatham House rule[28] to encourage free discussion and a more relaxed exchange of opinions. Moreover, depending on how sensitive the topic under discussion is, experts might prefer—for reputational concerns—to avoid a direct association of their names with what is publicly quoted.

Most of the expert gatherings established ad hoc would be convened by existing organizations or entities and have a political stake. Given their temporary nature, the working groups formed in a short time span would not challenge the position of the main actors in the IG field, nor would they propose radical reforms in terms of how the field was organized. The ideological struggle between a semi-privatized Internet model and an intergovernmental approach to it surfaced less and less in the reports issued by the ad hoc groups, despite the increasingly more sizeable mandates they were entrusted. An element of this was also reflected in the composition of the group, which was not open to public consultations. Senior members of the IG community and seasoned leaders with a broad understanding of the diplomatic and economic issues at stake constituted the large majority of ad hoc groups.

While the IG field had been at first dominated by computer scientists and engineers, subsequent developments around commercialization and litigation brought it closer to the community of entrepreneurs, investors, and lawyers. The structuration of the field was further enhanced with the contribution of the security community and with its opening up to a much wider audience following the WSIS. But crucial to the evolution of the field was the involvement of high-level figures from the political sphere, via explicit statements and positions, contributions to global agendas, and multifold participation in groups of experts, which became the established practice towards the end of the WSIS decade. Deployed as a meaning-making exercise, this anchoring practice led to iterative interactions shaping discourses and activities and supporting the enactment of constitutive rules by the most powerful. In this mutually enhancing exchange, the Internet became a public domain of action, whose global, regional, and national dimensions intersected.

---

[28] When a meeting, or part thereof, is held under the Chatham House rule, participants are free to use the information received, but neither the identity nor the affiliation of the speaker(s), nor that of any other participant, may be revealed.

Synopsis

As a policy field coming of age, the Internet faced a more reflexive turn post-WSIS. Concerns for authority, legitimacy, and accountability—expressed by different stakeholders—become central to the consolidation of this governance domain. A number of challenges, stemming from three diverse sources, were embedded therein: first, questions were spawn by the *modus operandi* of the *sui generis* institutions of the field, such as the international technical bodies exercising public governance functions for the Internet, in particular in connection to ICANN; second, demands for a broader space for regulatory intervention resulted from the gradual adaptation of intergovernmental organizations and their closer involvement in global Internet policymaking via the WSIS process; third, and perhaps most importantly, the role of private intermediaries started to be questioned as their financial and political power exceeded that of developing countries. Their relation to certain governments was also probed, in particular after the 2013 surveillance revelations. Never before was the centrality of US-based institutions more contested than throughout the WSIS decade.

The expansion of the concept of IG also brought in actors that did not participate in the early days. Further classification, segmentation, and clustering of stakeholders ensued. The institutionalization of representation procedures and the clear categorization of stakeholder groups solidified and the contestation that surfaced rarely addressed the WSIS definition of IG. But the strict categorization of stakeholder groups into government, civil society, business, technical, and academic community did not match the reality of fluid and evolving, issue-specific groupings. Nor did it reflect the distribution of power among stakeholders.

Like many other institutional innovations, non-binding forums such as the IGF offered an experimental venue for testing how IG might be conducted with the participation of dominant and marginal actors, with core or tangential interests. It also offered a vessel for easing the tensions between the two dominant governance approaches at the time: intergovernmental and private. The involvement of civil society and industry actors at various levels, alongside governments, and the opening-up of new negotiation arenas was unprecedented during this decade. Emblematic of multi-institutional IG *bricolage*, these dimensions uncovered new patterns and agents of structural change, the addressees of such changes and the conflicting sources of authority. But what will become permanent and what will dissolve in the near future?

6

Enacting Internet Governance: Power and Communities over Time

The previous chapters showed that the nascent order around Internet governance (IG)—mired in political stakes and built in distinctive phases—matured and crystallized as part of a global dialogue. The diversification of approaches to governance characterized the World Summit on Information Society (WSIS) decade phase of Internet development. Soft instruments, especially discursive and operative modelling tools, were deployed to influence the behaviour of others in this space, mobilized primarily around cybersecurity and civil liberties. Multiple sets of rules and norms discussed across partnerships, from the national to the global scale, entangled to shape the Internet as we know it today. The key transformation compared to previous decades was the understanding that the Internet was ultimately a social and political field of action.

In recent years, the underlying business structure of the Internet came on the radar of regulators more prominently. The oligopolistic position of dominant Internet companies has led to a so-called 'tech backlash' in public discourse: a more careful scrutiny of their activities and the imposition of financial sanctions. The potential for digital market dominance, be it by Western or by Chinese companies, had long been foreseen. In the words of Freedman (2012, 115), 'one thing that has remained constant on the Internet is the structure of a "winner takes all" market which systematizes the need for huge concentrations of online and offline capital'. The policy responses have ranged from imposing stricter taxation rules and defining employment rights in the platform economy to sanctioning anti-competitive behaviour and data protection breaches. Self-regulatory approaches continue to appeal in newer areas of fast technological development such as cloud computing, but all-encompassing regulation on issues such as data protection brings about a horizontal baseline.

Currently, the trust in the effectiveness and power of multi-stakeholder partnerships has diminished. The vision of a public Internet as a force for good

Negotiating Internet Governance. Roxana Radu © Roxana Radu 2019. Published 2019 by Oxford University Press.

and empowerment has grown to be more nuanced. 'From the Arab Spring to the Occupy movements, from Pegida and the jihadists to the European Indignados, the contemporary Internet is a space for commodification, a vehicle of propaganda, and a tool for political liberation, all at the same time', concluded Smyrnaios (2018, 6). Likewise, the credo of participatory politics via social platforms like Twitter and Facebook (Morozov 2013) was strongly challenged by the advent of algorithmic manipulation, considered a threat to democratic systems. The disclosures of electoral influencing in the campaigns leading up to the Brexit referendum and the US presidential elections in 2016 via algorithms raised concerns that 'filter bubbles' and mandated choices re-structure the public sphere, and in particular the deliberation space, in ways previously unaccounted for.

This chapter focuses on locating authority in the field: the first part pro-vides an analysis of the power drivers in a longitudinal perspective, followed by a reflection of the governance dynamics emerging since 2015, with an emphasis on the role of dominant Internet companies and influential states across multiple sub-fields; the strategies of China and India are then compara-tively discussed. The second part is dedicated to the formation and perpetu-ation of the IG community, its characteristics, and decision-making routines. It zooms in on the various meanings of the community referent across dif-ferent bodies, with the Internet Assigned Numbers Authority (IANA) stew-ardship transition as a case study, and reviews the three anchoring practices dominating the field.

Power Dynamics and Authority Locus

The diversification of venues for IG discussion that we witnessed starting in 2016 did not put an end to the contest over the re-balancing of power in the field. Once the debate over the management of critical resources ended in September 2016 with the withdrawal of the US government from its IANA stewardship function, the global focus shifted to the unfair distribution of benefits from the digital transformation, in economic, political, and social inclusion terms.

Institutional thickness reached a new height towards the end of 2015, but the phenomenon of multiplication and persistence of international bodies and global regulation did not necessarily result in increased legalization. In the era of cross-sectoral partnerships, soft instruments were preferred to hard law. The adherence to rules entered a new stage, with more frequent refer-ences to sanctions rather than norm coherence. As discussed in this section, rule-based outcomes are continuously sought in IG and the existing global governance structures might not provide satisfactory answers.

From 2015 onwards, power positions solidified. A few Internet companies became more powerful than ever in the field and in the world, topping the industry profits ranking and deciding on the future technical development of the Internet through their investments. Previously, the tensions around the unilateral imposition of rules by one state dominated the IG debates; more recently, emerging powers such as China, Russia, and India strengthened their national approaches and proposed alternative governance principles on the global scale. Other countries and regional blocs also increased their regulatory powers and passed a number of laws with extraterritorial effects, in particular in the areas of cybersecurity, data protection, and privacy. The IG community—made up of representatives of the various sectors—continued to diversify capturing some of these dynamics as they permeated the work of technical bodies and multistakeholder forums.

A Longitudinal Comparison

Looking comparatively at the three periods identified, from the invention of the network to the maturing of a field of action, it becomes apparent that the dominant mode of governance (which sets the tone in a specified time frame) represents only one alternative amid the many governance configurations possible. Arriving at global regulatory coordination via market and state modes, the contemporary IG landscape is unique. Among its most important transformations was the transition from informal to codified procedures and to solidified institutional forms reflecting the growing assortment of international, regional, and national stakeholders. Cybersecurity and civil liberties continue to stand out as two key areas in which cyber norms are still disputed. In the last decade, most efforts have been directed not towards drafting hard law instruments, but towards influencing other actors' behaviour in this space. The effect of modelling has been just as strong through codes of conduct and voluntary schemes stirred by actors operating either individually or in partnership.

Ideologically, two main positions solidified in IG discussions since the 1990s. The first one was built around the exceptionalism of the Internet. It postulated that a global network revolutionizing daily activities across most sectors required a fresh approach, in light of the de-territorialization it fostered. This argument was best expressed by John Perry Barlow in his famous Davos message to the governments of the world:

You are not welcome among us. You have no sovereignty where we gather. You have no moral right to rule us nor do you possess any methods of enforcement we have true reason to fear. Cyberspace does not lie within your borders. (Barlow 1996)

On the legal side, that translated into a pursuit of new regulations and 'cyber-laws' at the expense of adapting the existing legislation to tackle relevant on-line aspects. This approach has been revived several times throughout the 1990s and 2000s, going from a complete rejection of the applicability of 'old' laws (Post 2002) to designing exclusive online guarantees such as the 'right to be forgotten' (Chenou and Radu 2017). The development of an overarching governance system specific to the Internet continues to be an ideal for some of the members of the IG community. While more and more organizations have come to populate the field, there are only a handful core bodies with exclusive attributes for IG. As this study showed so far, the emergence of a highly complex field such as IG rests on a variety of forms of action—from hard law to discursive or operative modelling—implemented by a plethora of new and old institutions.

The second ideological position focused around the need to see the Internet as embedded in real law. This approach was built around understanding how the network has been anchored in geography and how the responsibilities of nation states can be redefined. National, regional, and transnational rules sustained the tremendous success of the Internet since the beginning, in particular as they were covered by the neoliberal mantra prioritizing market development. The new economic models fostered by the Internet were closely linked to the *laissez-faire* regulatory frameworks defined by the Pentagon, at times accepted tacitly, at times vocally contested by other nations. In recent years, the economic and sociopolitical dimensions of the Internet garnered unprecedented attention, challenging the leadership of the United States in the field through the adoption of stronger national regulation targeting data-driven business models.

Making sense of the interconnected code, law, and politics pertinent to IG is an ongoing struggle for anyone participating in these processes. It is thus crucial to understand how critical levers work at various points in time and how they come to define what matters for a community. For instance, in the work of the Internet Engineering Task Force (IETF) and via its Request for Comments (RFCs) practice, standard-making became public—at first out of sheer necessity, subsequently strongly re-enacted for accountability purposes. This set the tone for a series of developments emulating this model, pushing for the open participation of stakeholders across the board, with an implicit understanding of who gets to participate at what stage in the process.

It is thus timely to put into perspective the way in which two dominant actors—companies and states—have evolved in the post-2015 period. Their strategies and expressions of power are indicative of the changes ahead and of the potential for entering a fourth IG evolution phase, built on a new set of principles and introducing novel dynamics.

Private Giants on the Rise

Among the world's most valuable ten firms, seven are Internet giants: five American companies (Apple, Amazon, Alphabet, Microsoft, and Facebook) and two Chinese companies (Tencent and Alibaba). At the time of writing this book, Apple became the world's first public company to be worth $1 trillion (Johnson 2018). These tech companies have long competed for conquering emerging markets and the next generation of Internet users, but after a series of failed connectivity experiments, their attention has shifted towards crossing new frontiers in Internet services and in artificial intelligence (AI). Amazon, Alibaba, and Microsoft are also strengthening their position in cloud computing, a new direction of investments dominating the market.

Many of the top ten companies have introduced projects to bring connectivity to underserved areas of the globe, with mixed results. After a controversial Free Basics proposal that was rejected in India on net neutrality grounds, Facebook deployed the programme in sixty-three countries around the world in partnership with local telecom operators. Despite the explosion of its Space X satellite over sub-Saharan Africa in September 2016, the Facebook experiments continue with its plane-size, solar-powered Internet drone called Aquila. Alphabet's drone program, Project Titan, was terminated in 2017, but work continues for high-altitude balloons in the framework of Project Loon. Microsoft tests unused television airwaves (white space) to reach the unconnected with pilot projects in Jamaica, Namibia, the Philippines, Tanzania, Taiwan, Colombia, the United Kingdom, and the United States.

Technologies like the fifth generation (5G) of mobile networks are of close interest to Chinese companies, which are sending increasingly more representatives to related meetings organized by standardization bodies. They work closely with the government in the framework of China's Belt and Road Initiative, one of the largest ever infrastructure projects covering more than sixty-eight countries. The initiative comprises a 'digital Silk Road' ambitious plan to build anything from fibre-optic cables and mobile networks to smart cities on the multiple water and land corridors thus created. This is achieved with Chinese companies, engineers, and managers, with capacity building provided by Chinese experts.

At the level of Internet architecture, a fundamental change is underway in submarine cable investments. A number of hardware, software, and data-driven companies have participated in consortia to build a large number of the 448 undersea cables in use around the world (at the time of writing). Google, for example, invested in six cables since 2008. This space has been privately owned since the beginning and the telecom operators paying for the deployment of cables set up specific traffic exchange and power sharing arrangements in the 1990s. Since 2016, major investors in cables have been underway by new players: content providers such as Google, Facebook, or Amazon have joined the submarine connectivity race. More and more of these companies are buying important shares in the business or creating their own cables: Google owns 63,605 miles representing 8.5 per cent of the under cables worldwide, and will soon become the first content provider with sole ownership of submarine cables in the industry (BroadbandNow 2018). Facebook and Amazon, together with four more partners, jointly build the Jupiter cable to link the United States to Asia by 2020. These investments are alimenting the cloud computing business, which represents a $60 billion-a-year market, continuously growing with Amazon in the lead (33 per cent share), followed by Microsoft, Google, Alibaba, and IBM (Lohr 2018).

This change at the level of infrastructure has to do with a better quality of service, obtained by moving a copy of the content closer to the user, to avoid transit delays. Yet, according to Huston (2016), this imposes a degree of 'frag-mentation in the architecture of the Internet as a result of service delivery specialisation' and restructures the market according to new rules imposed by the big players. Standard-making may also depend entirely on these private content providers turned infrastructure providers in the near future.

Younger Silicon Valley companies, such as Airbnb and Uber, have made their fortune in the sharing economy. The second wave of promising Bay Area companies built their business around the collection and processing of real-time information of demand and supply. In the words of Tom Goodwin (2015):

Uber, the world's largest taxi company, owns no vehicles. Facebook, the world's most popular media owner, creates no content. Alibaba, the most valuable retailer, has no inventory. And Airbnb, the world's largest accommodation provider, owns no real estate.

Ridesharing, apartment or home lending, and re-selling are all peer-to-peer alternatives to owning the good or the service of interest. The difference lies in the use of data to provide added-value and comfort via an online platform. 'Uberisation'—a term derived from the name of an American ridesharing company, Uber—is now applied across the board to designate the transition to a new economic model based on digital technologies enabling direct exchanges between providers of services and potential customers at lower costs. These business models share three main features: a prevalence of contractual and temporary employment, a digital platform/app for peer-to-peer transactions, and a rating system for evaluating the quality of the service provided.

Examples of companies claiming to take part in the sharing economy abound across many sectors: entertainment (Spotify, Netflix, GameFly), transportation (Uber, Lyft, Zipcar), accommodation (Airbnb, HomeExchange), labour (Mechanical Turk, SkillShare, TaskRabbit), fashion (Fashionhire, Rent the Runaway), etc. According to Parker et al. (2016), the networked business model introduces two innovations: (1) the company no longer creates the end product or service, but focuses on making available a common infrastructure that matches consumers and producers using the knowledge of the market and imposing the rules of governance; (2) the producers of value and consumers of value come from outside the system. The expansion of the 'gig economy' model across different sectors introduced a wave a social experimentation indicative of the extensive power of corporations in the digital world, equalling or exceeding that of governments.

In a span of six years, the prospects of the sharing economy have been critically reassessed. Two dominant narratives have driven the debates on different value propositions: on the one hand, the bright future of automation promised further innovation and entrepreneurship opportunities, as well as flexible schedules and labour market activation, putting technology at work for delivering better products at a lower price. On the other hand, the narrative of medieval exploitation surfaced as an equally strong one: algorithmic ratings, consumer evaluations, and temporary tasks delivered on platforms led to an ever-expanding, precarious on-demand workforce, primarily underemployed (Prassl 2018). The shift from the first to the second narrative has revealed that innovations in the digital economy pose novel and more complex regulatory challenges, not only to the policymakers, but also to the companies themselves.

Uber's enormous exposure to litigation in the majority of jurisdictions in which it operates epitomizes broader dilemmas in assessing the effects of business models on society. Classifying the sharing economy services as information ones (providing the data necessary to link demand and supply) or as part of a regulated industry (transport, hospitality services, etc.) has been the crux of the matter, as it brings forward the applicable regulatory regime: most legal cases are about the employment and labour conditions of those gaining a living this way, as well as e-commerce and trade aspects, including competition, advertising, and licensing. Organizing the digital landscape while fitting the current societal structure has been an ongoing power struggle, in which the dominant businesses have predominantly argued for exemption from the rules applied to the industries they seek to displace. The gatekeeping function of giant technology companies limits access to alternative models of social and economic organization, although the Internet infrastructure itself does not, in principle, prioritize one over the other.

Alongside infrastructure and digital economy, the third subarea of unprecedented private sector development has been AI. This broad umbrella term refers to the latest and most successful wave of machine learning modelled on neural networks and deep learning. Deployed for purposes as diverse as advancements in medical diagnosis and autonomous driving, this technological breakthrough allowed a number of start-ups—mainly based in the United States, in India, and in China—to build up their profiles. The largest tech companies are either developing their own research unit on AI or acquiring the smaller companies thriving in the field.

In the data-driven economy and in the functioning of AI, algorithms are indispensable. They are deployed across a wide number of services, from technical ones (e.g. spam filtering and advertising) to those facing the user and influencing behaviour: search engines (e.g. Google search), news aggregation services (e.g. Google News), news feeds (Twitter Trending, Facebook's Trending Topics), prognosis/forecast (e.g. Google Trends), news scoring (e.g. Reddit, Digg), content production (e.g. Quakebot, Quill). Bias, discrimination, and the secret nature of data processing and algorithms (Pasquale 2015; Noble 2018) were originally discussed in the context of search engines and recommendation systems for shopping and for entertainment online, but the debacle expanded to large-scale electoral propaganda and public opinion influencing in 2016 and 2017, when data-sharing practices among companies started to be scrutinized.

Following the Facebook–Cambridge Analytica scandal, algorithm-driven decision-making is currently regarded as a threat to democratic processes, highlighting a number of concerns: the covert manner in which personal data is collected, processed, and rendered profitable by companies without the consent of the data subjects; the opacity of the data sharing practices in the private sector; the increasingly more sophisticated tools applied by self-learning algorithms in decision-making. Different from supervised machine learning, which predicts an output based on the data input, more responsibility is assigned to a computer program in unsupervised and in reinforced learning. The former is often deployed to structure large datasets based on pre-defined features, whereas the latter allows the computer to learn how to behave in a new environment, based on constant feedback (Article 19 and Privacy International 2018).

In his responses to the US Congress inquiry held in April 2018 on social media manipulation during the US 2016 presidential election, Facebook's CEO Mark Zuckerberg made frequent references to a solution his company invests in to tackle misinformation on its platforms: perfecting AI to automatically recognize and remove unwanted content. Using algorithms to police the Web, be it based on user feedback via flagging (Caplan and Boyd 2016) or in an automated manner, is in no way new to the operations of Internet companies. This practice is applied across the board to abide by national legislation or to address copyright infringement, among others. Yet deploying it uniformly for addressing social problems does not epitomize a solution-driven, people-centred approach, but reinforces the technological determinism credo dominating the Silicon Valley. This may do more harm in the long-term.

Distrust in the power of companies to protect their users' information first appeared as a generalized concern around the 2013 Snowden revelations and continued with a staggering number of data breaches over the following years, resulting in the disclosure or misuse of billions of online personal records. In 2017 alone, there were 5,207 breaches reported, exposing approximately 7.89 billion records, an increase of about 24 per cent compared to the previous year (Risk Placement Services 2018). Alongside hacks and accidental publications of data, personal information has also been progressively compromised in cyberattacks. In May 2017, the WannaCry ransomware attack affected more than 200,000 computers in 150 countries, followed by other attacks equally disruptive. The vulnerability exploited in this attack on Windows systems paralysed the National Health System in the United Kingdom, where an important number of hospitals were using an older, unpatched version of the operating system produced by Microsoft.

The call to restore trust in the Internet, first placed on the global agenda in 2013 by technical bodies and later by international organizations, was heard over and over again. Since 2015, it was in connection with cybersecurity norms. What was different this time was the authoritative proposal coming from companies to look for solutions together with governments. In addition to voluntary initiatives, corporations like Microsoft or Google provided unilaterally drafted norms for a Digital Geneva Convention and for digital security and due process, respectively. The role of Microsoft as a norm entrepreneur was highly prominent in the last two years, due in particular to its attempts to socialize the proposal in the UN framework and among industry players.

Proposing six security principles back in 2014, Microsoft moved in 2017 to a more comprehensive approach to limiting the stockpiling of cyber weapons, building on the humanitarian conventions (to protect civilians in times of war) signed in Geneva at the turn of the century. At a time when the perceived exceptionalism of the Internet sector is increasingly challenged, this proposal focuses on treating the industry as neutral in cyberattacks, thus permitting user-centred interventions. In his keynote at the UN in Geneva on 14 November 2017, Brad Smith, the President and Chief Legal Officer of Microsoft concluded his speech with the message: 'Cybersecurity needs to be a cause for our times; all communities must contribute and learn from each other to find solutions' (Radu 2017). The next step in Microsoft's efforts was the Cybersecurity Tech Accord introduced in April 2018, a voluntary industry initiative committing to protecting users from malicious attacks by states and criminals. As of June 2018, the Accord had forty-five signatories, including Microsoft, Facebook, LinkedIn, Nokia, Telefonica, Cisco, and Dell. States have so far been reluctant to endorse the Digital Geneva Convention proposal.

In the area of AI, a similarly powerful call has been made by industry players to governments around the world. In 2017, 116 technology leaders and founders of robotics and AI companies from twenty-six countries, including Google DeepMind's Mustafa Suleyman and Elon Musk, the American inventor and engineer behind Space X and Tesla, sent a petition to the UN to call for new regulation on the development of AI weapons and an explicit ban of lethal autonomous weapon systems (LAWS), or killer robots. Discussions on this are ongoing in the framework of the UN Group of Governmental Experts on LAWS, to which 125 countries (all high contracting parties to the Convention on Certain Conventional Weapons) are participating.

This new exercise of power, coalescing around the introduction of norms that can be agreed cross-sector, is indicative of the current search for basic consensus and norms around the conduct of war in the cyberspace. As of 2018, a form of legalization compatible with current business models continues to be sought by big Internet companies, but also by states, in a space dominated by limited means to attribute attacks, informal governance, and ad hoc arrangements. The next section turns to the position of governments in these discussions, presenting different and sometimes conflicting conceptions of power in IG, be it in material or social power terms.

Stronger National Approaches

The growth of the Internet has long been steered by the Pentagon and that represented one of the core power contests in IG. Post-2015, a differentiation of approaches is visible, in particular due to the increased prominence of regional groups and developing nations, in the context of the Trump-led withdrawal of the United States from Internet policy. Around the IANA stewardship transition, Powers and Jablonski assessed that 'the United States no longer has the diplomatic, military or economic capital to compel international compliance with its unilateral control over the world's most critical medium' (2015, 130). Cybersecurity is one of the fields where responsibilities have been re-assessed under President Trump. The position of US cybersecurity coordinator, introduced under President Obama in 2009, was abolished by the National Security Council in May 2018, when the portfolio was delegated to a deputy (Kornbluh 2018).

Importantly, as national governments have defined more clearly their interests, the interaction with the private sector has changed. Many states have increased their cyber capabilities for both offensive and defensive operations (Radunovic 2017a) and modelled their relationship with the private sector as a delegated authority one. Not only are companies policing the Web on behalf of states, but they also execute complete Internet shutdowns at the request of governments, a phenomenon ever more common after the Arab Spring. The NGO AccessNow (2018) documented 108 instances of blackouts in 2017, the majority of which took place in Asia and Africa. The reasons offered by governments for these intentional disruptions of service or connectivity range from ensuring public safety and limiting mobilization during election times to preventing cheating in school exams. In the first half of 2017, Google, Facebook, and Twitter received a total of 114,169 requests to remove content from seventy-eight countries and 179,180 requests for information about Internet users from 110 countries (Horejsova et al. 2018, 9).

Acting as a regional bloc, the EU introduced the General Data Protection Regulation (GDPR) governing the privacy, the protection, and the transfer of data of European citizens. The regulation entered into force on 25 May 2018 and harmonized the data regimes across all member states, setting a standard to be pursued inside and outside the European border by both public and private institutions. In effect, a number of countries such as Argentina, Brazil, South Korea, or Tunisia have adopted or are discussing the adoption of legislation similar to the GDPR, leading to an expansion of the model to the Global South.

Among the GDPR innovative aspects are: the focus on the explicit consent of the user, the right to rectification and erasure of information, as well as the right to explanation. The latter mandates that 'meaningful information about the logic' of automated systems is provided when a request is made by the data subject, together with an explanation of the significance and envisaged consequences of the processing thus implemented (Articles 21 and 22). Conceived as a framework for data minimization, the GDPR imposes an obligation to report breaches and introduces a two-tiered sanctions regime: for non-compliance with important data protection provisions, businesses risk fines imposed by data watchdogs of up to €20 million or 4 per cent of global annual turnover for the preceding financial year, whichever is the greater. For other breaches, fines of up to €10 million or 2 per cent of global annual turn-over of companies are envisioned.

In Europe, a strong regional approach was preferred by the Commission for privacy and data protection, whereas for other issue areas, such as the sharing economy, the Court of Justice of the European Union (CJEU) encouraged the development of national approaches. The CJEU judgment from December 2017 settled the long-standing issue of defining the legal status of Uber in an inquiry brought forward by the Barcelona taxi association over misleading practices and acts of unfair competition. Declaring Uber 'a service in the field of transport', rather than an information society one, the court decided that member states can regulate this business model as they see fit under their local laws. While the GDPR allows derogations by member states to fifty different provisions, enabling them to fit their local needs by adjusting certain parameters, the crux of it remains a Brussels-controlled regulation with extraterritorial effect.

On the surge lately, the trend of extraterritoriality derived from domestic regulation has touched the areas of cybersecurity, privacy, and data protection, as well as freedom of expression. More than thirty-five laws were passed since 2015 in thirty-four countries across Europe, Africa, the Americas, the Middle East, and Asia-Pacific (ISOC 2018) in these IG domains, a majority of which focuses on cybersecurity. This points to a move towards an increased securitization of the field worldwide. The international relations (IR) concept of securitization, developed by the Copenhagen School and understood to mean the process through which an issue is presented as posing an existential threat to a designated referent object (Buzan et al. 1998), explains how discursive politics around an issue might justify extraordinary measures to a legitimating audience (Balzacq 2011). Repeated attempts to galvanize support around cyber norms have led to the securitization of IG as a whole in the last couple of years, both rhetorically and in terms of physical changes to the network.

Technical modifications of the infrastructure performed in order to strengthen security and control at the national level have a considerable impact on the global Internet, engendering the long-feared prospect of fragmentation by creating several Internets. China, for example, uses the Source Address Validation Architecture for inspecting the source of the data packets forwarded on the Internet based on an authenticated Internet protocol address that must be authorized, unique, and traceable. This process, using network management, control, and malware avoidance techniques, stops any communication from unauthorized addresses. Since 2009, Chinese authorities have implemented a real-name registration policy for the country-code top level domain *.cn*, requiring citizens who register domains under *.cn* to provide prior passport identification. Iran and Russia have also announced similar plans to build their own infrastructure and impose strict restrictions on Internet exchanges.

Internationally, rules for the conduct of cyberwar remain a heated topic in state-led forums. Bilateral treaties opposing cyber-espionage and cyberattacks have been on the rise, with wide variations at the level of engagement: strategic partnerships (Canada–Israel), continuous dialogue (EU–Japan), or memorandums of understanding, such as the one between the United Kingdom and Singapore (Radunovic 2017b). Inter-governmental cooperation has been advanced in the framework of regional cooperation and cybersecurity capacity building now has a permanent place on the policy agenda of the Commonwealth, the African Union Commission, the European Union, or the Organization of American States. In the absence of a global consensus on norms of behaviour in the cyberspace, the staggering number of cyberattacks and state defence probing exercises have led different coalitions of states to design their own set of rules. Participation in internationalizing coalitions on security matters is not new, but the focus on cyber aspects has increased tremendously over the last three years. At the international level, both China and Russia have promoted the cyber-sovereignty principle, understood as the right to choose an own path of digital development and to participate on an equal footing in international Internet-related decision-making.

On the one hand, Russia has proposed an international code of conduct for information security, submitted to the UN General Assembly in 2011 and revised in 2015 in the framework of the Shanghai Cooperation Organization (SCO). Russia is expected to propose this code again in the UN in September 2018, following the failure of the dedicated UN Group of Governmental Experts to agree on language endorsing state responsibility and the right to self-defence. On the other hand, NATO recognized the cyberspace as an operational field in 2016; the expert revision of the voluntary Tallinn Manual laying down the applicable international legal norms in cyberspace was completed in 2017.

At the domestic level, Internet-related regulation used to be addressed as part of different ministerial mandates such as telecommunications, economy, foreign policy, or defence. For the longest time, these ministries worked in silos, without a unified approach to Internet policies and with little or no cooperation for deciding or implementing actions together.[1] Participation in

---

[1] A frequently cited exception was Brazil, where the coordination of most Internet-related activities was primarily achieved via a multi-stakeholder body, the Internet Steering Committee (Comitê

ITU and other international meetings lacked a unitary national vision, which resulted in adopting incoherent positions across subfields of digital policy during international negotiations. This is beginning to change as the Internet is placed higher up on the political agenda.

A number of states have also appointed cyber diplomats (the United States, the United Kingdom, Germany, and Finland were among the first) and have created specific agencies for IG-related actions (the United States, China) aiming to mitigate the lack of consistency in sectoral approaches. A preoccupation for digitization and new technologies has led to concrete frameworks and action plans. In 2017, the United Arab Emirates appointed the first minister for AI, the G20 held two summits for ministers in charge of the digital economy, and Denmark appointed its first ever digital diplomat in the Silicon Valley. IG has been a part of foreign policy for a much longer period of time, but the current developments indicate that—beyond an international (re) distribution of power—tech diplomacy nowadays is supported by domestic political structures.

Just like for companies, the next power struggle among states is leadership in AI. Russian President Vladimir Putin was quoted as saying, in September 2017: 'whoever becomes the leader in this sphere will become the ruler of the world' (RT 2017). By mid-2018, twenty-two countries have either started or completed a process to define their national AI strategies or frameworks with dedicated budgets, including Canada, China, France, India, Japan, Mexico, Singapore, South Korea, the UAE, the United Kingdom, and the United States.

In their report on the rise of the so-called 'techplomacy' in the Bay area, Horejsova et al. 2018 note an increased specialization in the field of diplomacy attuned to particular subfields, such as AI or cybersecurity. The current diplomatic presence in the Silicon Valley takes various forms, from a dedicated tech diplomat (e.g. Denmark), to consular representation and an innovation centre (e.g. Austria, Switzerland, the Netherlands), a state investment promotion agency (e.g. Czech Republic), an honorary consul (e.g. Hungary, Finland) or a separate branch of government (Japan). However, for the time being, most developing countries mediate their relations with the US-based tech industry from their embassy in Washington DC.

China and India, the two largest Internet markets by number of users, pursued different strategies in their profiling as leaders in the IG field. Both countries have seen government-backed progress in Internet technology, yet

Gestor da Internet no Brasil, or CGI.br). Due to the political turmoil in the country, CGI.br has recently come under attack and its approach is likely to suffer changes.

their approaches reflect different core values and future directions. The approaches taken by these two countries deserve a separate discussion below.

China and India

Poised to become the second largest contributor to the UN general budget for the 2019–2021 period, China exerts considerable influence in the key UN sub-agencies covering Internet-related aspects. India, caught in between a multi-stakeholder rhetoric and a state-based approach to IG, has yet to define a consistent approach in its international engagement, be it as part of G20, of the SCO or of the BRICS—Brazil, Russia, India, China, and South Africa.

Beijing has taken the route of trade and investment policies to influence global IG and gained considerable support from other countries via its Belt and Road Initiative. Moreover, in the e-commerce preparations ahead of the WTO Ministerial in 2017, China has co-sponsored (together with Pakistan) a proposal focused on the promotion and facilitation of cross-border trade in goods, payments, and logistics services, maintaining an emphasis on the development dimension. This vision of e-commerce is favourable to its platforms, currently among the largest in the world. The tech trinity known as BAT (Baidu, Tencent, and Alibaba) have recently started investing in or acquiring companies in other industries, including retail, sharing economy, or fintech (Liu 2018). China is also coming second after the United States in international patent applications, the two technology companies topping the global ranking being Huawei and ZTE Corporation (WIPO 2018).

India, on the other hand, has taken an inward look and focused on domestic technological upgrades. It opted for open-source technology in moving its governmental services online, to avoid dependence on private providers and adapt the specifications to the local context. The 'India stack' collection of digital platforms built by the government, together with the digital infrastructure on which it resides, are placed under public oversight. To provide an identification system for Indian residents and facilitate access to governmental services and social benefits, India introduced *Aadhaar*, the world's largest biometric ID system which has over 1.2 billion enrollees now (Nilekani 2018). The introduction of this system in 2009 was mired in fears of privacy breaches, convergence of the data collected across databases, increased surveillance, profiling and targeting, as well as vulnerability to fraud, all of which turned out to be real. More recent debacles drew attention to the use of Aadhaar by private companies (such as telephone companies and banks) and the case was presented in front of the Supreme Court.

A digital national identity card project is also underway in China, where Alibaba and WeChat compete for providing it. After passing strict regulation in areas such as social media or gaming, China is experimenting with a social credit programme, that rewards good behaviour online and sanctions unwanted behaviour, defined by the government and implemented with the help of companies. The score resulting from public and private records about a citizen's behaviour could be further used to determine opportunities for travelling or employment. Voluntary for the time being, the system will be mandatory as of 2020.

China's July 2017 comprehensive strategy entitled *A Next Generation Artificial Intelligence Development Plan* stresses the aspiration to become the 'world's primary AI innovation centre' by 2030, touching research and development, industrialization, talent development, education and skills acquisition, standard setting and regulations, ethical norms, and security. Deployments of AI are also tested in the military field, in particular for cybersecurity, surveillance, and autonomous drone swarms. For its near-future plan, India embraced the 'AI for all' approach stressing social inclusion alongside economic development. While rhetorically adopting a national approach closer to a public good vision of the Internet, India has yet to show how it can be deployed in a citizen-centred way. Preserving a socio-economic baseline at a time when its top firms providing technical services to brands all over the world—Infosys, Tata Consultancy Services, and Wipro—increasingly resort to automation might bring the country closer to some of the debates in Germany, where a 'third way' between market economy and social welfare is sought in designing the national AI strategy (Hoene 2018).

Preparing to become a 'cyber-superpower' as stressed by President Xi Jinping, China is harnessing the potential of quantum computing in addition to AI. Since the launch of the first ever satellite using quantum cryptography communication in 2016 and the opening of the Beijing-Shanghai Backbone Network (BSBN), the world's first long-distance quantum-secured communication route in 2017, China envisions working closely with its native companies to develop driverless cars, automated medical diagnosis, and smart city management systems.

Conventional approaches to power underline the material or the dominance dimension, but the manifold manifestations of power we have noted here show them alongside implicit or 'soft' forms, such as the ability to shape the agenda and the subsequent global discussions, as well as the ability to form identities and perpetuate communities over time. As far as the classical definition of power goes, the capacity to do something or determine others to do it might not tell the full story in IG. The technological breakthroughs to come and the new authority dynamics they will incorporate can help us develop novel understandings of IG power.

As it continues to transform, the Internet builds on its now-established governance patterns, confirming or dismissing various relations of power. This discussion shows how technology and dominant market positions intertwine to wield new forms of power, with intended and unintended effects. It provides evidence for how a collective representation of a technical project (Flichy 2007) is pre-defined politically and later encapsulated into a vision integrated across all relevant sectors of society. Beyond states and companies, a significant repository of power in the field is the IG community, an agency-loaded space where interests come together to be represented, mediated, heard, and legitimized.

The IG Community

What used to be a community in the hundreds now spans a few thousand people who regularly speak at multiple global events every year, attend most of the preparatory meetings, and participate actively in online discussions. The Internet community has expanded and diversified significantly after the WSIS process. The number of on-site Internet Governance Forum (IGF) participants has increased from around 600 in 2006 to more than 2,000 by 2017. The Internet Corporation for Assigned Names and Numbers (ICANN) and IETF meetings regularly gather about 2,000 people, a number of attendees similar to the annual WSIS Forum. The NetMundial event hosted by Brazil in 2014 brought together more than 1,200 representatives of different sectors, whereas the Wuzhen Internet Summit convened by the Chinese Internet Information Office had approximately 1,000 participants in 2014 and twice as many in 2015. Business-led events like the annual Mobile World Congress organized by the Global System for Mobile Communication Association (GSMA) in Barcelona every end of February, attract close to 100,000 attendees. The key players from the industry also participate as sponsors and send delegates to most Internet gatherings.

Apart from global events, active IG members are generally also involved in activities led by regional organizations like the Council of Europe, the Association of Southeast Asian Nations (ASEAN), the EU, or the African Union, and run or participate in the twelve regional and seventy-six national IGFs. While the target group for each of these meetings might differ, there is extensive overlap of participants, indicating that a core community has formed. The ability of participants with different skills and backgrounds to contribute to discussions on highly specialized IG topics was enhanced over time through better and easier access to resources, demands for more transparency in the process and, in some cases, financial support to attend face-to-face meetings.

In the early days of the Internet, following the wording of the RFCs, 'community' was the preferred referent for the grouping of volunteers, enthusiasts, and experts closely associated with a particular process. Generally, they were joining the discussion in an individual capacity. Currently, the term is used to refer to those professionally engaged in the development of the Internet, on the policy or technical side, in a wider sense or for delineating constituencies, as in the case of ICANN or Number Resource Organization (NRO). In conferences and meetings, it has become customary to use the stakeholder grouping to distinguish between participants belonging to various communities (governments, businesses, civil society and technical community, academia), often by assigning them different colour name tags. The representatives of these groups were self-selected in the beginning, yet procedures for nominations and approval have been subsequently institutionalized, spanning different degrees of formality.

Physical participation in IG meetings that rotate across the globe is highly valued, requiring significant commitment of time, energy, and resources. Despite the distributed, virtual modalities of work adopted in between meetings, the knowledge-sharing process and its socially situated nature is reinforced in face-to-face encounters. This results in a pattern of attendance favouring the 'information rich', which not only perpetuates, but also increases the inequality of power and influence. Moreover, this phenomenon tends to favour the over-representation of corporate actors, who are more incentivized to participate in physical meetings as part of their lobbying and marketing efforts. Despite repeated calls for inclusiveness, the under-representation of developing countries in the IG community remained a constant throughout the WSIS decade and it has only come to be addressed when formal mechanisms of selection were introduced to ensure a balanced representation of all regions. The unequal access was partly due to a reliance on volunteer work, the mark of native Internet institutions, as opposed to the principle of uniform representation of all member states in intergovernmental settings.

With the steady increase in the number of global meetings, patterns of participation are more difficult to distil, and it is oftentimes complicated to assign one pre-defined sector-based identity to some of the early participants in IG processes. After the creation of ICANN, when the meaning of 'community' was formalized, categorizations by sector and orientation were popular: for example, business community, non-commercial stakeholder community. In its communication related to the IANA stewardship transition in March 2014, the National Telecommunication and Information Administration (NTIA) referred to the 'global multistakeholder community', leaving it up to those involved in the process to specify what that might mean. Consequently, an intricate process to define the various interests, affected communities, and representatives was set in motion, which ultimately led to a proposal to form an 'empowered community' as a check-and-balance mechanism, discussed below.

Communities in the IANA Stewardship Transition

A new governance process was set in motion a month before NetMundial, on 14 March 2014, when the Department of Commerce's NTIA announced its intent to transition the IANA oversight function to the 'global multistakeholder community'. The US government contract with ICANN over the coordination of the Internet's technical resources specified the former's stewardship role over the domain name system (DNS)—a role entrusted to the NTIA. According to this agreement, for any change in the DNS root zone, such as the introduction of a new top level domain, ICANN would need a validation from the NTIA before execution. The NTIA, in turn, would check that ICANN's decision respected its policies and would ask Verisign (the private company maintaining the root zone) to implement. Importantly, the fact that there had not been any instances of non-approval by NTIA throughout the duration of the contract showed the political dimension of the discussion, building on the legacy of early-day discontent with ICANN.

What became known as the IANA stewardship transition process was initially intended to be finalized by 30 September 2015, but was extended until September 2016. Similarly to the 1998 process resulting in the creation of ICANN, the NTIA established a set of *sine qua non* conditions for the transition: first, to obtain a broad community support; second, to adhere to the following four principles: support and enhance the multi-stakeholder model; maintain the security, stability, and resiliency of the Internet DNS; meet the needs and expectations of the global customers and partners of the IANA services; and maintain the openness of the Internet. ICANN acted on this announcement by issuing a scoping document on 8 April 2014 and fostering a month-long consultation on the next steps.

Refocusing attention away from the surveillance debates and back to the legitimacy and accountability of ICANN, the IANA stewardship transition process involved a large number of active ICANN participants serving in a voluntary capacity, as well as a number of observers from different walks of life. Of the volunteers, thirty members joined the IANA Stewardship Transition Cooperation Group (ICG) and acted as liaisons for thirteen different stakeholder communities within the corporation. To agree on a final proposal for the review of the NTIA, the coordination body thus formed had the mission of compiling the proposals developed independently by the communities directly affected by the transition: the Protocol Parameters community, the Numbers Resources community, and the Domain Names community. Table 6 provides an overview of the proposals put forward.

Of these proposals, the most controversial was the naming-related one, which linked the transition to a planned ICANN accountability reform.

Table 6 Comparison of the proposals of ICANN communities for the IANA stewardship transition

	Protocol parameters community	Numbering resources community	Domain names community
Functions	IP parameters	Management and distribution of numbering resources	Naming-related
Proposal submitted	*6 January 2015*	*15 January 2015*	*25 June 2015*
Proposal issued by	IANAPLAN Working Group (IETF and IAB)	Consolidated RIR IANA Stewardship Proposal Team (NRO, ASO, and RIRs)	Cross Community Working Group (GNSO and ccNSO)
Substance of the final proposal	IANA protocol parameters registry updates to continue to function as before. To continue to rely on the system of agreements, policies, oversight mechanisms created by the IETF, ICANN, and IAB for the provision of the protocols parameters-related IANA functions.	ICANN to continue to serve as the IANA functions operator for number resources and perform those services under a contract with the five RIRs. A contractual Service Level Agreement (SLA) to be established between the Regional Internet Registries and the IANA Numbering Services Operator. A Review Committee (RC) to be formed (community representatives from each region) to advise the RIRs on the performance of the IANA functions operator.	Form a new, separate legal entity, Post-Transition IANA (PTI), as an affiliate of ICANN to enter into contract with ICANN for the operation of the IANA functions. Create a Customer Standing Committee (CSC) responsible for monitoring the operator's performance as per contractual requirements and service level expectations. Establish a multi-stakeholder IANA Function Review process (IFR) to conduct reviews of the performance of the naming functions. ICANN's legal jurisdiction remains unchanged.

Work on the latter started in May 2014 and led to the formation of the Cross-Community Working Group on Enhancing ICANN Accountability (CCWG-Accountability) in October that year. The group divided the work into two parallel streams, the first comprising the prerequisites for the IANA transition (to be completed before the end of the NTIA contract), and the second extending reforms beyond the transition. To establish a clear division between the technical and policymaking functions, the proposal submitted by the ICG to the NTIA recommended that a separate legal entity take over the role of IANA functions operator, back then referred to as Post-Transition IANA. When the entity was legally incorporated in California in August 2016, the name changed to Public Technical Identifiers. Two more committees were created ahead of the transition, namely the Customer Standing Committee and the Root Zone Evolution Review Committee, together performing the oversight function previously entrusted to the NTIA.

Different drafts for the accountability architecture proposed by the CCWG-Accountability were developed by the group and were open to public comment at different stages. The last one of them, further refined, proposed that a new entity, 'the empowered community', be created as a California unincorporated association, comprising all existing supporting organizations within ICANN, plus the Governmental Advisory Committee and the At-Large Advisory Committee—representing end-users. The envisioned empowered community, to be consulted before key pronouncements, would have a veto power over a number of decisions by the ICANN Board in case of dissatisfaction. Among these were: the budgets or strategic/operating plans, changes to ICANN standard by-laws and fundamental by-laws, status of individual Board members or the entire Board, and Board decision-making related to reviews of the IANA functions.

Despite a few legal challenges that made the transition uncertain until the day before,[2] the process leading up to the removal of the NTIA oversight over ICANN concluded on 1 October 2016, when the IANA contract between the two entities expired and the new IANA functions set-up was introduced. The added-value of the transition process was the initiation of a much broader dialogue on the accountability of ICANN. While the minimum accountability prerequisites materialized for the transition to happen,

---

[2] Among the most important of these was the lawsuit filed on 28 September by state attorneys general in Arizona, Texas, Oklahoma, and Nevada asking a federal district court to issue a temporary restraining order preventing the contract to expire on 30 September 2016. The arguments put forward revolved around considerations for potential freedom of speech risks and disposal of US property without congressional approval.

discussions continue around larger reforms and ways to strengthen ICANN's accountability towards the broader community.

In the IANA stewardship process, the role of the community was rethought and brought forward along new dimensions, unique in this space. It remains to be seen what power differentials emerge in the implementation of this ambitious project. This way of involving the transnational policy network formed around the technical management of the Internet builds on the grand collaboration that has been historically developed by technical bodies with volunteer support. Although ICANN remains under Californian jurisdiction, its legitimacy is no longer challenged in the IG architecture.

Various Meanings of Community

The World Wide Web (WWW) expanded and changed tremendously through the collective work of public interest groups, originally formed to tackle the technical issues emerging from networking. Later on, content and software developers employed by companies joined the initial groups to bring their contribution to the development of standards. Unpacking the community referent for the key Internet institutions shows that business orientation has remained strong in technical meetings dedicated to the Internet standards. In the work of the IETF, anyone could participate in the development or proposition of a standard, according to the published rules and procedures, by signing up as a volunteer to one of the working groups. However, technical expertise constituted an essential prerequisite for effective participation, and that indirectly led to an overrepresentation of participants regularly involved in its processes.

In recent years, a new significance has been attributed to the 'community' referent: dominant businesses such as Facebook have started employing it to designate the group of people drawing the rules of behaviour on its platforms. These standards are established by a 'faceless' group made up of content policy team members at Facebook in eleven offices around the world (Facebook 2018). The guidelines are revised regularly and implemented in the content moderation activities, including flagging content, filtering, or taking it down, tasks performed by combining AI tools, manual reviews, and reports from users. The Community Operations team implementing these standards works with more than 7,500 content reviewers in forty languages. But in spring 2018, the Community guidelines were deemed insufficient by many international organizations and governments, which started scrutinizing the role of Facebook in furthering abusive behaviour and hate speech, and inciting violence in a number of developing countries (Taub and Fisher 2018). In

Myanmar, Indonesia, India, and Mexico, the amplifying effect of hate speech on Facebook led to the murdering of tens of people.

Local values representation is the second point of contention towards the Facebook community. The unilateral definition of what is and what is not acceptable online by a company headquartered in the United States is harder to sustain as more than 2 billion people use the platform. Facebook's largest user base at the moment is in India, but little of the social and cultural norms there appear to transpire in the global policy of the company, despite the reinforced presence of Facebook's public policy team at all major IG events. In designing community standards, how much should reflect the community itself and be tailored to the local context? Will a global approach, designed by Facebook employees, together with invited experts and selected advocacy groups, be sufficient to avoid tragedies like the loss of human lives?

The initial Internet community was formed around a number of principles defined in a participatory manner by the contributors to the network. Their approach had little to do with form-filling and bureaucracy and more to do with achieving rough consensus by ignoring extreme views. However, the gradual institutionalization of the field resulted in having some of the early members in favour of (more) procedural approaches to designating representatives or appointing the leadership. The legitimacy and accountability discourses, more frequently heard in state-dominated forums, became central to the core Internet community, often with regards to the selection of delegates for higher fora.

At the outset, core communities were rather easy to identify through their membership arrangements and specified objectives, whereas nowadays the categorization is no longer as strict. The most active participants in ICANN and the Working Group on Internet Governance (WGIG) were also frequent speakers at the IGF and have been members of the Multistakeholder Advisory Group (MAG). Mueller (2006) provided a detailed summary of the ICANN-related appointees in the MAG for the organization of the first IGF:

Two (Alejandro Pisanty and Veni Markovski) are sitting ICANN Board members; one (Theresa Swineheart) is an ICANN staff member; two more (Nii Quaynor and Masanobu Katoh) are former ICANN Board members; two (Chris Disspain and Emily Taylor) represent ccTLD operators; two (Raul Echeberria and Adiel Akplogan) represent Regional Internet Address Registries (RIRs). Even the public interest or 'civil society' representatives are long time players in the ICANN sandbox: Adam Peake of Glocom, Robin Gross of IP Justice, Jeanette Hofmann of WZ Berlin, and Erick Iriarte of Alfa-Redi are all associated with either ICANN's At Large Advisory Committee or its Noncommercial Users Constituency (or both). To that one can add an IETF representative, Patrik Faltstrom, often utilised by ICANN as a consultant, and the Internet Society's public policy advocate. (Mueller 2006)

Twelve years later, the same participants are still highly active in multiple Internet processes. While asserting one identity is important within the community for guiding interpretation schemes, many in the core group wear 'different hats', that is, have multiple affiliations. Most of the time, especially in less formal venues, they start their introduction by mentioning that. Such instances have become widely common and widely accepted in the IG space. Independent of their affiliation, they remain highly vocal on IG issues and procedures no matter what 'hat' they put on. Over time, they have not only taken on board legal, social, and technical issues, but have also been involved in or contributed to defining the ethics of the community. The boundaries between individual and institutional identities are rather difficult to draw for some of the charismatic leaders in the broader IG community. Occasionally, the positions they take may be contradictory: critics of intergovernmentalism often actively participate in the work of the Organisation for Economic Co-operation and Development (OECD) or serve as experts for the ITU.

Among the technical bodies that refer to their communities, two stand out: the World Wide Web Consortium (W3C) and the IETF. The W3C has introduced the possibility of creating Community and Business Groups open to anyone willing to join, free of charge. To lower barriers to individual participation, this initiative addresses Web stakeholders that would connect to the well-established international W3C community for creating open Web technologies. Such Community and Business Groups can be started with a short scope statement and a minimum number of supporters; the general criteria to abide by are the following: open to all without a fee, publicly visible, without time limit, intellectual property rights balanced, and tuned for transition to standards.

The IETF, on the other hand, has built its identity around the values of volunteerism and collaboration, but also informality. Its three meetings held yearly are week-long 'gatherings of the tribes'. The Tao of the IETF, updated several times, even included in its 1993 version a dress code paragraph:

Many newcomers are often embarrassed when they show up Monday morning in suits, to discover that everybody else is wearing T-shirts, jeans (shorts, if weather permits) and sandals. There are those in the IETF who refuse to wear anything other than suits. Fortunately, they are well known (for other reasons) so they are forgiven this particular idiosyncrasy. (Malkin 1993)

While social interactions are important variables for collaboration, the guide for newcomers does more than simply outline the rules. It builds the expectations of similar practices being preserved in the future by shaping the behaviour of leaders selected among their younger attendees. As they are encouraged to volunteer to be part of working groups, observing closely the attire of the more senior members has had a long-lasting influence.

When it comes to decision-making, the IETF rule of approving standards only after having the rough consensus at meetings endorsed on working group mailing lists was not emulated in other forums. Decisions regarding the public policy aspects of IG remained mostly confined to face-to-face meetings, with a minimum use of online collaborative platforms bridging the different stakeholder groups (Radu et al. 2015, 5). Although there is an intense use of mailing lists and e-participation tools for the exchange of ideas and (statement) coordination, they remain limited to the internal workings of a specific community (e.g. IG Caucus, BestBits for civil society groups) or a specific process (e.g. one of the IGF Dynamic Coalitions, various ICANN-related initiatives). A number of attempts to enhance cross-community communication on broad IG discussions—such as the 1net or the NetMundial initiative—have been short-lived, failing to engage key actors and substantiate actions in the aftermath of the physical meetings they were created for.

Old-timers and Newcomers

By and large, in the group dynamics, the small number of active participants—primarily established players or 'old-timers'—defines the rules for the larger passive membership. Key individuals thus become cultural and social containers, who produce, perpetuate, restate, or transform discourse. They represent the locus of power and have extensive leverage over the relationships formed with the newcomers, in particular by recruiting some of the younger participants, having a say in structuring their access and defining the transparency procedures introduced by the group. Gaining full recognition in the community comes after following a well-defined trajectory in the group, which generally starts with smaller project involvement and ends with a move towards the centre of the community for those most motivated. Along the way, a gradual, but steady identification with the community practices and acquisition of the jargon and vocabulary becomes the norm.

The expansion of the IG communities is closely linked to the process of designing guidelines and codes of conduct for newcomers, as a way to bridge the constant tension between the insiders of a shared practice and newly arrived members. Modelling becomes the main vehicle for shaping the community: as procedures grow ever more complex, most organizations introduce (and fund) newcomer programmes, in most cases targeting participants from developing countries. Examples of such initiatives include the IETF and ICANN fellowships to their meetings and ISOC ambassadorships to the IGF, aiming to bridge the gap between the 'information rich' and the 'information poor' and to give a voice to regions and stakeholder groups that are underrepresented, but also to immerse novices in the work of these institutions. ICANN also runs a Community Onboarding programme, while ISOC funds travelling of young people to global events via its NextGen programme. These activities are supplemented by online courses—like the ones ran by DiploFoundation or Internet Society—and opportunities to be involved in regional events. As embedded experiences, these programmes not only inform about praxis, but also immerse the newcomers in full-fledged, continuous discussions, in particular as they encourage repeated participation.[3] In the process, the newcomers become practitioners themselves.

Early on, in the technical groups, maximizing inclusion was key for ensuring that the standards were interoperable and satisfactory for those most likely to make use of them. Similarly, the adherence to multi-stakeholder processes has since been fostered into community-building processes, for example, in the way in which the ICANN and ISOC fellowships are structured—members of different communities being funded to participate and spend a week together in formal and informal settings. The personal relations established this way increase the trust different stakeholders have in the people they have bonded with informally. Unlike meetings with binding outcomes, the IGF and the WSIS Forum running for a few consecutive days provide a more relaxed atmosphere conducive to personal discussions and informal consultations. Alongside workshops and sessions, participants can attend tutorials, presentations, and, most importantly, hallway conversations concerning actual decision-making processes at the national, regional, or global level.

It is important to note here that the intergovernmental arrangements no longer stand in opposition with the *sui generis* grouping of Internet organizations in their standard-setting procedures or in their operation. They often collaborate, exchange ideas, and check the activities of other organizations in order to improve their inclusiveness and participation practices. Sometimes, the same individuals are behind such initiatives as initiators or proposers. The development of the Internet's technical standards and protocols has been conducted in an open manner, with the involvement of an expanding community encouraged to participate at different levels, and bodies like the ITU-Telecommunication Standardization Sector (ITU-T) have followed suit in adopting a similar approach to tutorials for newcomers, while preserving the solid role for governments specific to state-led processes.

---

[3] First-time participants in an ICANN fellowship are eligible for two more fellowships to future meetings, whereas some of ISOC's IGF ambassadors are eligible for funding twice.

The interdependence of Internet activities and the increasingly diverse backgrounds of those carrying them out gradually made any idea of acting in isolation fade away. The complementary skills and knowledge of various members, as well as their multi-membership across IG groups were considered a gain for the community. The expansion of a distributed knowledge base and the continuous effort to promote a consistent vision is reflected in the shared praxis. Various communities have worked on historicizing their experience and have subsequently put in place a wiki or a webpage recounting their progress and influence since formation (ICANN's NCUC, Best Bits, etc.).

The need for cooperation to make the network function translated, at the community level, into the amalgamation of cultures and mindsets (organizational, sectoral, disciplinary, but also national or regional) in solution-oriented activities. The distinctiveness of specific etiquettes of interaction, ranging from a rough-consensus approach to extensive diplomatic deliberations over wording, started to blur as an unchanged core group met regularly around (negotiation) round-tables in different venues. The resulting system of norms and rules is a hybrid incorporating, in a unique mix, diplomatic procedures, private logics, and public interest discourses.

Internal Dynamics

Within the community, what becomes apparent is a clustering of members according to the meetings they attend—a grouping they would re-assert across different venues—further reflecting the close interaction and social ties developed over time. ICANN-goers meet three times a year on different continents, whereas active IGF-ers generally pass through Geneva for an agenda-setting consultation before heading to the global meeting in the host country. The WSIS Forum and the CSTD meetings are generally scheduled back-to-back in May every year, allowing some of the participants to attend both. Key members of the community generally take advantage of the IGF schedule to reserve Day 0 for strategic discussions, side events, or public forums, and similar actions have more recently been taken around global gatherings that have not traditionally dealt with the Internet, such as the Human Rights Council's periodic meeting in Geneva.

My immersion in community-building activities over the last eight years allowed me to assess, on multiple occasions, two sets of dynamics that became constitutive of the IG space. The first was the tacit knowledge that community members had about the topics discussed and about each other, visible in the limited explanation about the issues at hand and the use of first names in formal meetings. The second was the consolidation and repetition of values endorsed by the old-timers.

The absence of introductory preambles and a direct jump into the core discussion without extensive details points to the constant communication that goes on via mailing lists. In this approach, there is an implicit understanding of the knowledge that other members of the group have, their potential contribution, and oftentimes their position in the debate. Moreover, the personal relationships, rivalries, and ideological standpoints are clearly delineated and well-known to everyone in the group, making it easy to assess what coalitions might be formed. As Wenger (1998, 130–31) remarks, sustained mutual relationships—harmonious or conflictual—represent a mark of ongoing interactions; in the IG community, it is not uncommon to start a mailing list interaction by referencing, with minimum information, a long-standing dispute.

Throughout consultations and meetings in formal venues such as the UN headquarters in Geneva, the use of first names was often preferred in lieu of spelling out the full name and affiliation for those who have been involved in IG processes for a long time: Markus, Bertrand, Bill, Avri, Ayesha, etc. This informality made the atmosphere more personal, giving established participants ownership over particular processes. For newcomers though, the practice of calling out personal names indicated a nucleus they were outside of; understanding who the people called by first name were became a rite of passage; it was important to meet them, discuss with them, and eventually become known to them by first name in order to get closer to the nucleus. This applied across sectoral divisions, yet it is important to note that in addressing government representatives the generic delegation formula was preferred (e.g. 'the Chinese delegation'). There were, however, exceptions for the representatives of countries that were most active at the IGF and during its preparatory process: the United Kingdom, Switzerland, France, the United States, and Sweden, whose representatives were also easily recognized by their first names (Epstein 2012, 181).

The second habitual characteristic of the community structuration was the solidification of principles put forward by its key members. Among these, inclusiveness and multi-stakeholder participation were subsequently internalized by the rest of the community. The underlying tenets of the fast-growing Internet community were reproduced in various ways: at recurrent events and through newcomer programmes, through local and transnational anchors, but also through the reiteration of principles that its most influential members upheld. The length of career within the community became a highly valued source of authority, compatible with membership across many other sub-communities. It is from this position that established members promoted the core values. In their interventions and contributions, the most active individuals frequently referred back to previous meetings they attended, using formulations such as 'I was there when this was discussed/I was a member of the working group/I was chairing the meeting'. Such prefaces reflected different knowledge and commitment levels.

The insights of those more regularly involved gained more weight, not coming in contradiction with their multiple membership across groups endorsing different beliefs. Their ownership claim was rooted in the service done to the community on many other occasions and in their proximity to power structures across different venues, as well as the privileged knowledge they had access to. Importantly, in the IG space, the discussions remained open. The boundaries of the group were maintained insofar as formal representation was concerned, but the different communities acting in this space did not define themselves in contrast with other groups.

Partly explaining this was the far-reaching sharing practice among community members, not limited to work only. Physical meetings offered opportunities to socialize and develop interpersonal relations during lunches, receptions, day-long trips planned together. These informal occasions further contributed to the adoption of a similar vocabulary and the development of a communal knowledge repertoire, which included information about community members, viewpoints, and expectations. The spaces for interaction and the social practices for IG were thus mutually constituted. Socialization shaped the extent to which a shared mindset and the idea of a collective future were perpetuated. As Cohen observed:

the quintessential referent of community is that its members make, or believe they make, a similar sense of things either generally or with respect to specific and significant interests, and further, that they think that that sense may differ from one made elsewhere. (1985, 16)

Defining a common horizon also meant, in the IG case, an aversion to the exclusion of participants based on their affiliation. It was, for example, common to have business and technical community representatives regularly participating in discussions on the Civil Society Caucus mailing list. In an analysis of the IGF transcripts for the period of 2006 to 2012, DiploFoundation (2015) concluded that the verbal contributions during the annual meetings were divided as follows: 34.45 per cent made by government representatives, 17.23 per cent by NGO representatives, 15.47 per cent by business representatives, 14.60 per cent by the technical community, 11.68 per cent by IO representatives, and 6.57 per cent by academics. Semantically, the contributions of all stakeholders but IOs and academia members were similar, revealing analogous patterns of word usage by the technical community, business community, and NGOs. This was highly indicative of how relationships have been forged at the nucleus of the community and how daily practices embedded shared-learning processes.

Face-to-face learning, the moulding of a common perspective and the exchange of good practices at global forums also played key roles in shaping the Internet communities in-the-making because they acted as a self-fulfilling prophecy, reiterating the core values in which the identities of the community were rooted. The flexible, self-organizing, English-speaking, male-dominated group that participated in the early days—in ARPANET or in the WSIS process—ossified as a cluster of authoritative voices for the maintenance of the structures whose creation they contributed to. More than sharing similar views on the values to be promoted in IG, the nucleus actively used its high profile and influence to advocate for its vision, for example in pleading formally for a renewal of the IGF mandate back in 2014.

To this day, the multi-stakeholder construct remains deeply ingrained in the principles put forward for institutional design, as it was the case for the creation of the IGF, or for opposing initiatives for not being inclusive enough. Recurrent, structured interactions and interrelations define the core community and reiterate the principles that unite them, limiting the radical discourses. In that sense, multi-stakeholder processes are 'enabling and including, but also disciplining' (Raboy et al. 2010, 84). Actors construct themselves based on their acquired affiliation(s), but also as contributors to the community. They often sit on Advisory Boards together, being habituated into specialized practices in similar ways. Peer reviewers, often called in for collective drafting exercises, are appreciated for both subject-matter expertise and immersion in community practices.

Over time, the process of assigning fixed identities taking into account geographic and community representation was institutionalized. From the selection of ICANN board members to the WGIG members and to the Board of the NetMundial Initiative, the institutionalization of procedures became a central discussion in the community. Procedural design consolidated the claim to representativeness and gave the community a sense of the preferences, ideas, and principles selected individuals would stand for, rather than providing a clear understanding of the arguments that would be put forward in the negotiation. For example, the ample consultation processes taking place within civil society groups served a legitimating purpose, alongside the functional approach to selecting speakers and delegates. The nominations were usually put forward on the mailing list and there was a transparent candidature process, followed by the expression of support and endorsement from the other members of the group, most of the times taking the form of '+1' for the preferred candidate.

Socialized in this practice originally developed by the technical community, the younger active members of the core IG community reproduce and perpetuate it. As Djelic and Quack put it:

Ultimately, socialization can lead to a transparency of structuring and institutional frameworks and thus to 'invisible' reproduction. This is probably one of the most powerful kinds of stabilization mechanisms, suggesting profound entrenchment and generating great legitimacy. (2007, 165)

The discussion above indicates that neither the community, nor the group belongingness remains static. The meaning and the accepted forms of community participation have solidified and institutionalized in the process, but are by no means fixed. While deliberate effort was put into community expansion—through capacity building programmes, summer schools, newcomer guides, and the mutual orientation of members—social interactions and collective drafting of rules of conduct provided the basis for maintaining the core group. The dynamism of the IG nucleus stems, in part, from the continuous reiteration of common principles and aspirations. But it is also reactionary, as fast responses are required for technical developments and regulatory moves. To participate in fluid configurations of governance, the core community enacts structures of signification and legitimation by drawing on praxis, expertise and lengthy involvement in IG processes.

Anchoring Practices

As discussed in the opening chapter, the IG scholarship has spent considerable time focusing on institutions and novel mechanisms at the expense of comprehensive analyses of practices. This book breaks away with that tradition by integrating practices as an additional dimension of empirical investigation, to reveal how actors coalesce around routines and meanings in their daily work. Anchoring practices are solidified habits turned into pillars for community formation. They represent instances of power perpetuation, reinforcing broader governance structures. Each one of the three anchoring practices identified here is specific to a period, but it is perpetuated beyond, enduring over the years: by 2018, more than 8,400 RFCs had been issued, thousands of multi-stakeholder events took place, and hundreds of ad hoc expert groups completed their IG work.

Importantly, these three practices are also instances of co-regulatory routines consonant with broader contemporary governance arrangements. First, the RFCs emerged in the early days of the Internet and became authoritative in the 1980s to help standardize the first protocols and foster communication within the technical and academic community working on the precursor of the Internet. Moreover, they helped embed particular values about how things should be done, and what should be prioritized in the process. Second, multi-stakeholder routines were championed around the creation of ICANN and became dominant in the privatization decade up until 2003–2005, when they were sanctioned in the Tunis Agenda. Third, ad hoc expert bodies were more often deployed post-WSIS to legitimize a set of punctual solutions that generally did not challenge the status quo. While they all used to depend on a few active individuals, the anchoring practices explored here are now formalized and institutionalized. To a large extent, the move towards entrenching detailed procedures has shifted the focus from the substance and content of debates to the bureaucratic processes around them.

Influential routines generally enact ideological elements. The different mechanisms of governance at work become structural conditions for social practices framing the rules of the game. In that sense, routine interactions are guided by deeper political endeavours—be they reinforcing or breaking away with established rules—in daily enactments of governance. In the IG community, the neoliberal, market-enabling understanding of the space (Flichy 2007) stood at the basis of the multi-stakeholder discourse. In nascent issue domains, where no textbook approach is possible, substantive expertise is closely linked to the interaction with the groups which possess and produce the expert knowledge. This practice makes it difficult to draw the line between the embodiment of an ideological credo and a genuine participatory approach to governance, as it conflates various dimensions by legitimizing the presence and disciplining the actions of particular actors around the negotiation table.

The creation of ad hoc expert groups speaks to the hierarchy of knowledge established in the community. It therefore performs a separation between those who possess the expertise and are entitled to speak on behalf of different groups and the rest of the community members. While the selection would also be driven by formal considerations such as the representation of different geographical areas and sectors, the expectation of having political stances represented is taken for granted. The practice has become widespread within the EU, with a number of high-level expert groups being formed since 2016: High Level Group on Internet Governance (2016), on Radicalisation (2017), on Fake News (2018), and on Artificial Intelligence (2018). In the same vein, the International Labour Organization (ILO) has established a Global Commission on the Future of Work, chaired by Ameenah Gurib-Fakim, President of the Republic of Mauritius, and by Stefan Löfven, Prime Minister of Sweden. The Commission is expected to produce an independent report in 2019 on digitalization, jobs and social justice. Most prominent among this new set of initiatives is that of the UN Secretary General António

Guterres, who appointed in July 2018 a High-Level Commission on Digital Cooperation, chaired by Melissa Gates and Jack Ma, for a nine-month-long mandate.

Encoding the dominant meanings, anchoring practices are key to understanding the evolution of an issue domain, in particular as they embody rules which are not codified as such formally. They rely on common knowledge, which implies that they 'do not require the time or repetition that habits require, but rather the visible, public enactment of new patterns so that "everyone can see" that everyone else has seen that things have changed' (Swidler 2001, 87). The way communities reiterate practices of recognition and celebrate their members is a case in point here. Starting in 1999, ISOC has been awarding, on an annual basis, the Jonathan B. Postel Service Award. The award, presented at an IETF meeting, goes to an individual or organization with an outstanding contribution to the data communications community. In the selection of the awardee, particular attention is paid to 'candidates who have supported and enabled others in addition to their own specific actions' (ISOC 2015b). Similarly, ICANN's Multistakeholder Ethos Award was launched in June 2014 in London to recognize the leaders of the community promoting multi-stakeholderism within the organization by serving it—for at least five years—in different roles and collaborating across supporting organizations and/or advisory committees.

As the call for nominations details, the Multistakeholder Ethos Award 'recognises ICANN participants who have deeply invested in consensus-based solutions, acknowledging the importance of ICANN's multistakeholder model of Internet governance, and contributed in a substantive way to the higher interests of ICANN's organisation and its community' (ICANN 2015). This annual practice reiterates the need to strive for consensus in ICANN-related activities; but it goes further than that. Just like the ISOC award, it also upholds peer recognition as highly valuable, since the nomination and the review of candidate profiles is done by (a panel of) community members.

Anchoring practices in IG, as evidenced throughout the evolution of the field, reflect the merging of two forms of authority: social and epistemic. On the one hand, group belongingness entitles certain individuals to take part in Internet-related processes. On the other hand, expertise grounded in subject-matter knowledge becomes more appreciated over time. Different IG groups are both rule-makers and targets of rules. In a nutshell, anchoring practices are also an important proxy for ideological cohesion and community support. A plethora of consultation mechanisms and channels of input exist, both formally and informally, to bridge the divide between the private and the public realms. This provides evidence for the consolidation of a hybrid environment, in which the boundaries of the community are no longer drawn solely in accordance with the position taken by key actors. In part, it is due to the reproduction of practices of collaboration that have become the 'invisible thread' behind the way in which the community is organized.

Synopsis

Nowadays, the Internet presents multiple sites of authority at different levels, from national to global. While some of the developments that marked the IG evolution post-2015 were direct continuations of processes started before, such as cross-sectoral convergence facilitated by Internet technology, new concerns surfaced as fresh political and legal endeavours to tackle, such as the pursuit of cybersecurity norms or AI. The first part of this chapter investigated the power dynamics at play post-2015, putting into perspective the key governance transformations.

Dominant private companies, on the one hand, and influential governments, on the other, are currently restructuring the debates along realpolitik and economic dimensions. Their actions impose, legitimize, and strengthen what appears to be a contested re-arrangement of power. Carving out a clear-cut regulatory space in a dense institutional ecosystem has long been a national priority, but the stakes increased amidst technological innovation and diversification. A product of public and private collaboration, the Internet does not cease to be a field in search of ethical and legal guiding frameworks as its political standing continues to rise. The repeated calls to develop rules, in particular on cyber-operations and AI, point to the securitization of a significant part of the field.

Shifting attention to agency, the second part of this chapter brought into sharper focus the role of the IG community in structuring a unique field of governance. From the introduction of specific guidance for newcomer programmes to the perpetuation of decision-making processes and the enactment of anchoring practices, the core values passed on reflect the characteristics of the initial group of technical bodies, formalized and politicized over time. The dynamics within the community, however, present their own patterns and specificities. In this longitudinal perspective, abstract oppositions frequently applied to IG, such as bottom-up versus top-down, public versus private, state versus market, took on a new meaning. More than articulating a functional, solution-oriented approach to problems, the community patterns identified here are tightly linked to ideological positions, as well as social and epistemic authority. The global IG regime is built on both disruptions and continuities and many different legitimation routes open up in its restructuring.

7

Conclusion: Reflections on a Global
Issue Domain

More than half a century after the deployment of the packet switching technology and twenty-plus years after the rollout of the World Wide Web and the rise of e-commerce, the Internet is a constant of modern life. Enticing and convoluted, its evolution from a technical experiment in internetworking to a ubiquitous presence encapsulates the tensions of globalization in the most concrete manner. The global governance of the Internet remains at odds with the research traditions of international relations (IR), none of them fully accommodating this new issue domain. As this study has shown, the Internet presents us with a 'bricolage' picture: different forms and varieties of governance emerging, with various degrees of institutionalization, at different stages and degrees of (re)negotiation, with varying degrees of success in addressing global concerns.

The prime objective of this analysis was to unpack the complexity of Internet governance (IG) and present a new analytical perspective for examining its genesis and structuration as a domain of global governance. This perspective, derived from the constructivist approach to IR, places IG amidst a changing global order and takes into account the broader context in which the debates over global rules regulating the network of networks are framed. Whether we discuss cybersecurity or an ethical framework for artificial intelligence (AI), it is the characteristics of the governance system in place that shape future decision-making processes.

The dataset constructed for this study—consisting of 311 governance instruments—provided a unique entry point for mapping and assessing the mechanisms and actors in the field. Spanning more than four decades, the governance instruments recorded here were assessed in interaction with external driving forces and with power positions specific to the field. The enactment of governance in this issue domain was further deconstructed along a praxis dimension, exploring dominant routines adopted by the core

Negotiating Internet Governance. Roxana Radu © Roxana Radu 2019. Published 2019 by Oxford University Press.

community forming around IG. This holistic account, grounded historically, helps us understand the totality of debates constructing the Internet.

In the periodization exercise, three phases were identified as key to the evolution of the field. For each of these stages, specific governance patterns surfaced: (1) the early days of the Internet were dominated by informal governance and focused on technical standards (1970s to 1994); (2) the globalization of the Internet was closely linked to an increasing role of private actors and the salience of the market-oriented approach (1995–2004); and (3) the decade of global regulatory arrangements (2005–15) brought hybrid configurations to the fore, privileging cross-sectoral partnerships. Post-2015, new power trends indicate a stronger position of a limited number of companies and states, clashing more frequently over the fundamentals of governing the field. Across various subfields, whether related to infrastructure and critical resources, cybersecurity, legal issues, digital economy, ICT for development (ICT4D), or civil liberties, legacy configurations and specific patterns of community development predefine the terms on which governance is exercised.

This chapter presents comparatively the findings of this research covering more than four decades. An evolutionary perspective is offered for the IG community-building practices and internal dynamics. The empirical analysis brings us back to normative questions related to the creation of systems of global rule and opens a theoretical reflection on the constitution of IG as a global power field. The remainder of this chapter explores implications beyond this issue domain for the research agenda proposed here and potential future directions.

Findings

Originally designed as a technological facility for the use of academics and researchers, the NSFNET became the backbone of the global network which is currently an integral part of our social life. Coupled with a deregulatory approach, the worldwide development of the Internet led to a strong focus on legal, economic, and developmental aspects, subsequently reaffirmed at the UN-organized World Summit on Information Society (WSIS) in 2003 and 2005. The fast and substantial growth of the issue domain was fomented by technical developments and by an unprecedented institutional expansion. As the network grew manifold, the range of actors interested in its governance diversified; from the small group of individuals operating in loose structures at the outset, we nowadays have a highly diverse set of actors and a formalized system of rules (re)defined in numerous settings.

Illustrative of this transformation is also the rising number of governance mechanisms applicable to the Internet, as summarized in Table 7. These take three main forms: legal enshrinement, institutional solidification, and modelling. In the last decade, the majority of these were specifically designed for the Internet. As for their binding power, the predominance of soft law instruments over hard law is hardly surprising: treaties and conventions are generally signed by governmental actors and are not open to new(er) actors in the international system, such as civil society groups or businesses. In IG, there has been intense political contestation surrounding legally binding agreements, revealed, for instance, in the lengthy negotiations around the specific wording of the WSIS outcome documents in 2003 and 2005, but also in 2012 at the World Conference on International Telecommunication. For the majority of concerned stakeholders, preference appears to be given to modelling activities, be they discursive or operational, in order to influence

Table 7 Overview of IG issues, instruments, and mechanisms over time

Timeframe	No. of instruments recorded	Broad vs. specific	Salient issues	Dominant Mechanisms	Dominant instruments
1969–93	25	90% vs. 10%	Infrastructure and technical standards	Legal enshrinement	Treaties
			Security	Operative modelling	Guidelines
				Institutional solidification	Specialized bodies
1994–2004	74	45% vs. 55%	Legal	Operative modelling	Model law, guidelines
			Cybercrime	Discursive modelling	Recommendations, charters
			Digital economy	Legal enshrinement	Treaties and conventions
2005–15	212	34% vs. 66%	Cybersecurity	Discursive modelling	Guiding principles
			Civil liberties	Operative modelling	Model laws
				Institutional solidification	Global agendas

the behaviour of other actors in this space. This deliberate choice signals their positioning in a field under construction in which priorities change fast.

The extent to which soft and hard law mechanisms coexist brings forward two important insights: the first is the fact that the logics of action pertaining to different actors involved in IG constrain the design of new rules; the second is the reality of multiple governance negotiations held simultaneously in different venues with minimum interaction across. The latter results in contestation at various levels, ranging from street protests (as in the case of ACTA) to the initiation of UN resolutions. Among the most salient issues in Internet-related discussions and governance actions, cybersecurity was a constant preoccupation for the main actors. It is in this area that all the different types of governance instruments were concentrated over the last two decades, but the search for cyber norms is not yet over. A securitization approach continues to be noticeable post-2015, especially as some initiatives involve more closely the private sector or are indeed proposed by companies. A similar level of concern could be observed in the 1990s for legal and economic developments, or for the promotion of civil liberties in the WSIS decade, setting the foundations for the structuration of the field.

Since its early days, authority remained embedded in horizontal structures such as technical communities, and in hierarchical ones, creating a decentralized system with one point of final control: the US government. Gradually, the hierarchical relations reconfigured as more and more governments started to participate actively in ruling the network by introducing domestic changes or by defining mandates inside international organizations and establishing specialized bodies.

Developing countries versus developed countries, smaller business players versus market dominant ones, and governments versus corporations are dichotomies that still apply to IG, adding to the specific tensions inherent to the maturation of the field. As this book shows, the rules designed for the Internet cannot be secluded from power plays, ultimately resulting in a certain variability of authority structures and exhibiting a hybrid character.

In addition to divergences over technical challenges, such as the need to maintain a unique, reliable, and resilient network, conflict over an appropriate model of IG has been recurrent, demonstrating the perpetuation of the high political stakes attached to this domain. The informal management of the Internet at the outset nurtured a culture of consensus that became dominant in the technical community. Negotiations on Internet matters outside these bodies remained, however, circumscribed to 'politics as usual', introducing a diversity of perspectives grounded in socioeconomic and power logics that have over time permeated the discussions on infrastructure, standards, and management of critical resources. The global rise of the commercial network and related controversies in the late 1990s led to a formalization of practices and subsequently to their institutionalization. The anchoring practices discussed here—Request for Comments, multi-stakeholder participation, and ad hoc expert groups—reinforced the power distribution on two levels: the first was the global ordering reflecting who gets to govern and on what terms; the second pertained to the specific praxis among active IG participants, delineating volunteers from professionals, experts from non-experts, and last but not least, reaffirming categories of stakes.

This book's historical approach uncovered the way in which personal interactions played out in the construction of a governance regime for the precursor of the Internet, ARPANET. The individuals with a critical role in sowing the seeds of institutional design remained highly influential throughout the following decades, either as community leaders or as corporate actors. Among these, Steve Crocker, Jon Postel, Robert Kahn, and Vint Cerf led a series of institutional developments that left an authoritative legacy. Similarly, the small group of people involved in negotiating the creation of ICANN became highly influential in discussions at WSIS and continues to form the core of the IG transnational network. Elements of informality continue to structure this issue domain, and ad hoc formations remain a constant, be it in the specialized work of technical bodies or as part of expert groups in various policy processes.

With the growing importance of the field emerged a set of tensions which called into question the fragmented approach to IG rule-making. Two main alternatives were debated: on the one hand, the private-sector led processes were strongly supported by the United States, which retained an authoritative role; on the other hand, the intergovernmental option increasingly came to the fore as governments sought to strengthen control beyond the national level. A basic point of divergence for power dynamics has been the position of the US government. Providing the funding for the development of ARPANET and, subsequently, the NSFNET, the US administration designed a private regime for the management of unique identifiers and the Internet addressing system. In the process, it retained oversight over a critical part of DNS management, namely the Internet Assigned Numbers Authority (IANA) function. This tension underlined the negotiations at WSIS and, post-Snowden, globalized the debate.

On critical Internet matters, the position of the state (fluctuating between central and marginal) among market-based governance modes and hybrid configurations has brought new perspectives to the fore. For scholars of globalization, the longitudinal perspective presented here is particularly relevant as it demonstrates the reversibility of authority from governments to non-state actors, which is not only possible and deliberate, but also unfolding in ways previously understudied. The undermining of democratic practices, under discussion following the 2018 Facebook–Cambridge Analytica scandal (around algorithmic manipulation of voters in the Brexit referendum and US elections in 2016), or the future of AI systems are just two of the many elements that restructure the debate around defining societal priorities before pursuing market and technological ones. Via institutional solidification efforts, these choices lead to path dependency and become a permanent feature of global governance.

Rather than fostering an array of separate initiatives, a relatively cohesive community coalesces around an ever-growing scope of IG. A stable group of experts, helping to spur interest in transborder solutions, has formed over time and continues to meet to enact governance in all its forms, from providing guidance in policy processes to moulding the next generation of community leaders. Generally grouped according to the stakeholder categories sanctioned in the Tunis agenda, participants in these processes are agenda-setters and legitimizers of discursive modelling actions, encapsulating unique expertise and know-how. By 2015, the majority of actors involved in IG acted in more than one policy field and community representatives regularly engaged in multiple governance processes simultaneously. The public–private restructuring of the digital markets (observed at the structural level) had a corresponding effect at the community level, bringing together a growing number of interests.

Understanding New IG Trends

The standing of IG grew over time from a technical area to a 'new foreign policy imperative'.[1] Yet a consensus of key stakeholders on issues of importance to the development of the field continues to be avidly sought. Policymakers are now confronted with cross-sectoral concerns combining socioeconomic, political, and ethical dilemmas simultaneously, for example in addressing the challenges of the sharing economy or in advancing digital rights. Cybersecurity and data protection continue to be critical points of deliberation, while technology-driven transformations, such as the Internet of Things (IoT) and AI, have imposed a wider public debate. If the three historical phases showed us that changes in the scope, size, and scale of the network were enthusiastically welcomed, the fourth period we see emerging might be driven by scepticism. Can and should this mature phase reached by

---

[1] As referred to by Hillary Clinton (Jamart 2014).

the Internet be sustained? Should the fundamentals be reconsidered? The first insights post-2015 bring mixed evidence.

The unprecedented level of global interconnectedness we have reached due to the Internet continues to be perceived as one of the main drivers of global governance, but the capacities of the current institutional patchwork to deliver on transborder challenges are called into question. Alongside other global governance challenges, such as international migration flows, water scarcity, or climate change, the collective management of Internet resources is premised on a cohesive vision pursued by a diverse, cross-sectoral leadership group. Nowadays, efforts by governments and international organizations to define governance norms are regularly paralleled by civil society and business sector actions aimed at modelling behaviour, exchanges, and responsibilities at the global level.

For the first time in the history of the Internet, an increasing number of tech companies have revenues that exceed the GDP of many countries; unprecedented cross-border influence in negotiations comes with this newly-acquired financial power. The friction between governments and industry, or the so-called 'techlash', started to profile itself as a tension likely to define the fourth phase in the development of the Internet. While the companies' responsibility to abide by national laws goes back a long way, recent technological developments such as encrypted apps or self-learning algorithms have reframed the debate from 'who should govern' to 'how and on what terms' could the field be governed. On their side, legislators turned to monetary sanctions and laws with extraterritorial provisions for ruling on key matters, while the top companies decided to explore new investment opportunities in areas of no regulation. As Chapter 6 discussed, internationalizing coalitions promoting the Chinese or the Russian understanding of 'cyber sovereignty' are increasingly more vocal in IG spaces, where alternatives to the status quo continue to be sought.

Amidst these transformations, the power of multilateralism, which constituted a foundation for the neoliberal regime established in the 1990s, appears to weaken in IG processes. Three recent instances of failure to achieve consensus in different subareas attest to that and are indicative of dominant tensions. In light of more influential roles played by the business sector in IG, be it at the level of infrastructure or content, and the stronger national approaches adopted recently, will the Internet move closer to or further away from being understood as a global commons?

In the area of cybersecurity, the search for global norms becomes ever more intricate. The UN Group of Governmental Experts on Developments in the Field of Information and Telecommunications in the Context of International Security, meeting in its fifth working group since 2004, failed to find a common ground for rules of state behaviour in the digital space. After defining the global cybersecurity agenda, and socializing the principle of international law applicability to cyberspace in its previous reports, the group met in 2016–17 to discuss how neutrality, proportionality, the right of self-defence, and other concepts from international law could apply to cyberconflicts. Despite the progress made on cyber-capacity building by the twenty-five UN member states participating in the negotiations, the process unearthed major disagreements over state responsibility, dispute settlement, and the potential militarization of cyberspace.

The main positions delineated in these debates reflected the deeply entrenched disagreements between the United States, Canada, and European countries, on the one hand, and Russia and China on the other, with developing countries placed in the middle. As discussed in Chapter 6, on the margins of this UN process, a proposal for a Digital Geneva Convention was put forward by Microsoft, representing a first attempt by a private actor to define an overarching set of norms for the field of cybersecurity, oriented not only at companies, but also at states. So far, this proposal has received limited support, but a related, voluntary industry Tech Accord has been signed by forty-five firms.

In the sphere of digital economy, the eleventh WTO Ministerial Conference held in December 2017 in Buenos Aires ended without a consensus on redefining e-commerce rules. The memorandum of understanding dating back to 1998 remained in place. The consultations leading up to the meeting were particularly heated, revealing a clear perception of unequal distribution of the digital transformation benefits. Some developing countries proposed that the issue is tackled as part of the Doha development round negotiations once they are set on track, while others found it necessary to have agreement on other important matters first, such as access to infrastructure, capacity development, and digital skills (Geneva Internet Platform 2017).

Beyond selling and buying goods online, the issues put forward ahead of the negotiations touched on the free flow of data, removal of localization demands, and technology transfer requirements. All of these raised concerns among IG civil society groups, which argued against a potential expansion of the WTO mandate into regulating issues such as privacy and cybersecurity. The second instance of contestation emerged around the lack of legitimacy that intergovernmental venues have for Internet-related decision-making, reiterating the need for a more inclusive approach with the participation of different stakeholders. Following the WTO Ministerial, work on an e-commerce reform continues both informally and formally, as plurilateral solutions have started being discussed by WTO member states.

The third recent process that ended without a consensus was conducted within the Working Group on Enhanced Cooperation (WGEC) hosted by the UN Commission on Science and Technology for Development (CSTD). Derived from the WSIS process, enhanced cooperation represented a Gordian knot in IG discussions since the introduction of the Internet Governance Forum (IGF), that many saw was a venue for exercising precisely that. Other pundits assessed the need for a separate track of negotiations. The WGEC was consequently entrusted to find a definition for enhanced cooperation in its meetings in 2013–14. A new iteration of the working group, this time comprising twenty-two national representatives from different regions, five representatives each from business, civil society, academic and technical communities, and international organizations met five times between September 2016 and January 2018. The goal of these diplomatic negotiations was to agree to advance a set of recommendations on public policy issues to the UN General Assembly through its Economic and Social Council. Two unresolved matters blocked the consensus: (1) proposals for the creation of a new institutional mechanism; (2) proposals for addressing enhanced cooperation within existing bodies, like the CSTD/UN Economic and Social Council (ECOSOC) or the IGF.

At the core of the disputes was the idea of governments exercising control over international Internet public policy issues, which was opposed by Western countries and Japan, as well as by the majority of non-state actors involved in the process. The supporters of this proposal included countries such as Cuba and Saudi Arabia, which refused compromise on a middle-ground solution such as continuing to discuss Internet-related matters within the CSTD (Olufuye 2018). The enhanced cooperation track of negotiations broke down over the nature of the mechanism envisaged to take it forward and its different interpretations by UN member states, but its significance goes beyond this single process.

At a critical junction for IG, this reflective turn towards key evolutionary matters for the field, such as establishing definitions or creating new institutional venues, is reminiscent of the WSIS tensions in 2003 and 2005. The demand for a body in charge of Internet-related matters with equal-footing representation for all states, tabled several times since 2010, remains a fundamental rift in IG. In the three processes discussed above, the growing gap between the priorities of advanced economies and the Global South has become more obvious. The Chinese, Russian, Cuban, Iranian, and Saudi Arabian governments have repeatedly blocked consensus-driven deliberations in global venues. Other meetings, built around multi-stakeholder values, such as the IGF, have also seen a stronger presence of dissenting voices from these countries.

Ensuring a stable, functional, and reliable use of the Internet became a completely different endeavour in 2018. Institutional and stakeholder diversity represents a key characteristic of contemporary Internet governance, but it does not go uncontested. The opening up of technical bodies to civil society has been a welcomed development, in stark contrast to the disputes over the participation constraints imposed in intergovernmental processes. In recent years, legitimacy, but also accountability have come more prominently to the public fore. The new dynamics formed around the strain of final decision-making in Internet public policy show that long-standing concessions may still be overturned. The alternative route pursued in the absence of global consensus is intervention outside an established framework, in informal settings, and among like-minded groups.

The search for global norms and rules for the Internet continues. As some processes have shown their limitations, others emerged to foster the supremacy of national approaches or, on the contrary, the vitality of the pluralist environment with multiple stakeholders represented. From basic connectivity restrictions to algorithmic injustice and invasive AI tools, the future IG struggles will make the definition of the field ever more challenging. IG is affected by national and transnational developments, but it also continues to impact development in others fields, such as global security, finance, or the environment. Absent new institutional reforms and innovations at the global level, the search for an inclusive power-sharing arrangement solely within IG is not likely to be successful.

Theoretical Implications

The genesis and structuration of a global field of action can be compared with the construction of a unique architectural site, which needs to preserve both its functionality and its appeal over time. Laying the foundations without a perfect understanding of what comes next and how the complete work would look like is the task at hand in the constitution of IG as a global domain. This analysis has shown that the tools available for construction are mostly defined by those who would be involved in the building process, based on a range of design choices partly inherited from other governance systems and partly developed as unique adjustments. While the genesis of a field might be the result of contingency and spontaneous action, its long-term structuration is a political endeavour par excellence.

The evolution of a global power field is governed by internal dynamics and responses to external factors, determining its salience. By definition, the latter is irregular and relative to other policy fields. In turn, a nascent field influences or steers broader global changes, placing it in a dialectic relation with other, more-established policy areas. This reciprocity is central to conceptualizing an emerging domain on a broader governance spectrum. The interaction of powerful actors in this space can be disentangled by observing various phases in the evolution of a field, which might reveal common visions or contestation instances. For domains in the making, the structuration phase is open-ended and we can only speculate about its potential demise. It is worth exploring as we advance a research agenda on new global governance fields.

A structural constructivist understanding of the process of differentiation allows us to distinguish between different phases in the constitution of a new issue domain without neglecting the role of human agency. The Bourdieu-inspired analysis offered here presents individuals and institutions as interconnected and takes anchoring practices as a starting point for understanding how systems of rules are perpetuated. Governance articulation brings into focus pluralist explanations of authority and legitimacy, as various decision-making processes (generally driven by a few actors) overlap. Yet, to understand the different phrases in the evolution of a field, it is necessary to first disentangle the origins of governance and the structural conditions they enable.

Among the many insights derived from this study, three stand out as highly relevant for laying the theoretical foundations for understanding the lifecycle of new issue domains. The first is the drive for self-organization at the genesis stage, followed by adaptation and co-evolution in a more complex institutional arrangement. The second is the fluidity of developments and the vulnerability to changes, intrinsic to an emergent field of governance; unlike more established domains of action such as international trade, new fields are susceptible to a wide range of external variation, which may affect the power distribution among players. Third, while the demarcation line between different mechanisms of governance is constantly redrawn via changing political relations, the attention paid to defining principles for rule-setting emerges as a constant. Significant effort is put into designing codes of conduct, shared norms, and practices that inhibit the current balance of power or, as it is more often the case, uphold it.

Beyond the IG specific insights covered in this research, one question remains: Do the meanings derived here contribute to the development of an integrated framework for understanding global issue domains? As this study shows, the design of a governance system for an emerging issue domain is not the result of intent only. Contingency and technological advances also play an important role in the evolution of the field. Integrating the technical and the policy side of the discussions—a merger observed more frequently after the WSIS Summit of 2003 and 2005—leads not only to a diversification of governance approaches, but also to the expansion of the field as a whole.

An emerging issue domain has a lifecycle of its own. Rather than developing linearly, new policy fields are built around underlying tensions that may be displayed continuously or only surface in crisis moments. This ordering in-the-making implies steering of processes, but also 'rowing', or the perform-ance of specific functions for economic, social, political, environmental, administrative, or adjudicative purposes. The central role of states, empha-sized by students of IR and IG, continues to inform global politics, but it is no longer the only authoritative source of power. As the number of actors involved in global governance grows steadily, defining their roles and agreeing on the basic rules for their engagement is the priority.

A new area of investigation in IR, issue domains that are by definition global—like the Internet—pose a set of distinct challenges to the theorization of governance. Not only are they fragile realities of global governance, but they also (re)present distinctive, partial spheres of authoritative rule-making. Early work on environmental, financial, or health governance provided useful reflections for tackling emerging policy issues, but their insights remained rather scattered. The practice-based theoretical turn, drawing on European critical theory and in particular on the work of Bourdieu, added the dimen-sion of praxis to solving contemporaneous puzzles rooted in nascent fields of governance. This book took on the challenge of exploring what constitutes IG, how it emerges, and how it gets (better) articulated over time.

As posited in Chapter 1, the lack of a systematic focus on comprehensive, longitudinal analyses of the evolution of issue domains has obscured founda-tional subjects of inquiry, such as the emergence and articulation of govern-ance. A permissive agenda spanning different theoretical paradigms, the IR literature has offered, so far, only limited empirical studies on the workings of global governance, the 'who', 'why', and 'how' questions remaining insuffi-ciently addressed. To build a stronger conceptual and empirical link between governance enactment and the forms it takes, this study unpacked the global structuring for new issue domains, distinguishing between different evolu-tionary phrases.

An inward look at a global domain reveals a fragmented picture, with subfields developing their own specificities and institutional configurations. The conceptualization of the issue domain itself is partly the result of the governance patterns and power dynamics forming over time. From key decision-making to daily routines, points of control and inherent tensions around them drive both the cross-sectoral arrangements and the definition of spheres of authority. To explore the interaction at the heart of develop-ments, the three-dimensional framework of analysis proposed here was highly valuable: mechanisms, actors, and practices each reveal a crucial aspect for the formation and evolution of the field.

This study made four important contributions to IR and public policy: first, it helped close the gap between the conceptual and the empirical evidence for the origin and articulation of governance; second, it investigated the evolution of the Internet taking into account the underexplored dimension of dominant practices, alongside mechanisms and actors; third, it showed how continuity and change can be explained in a longitudinal analysis of over forty years; fourth, it laid the foundations for a new research agenda focused on the constitution of new issue domains. To take the latter forward, a comparison with governance patterns in other global domains (such as climate change, health, or global financing) could provide a useful avenue for assessing similarities and differences, unique features, and isomorphism instances. It would also help us grasp, in a more comprehensive manner, what challenges emerge for legitimacy and accountability in global governance when new policy fields become permanent features of the international system.

Future Research Directions

Theorizing the lifecycle of an issue domain in the making is an incomplete endeavour. In contemporary governance, just like in policymaking, we follow moving targets: the Internet is an eloquent example of that. The attention given to an issue domain varies in time, and may range from being assigned a global priority status to its obsolescence. The consolidation of a global institutional architecture and the political salience accorded to IG, as contested as it may be, indicates that the demise of this field is nowhere in sight. The reforms, adjustments, and adaptations it may undergo in the near future will determine which system of rules can effectively address the challenges facing users, governments, international organizations, business actors, civil society, and technical bodies.

This book investigated the collaboration and contention emerging over time in structuring a unique field of governance, providing a timely account of ongoing debates and their origins. Using many of the conceptual and empirical tools set out in the earlier discussion, complementary analysis can go deeper into theorizing the constitution of other new issue domains on the international agenda, such as global health, international finance, health, or environmental governance. The exploration of highly complex, cross-sector and cross-organizational policy arenas is a much-needed contribution to understanding contemporary global governance.

At the outset, I noted that we lack a coherent theoretical approach to grasp the evolution of issue domains beyond fragmentary glimpses at key developments in specific policy areas. When analysing nascent issue domains, new opportunities emerge to unpack complexity and revisit theoretical foundations in IR. Regime theorists came closest to defining the conditions under which a domain of governance is constituted, but presupposed an agreement on norms and principles comes first. This longitudinal analysis of Internet governance showed that principles and values may remain subject to debate as work gets completed in a number of subfields.

A study employing both historical and empirical grounding helps us refine explanations for the continuity and change trajectories observed in international affairs. The research agenda proposed here could be further pursued by concentrating efforts in two directions. To begin with, the dimensions analysed in this book (cross-sectoral mechanisms, actors, and dominant practices) provide the first inroads and are limited to IG-specific dynamics. They could be further expanded to better capture informal relations that are authoritative. Second, more comparative research is needed, in particular for issue domains for which we can locate genesis around the same time. Unquestionably, such comparisons would provide a fruitful ground for furthering the theorization of global governance.

What this book has shown is the complex constitution of a convoluted system of global rules. It has thus opened the door for a fascinating, multifaceted inquiry into governance processes in-the-making. The decentralized nature of the Internet has been mirrored in the intricate configurations for its governance, but also in the attempts to override it. Collaboration, competition, and contestation lie at the core of this new domain of power and continue to drive its development.

Bibliography

Aaronson, Susan Ariel. 2015. The Digital Trade Imbalance and Its Implications for Internet Governance. GCIG Paper No. 25. https://www.cigionline.org/sites/default/files/gcig_no25_web_0.pdf

Abbate, Janet. 1999. *Inventing the Internet*. Cambridge, MA: MIT Press.

Abbott, Kenneth W. and Duncan Snidal. 2000.Hard and Soft Law in International Governance. *International Organization* 54, pp. 421–56.

Abbott, Kenneth W. and Duncan Snidal. 2009. The Governance Triangle: Regulatory Standards Institutions and the Shadow of the State. In *The Politics of Global Regulation*, edited by Woods, Ngaire and Walter Mattli, pp. 44–88. Princeton: Princeton University Press.

Abbott, Kenneth W. and Duncan Snidal. 2013. Taking Responsive Regulation Transnational: Strategies for International Organizations. *Regulation & Governance* 7(1), pp. 94–112.

Abbott, Kenneth W., Philipp Genschel, Duncan Snidal, and Bernhard Zangl. 2015. *International Organizations as Orchestrators*. Cambridge: Cambridge University Press.

AccessNow. 2018. #KeepItOn campaign. https://www.accessnow.org/keepiton/

Adler, Emanuel. 2013. Resilient Liberal International Practices. In *Liberal World Orders*, edited by Dunne, Tim and Trine Flockhart. Oxford: Oxford University Press.

Anderson, Benedict. 2006. *Imagined Communities*. London: Verso.

Andonova, Liliana. 2010. Public-Private Partnerships for the Earth: Politics and Patterns of Hybrid Authority in the Multilateral System. *Global Environmental Politics* 10(2), pp. 25–53.

Andonova, Liliana. 2014. Boomerangs to Partnerships? Explaining State Participation in Transnational Partnerships for Sustainability. *Comparative Political Studies* 47(3), pp. 481–515.

Antonova, Slavka. 2007. The Global in the Internet Governance Regime: Fora, Stakeholders, and Policy Networks. *International Journal of Technology, Knowledge and Society* 2(7), pp. 15–24.

Aradau, Claudia, Jef Huysmans, Andrew Neal, and Nadine Voelkner. 2015. *Critical Security Methods: New Frameworks for Analysis*. London: Routledge.

Article 19 and Privacy International. 2018. *Privacy and Freedom of Expression in the Age of Artificial Intelligence*. London: Article 19 and Privacy International.

Autesserre, Séverine. 2014. *Peace and Conflict Resolution and the Everyday Politics of International Intervention*. Cambridge: Cambridge University Press.

Baldwin, Robert, C. Scott, and C. Hood. 1998. *A Reader on Regulation*. Oxford: Oxford University Press.

Balzacq, Thierry. 2011. A Theory of Securitization. Origins, Core Assumptions, and Variants. In *Securitization Theory. How Security Problems Emerge and Dissolve*, edited by Balzacq, Thierry, pp. 1–30. London: Routledge.

Barlow, John P. 1996. Declaration on the Independence of the Cyberspace. https://www.eff.org/cyberspace-independence.

Barnett, Michael and Martha Finnemore. 2005. *Rules for the World: International Organizations in Global Politics*. Ithaca, NY: Cornell University Press.

Bendrath, Ralf. 2003. The American Cyber-Angst and the Real World: Any Link? In *Bombs and Bandwidth: The Emerging Relationship between Information Technology and Security*, edited by Latham, Robert, pp. 49–73. New York: New Press.

Benkler, Yochai. 2006. *The Wealth of Networks*. New Haven: Yale University Press.

Beranek, L. 2005. BBN's Earliest Days: Founding a Culture of Engineering Creativity. *IEEE Annals of the History of Computing* 27(2), pp. 6–14.

Bergman, Michael K. 2001. White Paper: The Deep Web: Surfacing Hidden Value. *Journal of Electronic Publishing* 7(1). https://quod.lib.umich.edu/j/jep/3336451.0007.104?view=text;rgn=main

Best, Jacqueline and Alexandra Gheciu. 2014. *The Return of the Public in Global Governance*. Cambridge: Cambridge University Press.

Biermann, Frank, Philipp Pattberg, Harro van Asselt, and Fariborz Zelli. 2009. The Fragmentation of Global Governance Architectures: A Framework for Analysis. *Global Environmental Politics* 9(4), pp. 14–40.

Biersteker, Thomas. 1999. Eroding Boundaries, Contested Terrain. *International Studies Review* 1(1), pp. 3–9.

Biersteker, Thomas. 2010. Global Governance. In *Routledge Handbook of Security Studies*, edited by Dunn-Cavelty, Myriam and Victor Mauer, pp. 439–51. London: Routledge.

Biersteker, Thomas. 2014. Transnational Policy Networks. Paper delivered at the International Studies Association Annual Meeting, Toronto, Canada.

Bing, Jon. 2009. Building Cyberspace: A Brief History of Internet. In *Internet Governance: Infrastructure and Institutions*, edited by Bygrave, L. A. and Jon Bing, pp. 8–48. Oxford: Oxford University Press.

Bjola, Corneliu and Markus Kornprobst. 2010. *Understanding International Diplomacy: Theory, Practice and Ethics*. Hoboken: Routledge.

Black, Julia. 2008. Constructing and Contesting Legitimacy and Accountability in Polycentric Regulatory Regimes. *Regulation & Governance* 2(2), pp. 137–64.

Blackman, C. 2013. The Future of Multilateralism in the Governance of Communications. *Info* 15(1), editorial.

Boerzel, Tanja and Thomas Risse. 2005. Public–Private Partnerships: Effective and Legitimate Tools of International Governance. In *Complex Sovereignty: On the Reconstitution of Political Authority in the 21st Century*, edited by Grande, E. and L. Pauly, pp. 195–216. Toronto: University of Toronto Press.

Boerzel, Tanja A. and Thomas Risse. 2010. Governance without a State: Can it Work? *Regulation and Governance* 4(2), pp. 113–34.

Bourdieu, Pierre. 1976. Le sens pratique. *Actes de la recherche en sciences sociales.* (February) Vol. 1, pp. 43–86.

Bourdieu, Pierre. 1991. *In Other Words: Essays toward a Reflexive Sociology.* Stanford, CA: Stanford University Press.

Bourdieu, Pierre. 2000. *Pascalian Meditations.* Cambridge: Polity Press.

Bourdieu, Pierre and Loïc Wacquant. 1992. *An Invitation to Reflexive Sociology.* Chicago: The University of Chicago Press.

Braithwaite, John and Peter Drahos. 2000. *Global Business Regulation.* Cambridge: Cambridge University Press.

Broad, William. 1992. Clinton to promote high technology, with Gore in charge. *New York Times.* 10 November. https://www.nytimes.com/1992/11/10/science/clinton-to-promote-high-technology-with-gore-in-charge.html?pagewanted=print

Broadband Commission for Digital Development. 2015. *The State of Broadband 2015.* Geneva: ITU and UNESCO. https://www.itu.int/pub/S-POL-BROADBAND.13-2015

Broadband Commission for Digital Development. 2018. *The State of Broadband 2018: Broadband Catalyzing Sustainable Development.* Geneva: ITU and UNESCO. https://www.itu.int/pub/S-POL-BROADBAND.19

BroadbandNow. 2018. Google Owns 63,605 Miles and 8.5% of Submarine Cables Worldwide. 12 September. https://broadbandnow.com/report/google-content-providers-submarine-cable-ownership/

Brousseau, Eric and Meryem Marzouki. 2013. Internet Governance: Old Issues, New Framings, Uncertain Implications. In *Governance, Regulations, and Powers on the Internet,* edited by Brousseau, Eric, Meryem Marzouki, and Cécile Méadel, pp. 368–97. Cambridge: Cambridge University Press.

Brown, Ian and Christopher Marsden. 2013. *Regulating Code. Information Revolution and Global Politics.* Cambridge, MA: MIT Press.

Bueger, Christian. 2016. *International Organizations in Practice: The United Nations, Peacebuilding and Praxiography.* London: Routledge.

Bulkeley, Harriet, Liliana Andonova, Michele Betsill, Daniel Compagnon, Thomas Hale, Matthew Hoffman, Peter Newell, Matthew Paterson, Charles Roger, and Stacy Vandeveer. 2014. *Transnational Climate Change Governance.* Cambridge: Cambridge University Press.

Bush, Vannevar. 1945. As we may think. *Atlantic Monthly,* July issue. https://www.theatlantic.com/magazine/archive/1945/07/as-we-may-think/303881/

Buzan, Barry, Ole Waever, and Jaap De Wilde. 1998. *Security: A New Framework for Analysis.* Boulder: Lynne Rienner Publishers.

Bygrave, Lee A. and Jon Bing. 2009. *Internet Governance: Infrastructure and Institutions.* Oxford: Oxford University Press.

Caplan, Robyn and Danah Boyd. 2016. *Who Controls the Public Sphere in an Era of Algorithms? Mediation, Automation, Power.* Data & Society, New York: Data & Society.

Carr, Madeline. 2015. Power Plays in Global Internet Governance. *Millennium— Journal of International Studies* 43(2), pp. 640–59.

Carr, Madeline. 2016. *US Power and the Internet in International Relations: The Irony of the Information Age.* Houndsmills: Palgrave.

Cassidy, John. 2002. *Dot.Con: The Greatest Story Ever Sold.* Allen Lane: Penguin Press.

Castells, Manuel. 1996. *The Information Age: Economy, Society and Culture.* Cambridge, MA: Blackwell.

Castells, Manuel. 1997. *The Information Age: Economy, Society and Culture: The Power of Identity.* Vol. 2, Cambridge, MA: Blackwell.

Castells, Manuel. 2001. *The Internet Galaxy.* Oxford: Oxford University Press.

Cerf, Vint. 2013. *Marking the birth of the modern-day Internet.* Google Blogpost. https://googleblog.blogspot.ch/2013/01/marking-birth-of-modern-day-internet.html

Cetina, Katrin Knorr. 1981. *The Manufacture of Knowledge.* GB: Pergamon Press.

Chenou, Jean-Marie. 2014. *The Role of Transnational Elites in Shaping the Evolving Field of Internet Governance.* PhD Thesis. Lausanne: UNIL.

Chenou, Jean-Marie and Roxana Radu. 2015. Beyond Turf Wars in Internet Governance: The Relationship between Internet Organizations and IGOs. In *Global Governance Facing Structural Changes,* edited by Rioux, Michele and Kim Fontaine-Skronski, pp. 37–58. Berlin and New York: Springer.

Chenou, Jean-Marie and Roxana Radu. 2017. The 'Right to be Forgotten': Negotiating Public and Private Ordering in the European Union. *Business & Society,* https://doi.org/10.1177/0007650317717720

Chesnoy, Jose. 2015. *Undersea Fiber Communication Systems.* 2nd ed. GB: Academic Press.

Choucri, Nazli. 2012. *Cyberpolitics in International Relations.* Cambridge, MA: MIT Press.

Christiansen, Thomas, Andreas Follesdal, and Simona Piattoni. 2003. Informal Governance in the European Union: An Introduction. In *Informal Governance in the European Union,* pp. 1–21. Cheltenham: Edward Elgar.

Cisco. 2017. Cisco Visual Networking Index: Global Mobile Data Traffic Forecast Update, 2016–2021 White Paper https://www.cisco.com/c/en/us/solutions/collateral/service-provider/visual-networking-index-vni/mobile-white-paper-c11-520862.html

CJEU. 2014. Judgment of the Grand Chamber of 13 May 2014. *Google Spain SL and Google Inc. v Agencia Española de Protección de Datos (AEPD) and Mario Costeja González.* http://bit.ly/1AUdKN6

Clinton, Hillary. 2010. Remarks on Internet Freedom. *The Newseum,* 21 January, Washington DC. https://2009-2017.state.gov/secretary/20092013clinton/rm/2010/01/135519.htm

Coates, Kevin. 2011. *Competition Law and Regulation of Technology Markets.* New York: Oxford University Press.

Cohen, Anthony. 1985. *The Symbolic Construction of Community.* Chichester: Horwood.

Cohen, Benjamin. 2014. *Advanced Introduction to International Political Economy.* Cheltenham: Edward Elgar.

Compaine, Benjamin M. ed. 2001. *The Digital Divide: Facing a Crisis or Creating a Myth?* Cambridge, MA: MIT Press

Crain, Matthew. 2014. Financial Markets and Online Advertising: Reevaluating the Dotcom Investment Bubble. *Information, Communication & Society* 17(3), pp. 371–84.

Crocker, Stephen. 1969. RFC 3: Documentation convention. Network Working Group. http://www.faqs.org/rfcs/rfc3.html

Crocker, Stephen. 2009. How the Internet Got its Rules. *New York Times.* 6 April. http://www.nytimes.com/2009/04/07/opinion/07crocker.html.

Crocker, Stephen. 2012. Testimonial at the Internet Hall of Fame. *Internet Society* https://www.youtube.com/watch?v=vRuXFjQl7n8

Cutler, A. C., Virginia Haufler, and Tony Porter. 1999. *Private Authority and International Affairs.* Albany: State University of New York Press.

De Burca, Gráinne, Robert O. Keohane, and Charles Sabel. 2014. Global Experimentalist Governance. *British Journal of Political Science* 44(3), pp. 1–10.

De La Coste, Pierre. 2006. La gouvernance internationale de l'Internet. *Politique étrangère* 3, pp. 507–18.

Deibert, Ronald J. 2015. Authoritarianism Goes Global: Cyberspace Under Siege, *Journal of Democracy* 26(3), pp. 64–78.

Deibert, Ronald J. and Rafal Rohozinski. 2010. Risking Security: Policies and Paradoxes of Cyberspace Security. *International Political Sociology* 4(1), pp. 15–32.

Demchak, Chris. 2003. Creating the Enemy: Global Diffusion of the Information Technology-Based Military Model. In *The Diffusion of Military Technology and Ideas*, edited by Goldman, Emily and Leslie Eliason. Stanford, CA: Stanford University Press.

Dencik, Lina and Oliver Leistert. 2015. *Critical Perspectives on Social Media and Protest.* US: Rowman & Littlefield.

DeNardis, Laura. 2009. *Protocol Politics: The Globalization of Internet Governance.* Cambridge, MA: MIT Press.

DeNardis, Laura. 2014. *Global War for Internet Governance.* New Haven: Yale University Press.

DeNardis, Laura, Christian Sandvig, and William H. Dutton. 2013. The Emerging Field of Internet Governance. In *The Oxford Handbook of Internet Studies*, edited by William H. Dutton, Vol. 1, Oxford: Oxford University Press.

Desai, Nitin. 2005. Preface. In *Reforming Internet Governance: Perspectives from the Working Group on Internet Governance (WGIG)*, edited by William J. Drake, pp. vii–x. Geneva: United Nations.

DiploFoundation. 2015. Multistakeholderism in IGF Language, http://www.diplomacy.edu/IGFLanguage/multistakeholderism

Djelic, Marie-Laure and Sigrid Quack. 2007. Overcoming Path Dependency: Path Generation in Open Systems. *Theory & Society* 36(2), pp. 161–86.

Djelic, Marie-Laure and Sigrid Quack. 2010. *Transnational Communities.* Cambridge: Cambridge University Press.

Doria, Avri. 2014. The Use [and Abuse] of Multistakeholderism in the Internet. In *The Evolution of Global Internet Governance: Principles and Policies in the Making*, edited by Radu, Roxana, Jean-Marie Chenou, and Rolf H. Weber, pp. 115–39. Berlin and New York: Springer.

DOT Force. 2002. *Report Card: Digital Opportunities for All.* Ottawa, Canada.

Drahos, Peter and John Braithwaite. 2001. The Globalisation of Regulation. *Journal of Political Philosophy* 9(1), pp. 103–28.

Drake, William. 2005. *Reforming Internet Governance: Perspectives from the Working Group on Internet Governance.* New York: United Nations.

Drake, William J. and Ernest J. Wilson. 2008. *Governing Global Electronic Networks.* Cambridge, MA: MIT Press.

Dunn-Cavelty, Myriam and O. Rolofs. 2010. From cyberwar to cybersecurity: proportionality of fear and countermeasures, paper presented at the Munich Security Conference, 5 February, http://www.securityconference.de/Program.638+M5183285721d.0.html

Dutton, William, John Palfrey, and Malcolm Peltu. 2007. Deciphering the codes of Internet governance: Understanding the hard issues at stake, *Oxford Internet Institute and e–Horizons Institute, Forum Discussion Paper*, number 8, http://www.e-horizons.ox.ac.uk/pdfs/FD8.pdf

Dyson, Esther. 1999. Esther Dyson's Response to Ralph Nader's Questions. *ICANN website*, 15 June. https://www.icann.org/resources/unthemed-pages/dyson-response-to-nader-1999-06-15-en

Eagleton-Pierce, Matthew. 2013. *Symbolic Power in the World Trade Organization.* Oxford: Oxford University Press.

The Economist. 2012. A Digital Cold War? *The Economist* [online], 14 December. http://www.economist.com/blogs/babbage/2012/12/internet-regulation

Epstein, Dmitry. 2012. *The Duality of Information Policy Debates: The Case of the Internet Governance Forum.* PhD Thesis. Cornell University.

Epstein, Dmitry. 2013. The Making of Institutions of Information Governance: The Case of the Internet Governance Forum. *Journal of Information Technology* 28(2), pp. 137–49.

Facebook. 2018. Publishing Our Internal Enforcement Guidelines and Expanding Our Appeals Process. https://newsroom.fb.com/news/2018/04/comprehensive-community-standards/

Feinler, Elizabeth. 2012. Testimonial at the Internet Hall of Fame. *Internet Society.* https://www.youtube.com/watch?v=WLaOKfVssTU&feature=youtu.be

Finnemore, Martha and Kathryn Sikkink. 1998. International Norm Dynamics and Political Change. *International Organization* 52(4), pp. 887–917.

Flichy, Pierre. 2007. *The Internet Imaginaire.* Cambridge, MA: MIT Press.

Flyverbom, Mikkel. 2011. *The Power of Networks.* Cheltenham: Edward Elgar.

FNC. 1990. *Mission statement.* https://www.nitrd.gov/archive/fnc-material.aspx

Foucault, Michel. 1965. *Madness and Civilization: A History of Insanity in the Age of Reason.* New York: Pantheon Books.

Freedman, Des. 2012. Outsourcing Internet Regulation. In *Misunderstanding the Internet*, edited by Curran, James, Natalie Fenton, and Des Freedman, pp. 95–120. New York: Routledge.

Fyfe, Toby and Paul Crookall. 2010. *Social Media and Public Sector Policy Dilemmas Institute of Public Administration of Canada.* Toronto. http://ipac.ca/documents/correctionJune10.pdf

G8. 2000. MOFA: Okinawa Charter on Global Information Society. http://www.mofa.go.jp/policy/economy/summit/2000/documents/charter.html

Gaddis, John Lewis. 2001. Generalization: Rewriting Cold War history, Rethinking International Relations Theory. In *Bridges and Boundaries: Historians, Political Scientists, and the Study of International Relations*, edited by Elman, Colin and Miriam Colin. Cambridge, MA: MIT Press.

GAO. 2000. *Department of Commerce: Relationship with the Internet Corporation for Assigned Names and Numbers Report.* http://www.gao.gov/products/GAO/OGC-00-33R

Geertz, Clifford. 1973. *The Interpretation of Cultures; Selected Essays.* New York: Basic Books.

Gellman, Barton and Ashkan Soltani. 2013a. NSA Tracking Cellphone Locations Worldwide. *Washington Post.* https://www.washingtonpost.com/world/national-security/nsa-tracking-cellphone-locations-worldwide-snowden-documents-show/2013/12/04/5492873a-5cf2-11e3-bc56-c6ca94801fac_story.html

Gellman, Barton and Ashkan Soltani. 2013b. NSA Infiltrates Links to Yahoo, Google Data Centers Worldwide, Snowden Documents Say. *Washington Post.* https://www.washingtonpost.com/world/national-security/nsa-infiltrates-links-to-yahoo-google-data-centers-worldwide-snowden-documents-say/2013/10/30/e51d661e-4166-11e3-8b74-d89d714ca4dd_story.html

Geneva Internet Platform. 2017. WTO Public Forum summary report. 30 September. https://dig.watch/events/wto-public-forum-2017

Gibson, William. 1984. *Neuromancer.* New York: Penguin Putnam, Inc.

Giddens, Antony. 1984. *The Constitution of Society: Outline of the Theory of Structuration.* Berkeley and Los Angeles: University of California Press.

Gisselquist, Rachel M. 2012. What does Good Governance Mean? *WIDER Angle*, 1 January. http://unu.edu/publications/articles/what-does-good-governance-mean.html

Globo. 2013. NSA Documents show United States Spied Brazilian Oil Giant. http://g1.globo.com/fantastico/noticia/2013/09/nsa-documents-show-united-states-spied-brazilian-oil-giant.html

Goldsmith, Jack and Tim Wu. 2006. *Who Controls the Internet?* Oxford: Oxford University Press.

Goodwin, Tom. 2015. The battle is for the consumer interface. TechCrunch, 4 May. https://techcrunch.com/2015/03/03/in-the-age-of-disintermediation-the-battle-is-all-for-the-customer-interface/

Graz, Jean-Christophe. 2006. Hybrids and Regulation in the Global Political Economy. *Competition and Change* 10(2), pp. 230–45.

Graz, Jean-Christophe. 2014. New Players and New Processes in Global Governance: Theorising Hybrid Governance, IPSA paper presented in Montreal, 20–24 July.

Gross, Robin. 2011. Civil society involvement in ICANN. Strengthening future civil society influence in ICANN policymaking. *Association for Progressive Communications.* https://www.apc.org/en/system/files/Civil-Society_ICANN.pdf

Gunkel, David. 2003. Second Thoughts: Toward a Critique of the Digital Divide. *New Media & Society* 5(4), pp. 499–522.

Gupta, Jozeeta, and Claudia Pahl-Wostl. 2013. Global Water Governance in the Context of Global and Multilevel Governance: Its Need, Form, and Challenges. *Ecology and Society* 18(4), pp. 53–63.

Gurstein, M. 2013. Multistakeholderism vs. Democracy: My Adventures in ' Stakeholderland'. https://gurstein.wordpress.com/2013/03/20/multistakeholderism-vs-democracy-my-adventures-in-stakeholderland/

Haas, Ernst B. 1980. Why Collaborate? Issue-Linkage and International Regimes. *World Politics* 32(3), pp. 357–405.

Hafner, Katie and Matthew Lyon. 1999. *Where Wizards Stay Up Late: The Origins of the Internet*. New York: Simon & Schuster

Hall, Peter A. and David Soskice. 2001. *Varieties of Capitalism*. Oxford: Oxford University Press.

Hall, Rodney Bruce and Thomas J. Biersteker. 2002. *The Emergence of Private Authority in Global Governance*. Cambridge: Cambridge University Press.

Hansen, Lene and Helen Nissenbaum. 2009. Digital Disaster, Cybersecurity and the Copenhagen School. *International Studies Quarterly* 53, pp. 1155–75.

Hart, Keith. 2004. Notes towards an Anthropology of the Internet. *Horizontes Antropológicos*, 10(21), pp. 15–40.

Haufler, Virginia. 2001. *A Public Role for the Private Sector: Industry Self-Regulation in a Global Economy*. Carnegie Endowment for International Peace Report.

He, Bin, Mitesh Patel, Zhen Zhang, and Kevin Chen-Chuan Chang. 2007. Accessing the Deep Web: A Survey. *Communications of the ACM* 50(2), pp. 94–101.

Helfer, Laurence. 2004. Regime Shifting: The TRIPs Agreement and New Dynamics of International Intellectual Property Lawmaking. *Yale Journal of International Law* 29(1), pp. 1–83.

Héritier, Adrienne and Sandra Eckert. 2008. New Modes of Governance in the Shadow of Hierarchy: Self-Regulation by Industry in Europe. *Journal of Public Policy* 28(1), pp. 113–38.

Hern, Alex. 2015. Facebook criticised for creating 'two-tier Internet' with Internet.org programme. *The Guardian*. 19 May. https://www.theguardian.com/technology/2015/may/19/facebook-criticised-for-creating-two-tier-internet-with-internetorg-programme

Higgott, Richard, Geoffrey Underhill, and Andreas Bieler. 2000. *Non-State Actors and Authority in the Global System*. Hoboken: Routledge.

Hill, Richard. 2014. Internet Governance: The Last Gasp of Colonialism, or Imperialism by Other Means? In *The Evolution of Global Internet Governance: Principles and Policies in the Making*, edited by Radu, Roxana, Jean-Marie Chenou, and Rolf Weber, pp. 79–94. Berlin: Springer.

Hintz, Arne and Stefania Milan. 2009. At the Margins of Internet Governance: Grassroots Tech Groups and Communication Policy. *International Journal of Media and Cultural Politics* 5(1&2), pp. 23–38.

Hoene, Katharina. 2018. Ready for the future? Germany's emerging AI strategy. DiploFoundation blog. 3 September. https://www.diplomacy.edu/blog/ready-future-germanys-emerging-ai-strategy

Horejsova, Tereza, Pavlina Ittelson, and Jovan Kurbalija. 2018. The rise of techplomacy in the Bay Area. Geneva: DiploFoundation and the Geneva Internet Platform.

Hughes, John and Wes Sharrock. 1997. *The Philosophy of Social Research.* 2nd edn. London: Longman.

Huizer, E and S. Crocker. 1994. RFC 1603: IETF Working Group guidelines and procedures. Network Working Group. http://www.faqs.org/rfcs/rfc1603.html

Huston, Geoff. 2016. The death of transit? APNIC blog. 28 October. https://blog.apnic.net/2016/10/28/the-death-of-transit/

ICANN. 2002. *Bylaws for Internet Corporation for Assigned Names and Numbers. A California Nonprofit Public-Benefit Corporation.* Internet Corporation for Assigned Names and Numbers.

ICANN. 2009. Affirmation of Commitments by the United States Department of Commerce and the Internet Corporation for Assigned Names and Numbers. https://www.icann.org/en/system/files/files/affirmation-of-commitments-30sep09-en.pdf

ICANN. 2015. ICANN Multistakeholder Ethos Award. https://www.icann.org/news/announcement-2015-12-10-en

Irion, Kristina and Roxana Radu. 2013. Delegation to Independent Regulatory Authorities in the Media Sector: A Paradigm Shift Through the Lens of Regulatory Theory. In *The Independence of the Media and its Regulatory Agencies,* edited by Schulz, Wolfgang, Peggy Valcke, and Kristina Irion, pp. 15–54. Chicago: Chicago University Press.

ISOC. 2013. Statement on the Importance of Open Global Dialogue Regarding Online Privacy [online], 12 June. http://www.internetsociety.org/ news/internet-society-statement-importance-open-global-dialogue-regarding-onlineprivacy

ISOC. 2015a. WSIS+10 matrix. 16 October. https://www.internetsociety.org/re-sources/doc/2018/wsis10-matrix/

ISOC. 2015b. Postel Service Award. http://www.internetsociety.org/what-we-do/grants-and-awards/awards/postel-service-award

ISOC. 2018. The Internet and extra-territorial effects of laws. Concept note (September draft). Geneva: Internet Society.

Jackson, Patrick and Daniel Nexon. 1999. Relations Before States: Substance, Process and the Study of World Politics. *European Journal of International Relations* 5, pp. 291–322.

Jamart, Anne-Claire. 2014. Internet Freedom and the Constitutionalization of Internet Governance. In *The Evolution of Global Internet Governance: Principles and Policies in the Making,* edited by Radu, Roxana, Jean-Marie Chenou, and Rolf H. Weber, pp. 57–78. Berlin and New York: Springer.

Jerbi, Scott. 2012. Assessing the Roles of Multi-Stakeholder Initiatives in Advancing the Business and Human Rights Agenda. *International Review of the Red Cross* 94(887), pp. 1027–46.

Jerbi, Scott. 2015. *State 'Orchestration' in Transnational New Governance: What Roles Do Governments Play?* PhD Thesis. Geneva: Graduate Institute of International and Development Studies.

Jessop, Bob. 1998. The Rise of Governance and the Risks of Failure: The Case of Economic Development. *International Social Science Journal* 50(155), pp. 29–45.

Johnson, Chris. 2018. Apple is first public company worth $1 trillion. BBC News, 2 August. https://www.bbc.com/news/business-45050213

Kennard, William. 1999. Vision to mission: a blueprint for architects of the global information infrastructure. Speech before the World Economic Development Forum, 23 September.

Keohane, Robert and David Victor. 2010. *The Regime Complex for Climate Change*: Belfer Center for Science and International Affairs.

Kirton, J. and M. Trebilcock. 2004. *Hard Choices, Soft Law: Voluntary Standards in Global Trade, Environmental and Social Governance.* Aldershot: Ashgate.

Kleinrock, Leonard. 1962. *Message Delay in Communication Nets with Storage.* PhD Thesis. Cambridge, MA: MIT.

Kleinwaechter, Wolfgang. 2003. From Self-Governance to Public-Private Partnership: The Changing Role of Governments in the Management of the Internet's Core Resources, *Loyola of Los Angeles Law Review* 36(3), pp. 1103-1126.

Kleinwaechter, Wolfgang. 2004. Beyond ICANN vs ITU? *Gazette* 66(3–4), pp. 233–51.

Kleinwaechter, Wolfgang. 2008. *Internet Governance and the Information Society: Global Perspectives and European Dimensions.* Portland: Eleven International Publishing.

Kleinwaechter, Wolfgang. 2009. The History of Internet Governance. *Internet Governance*, 20 October. http://www.intgov.net/papers/35

Knight, Jack. 1992. *Institutions and Social Conflict.* Political Economy of Institutions and Decisions. Cambridge: Cambridge University Press.

Kooiman, Jan. 2003. *Governing as Governance.* London: Sage.

Koppell, Jonathan. 2005. Pathologies of Accountability: ICANN and the Challenge of 'Multiple Accountabilities Disorder'. *Public Administration Review* 65, pp. 94–108.

Koppell, Jonathan G. S. 2010. *World Rule: Accountability, Legitimacy, and the Design of Global Governance.* Chicago: University of Chicago Press.

Kornbluh, Karen. 2018. The Internet's lost promise and how America can restore it. *Foreign Affairs.* September/October issue. https://www.foreignaffairs.com/articles/world/internets-lost-promise

Kranzberg, Melvin. 1986. Technology and History: 'Kranzberg's Laws'. *Technology and Culture* 27(3), pp. 544–60.

Krasner, Stephen D. 1983. *International Regimes.* Ithaca, NY: Cornell University Press.

Kummer, Markus. 2007. The Debate on Internet Governance: From Geneva to Tunis and Beyond. *Information Polity* 12(1/2), pp. 5–13.

Kurbalija, Jovan. 2005. *An Introduction to Internet Governance.* Msida, Malta: DiploFoundation.

La Rue, Frank. 2011. Report of the Special Rapporteur on the promotion and protection of the right to freedom of opinion and expression. A/HRC/17/27. Human

Rights Council. Seventeenth session, 16 May. http://www2.ohchr.org/English/bodies/hrcouncil/docs/17session/A.HRC.17.27_en.PDF

Leiner, B. M., V. G. Cerf, D. D. Clark, R. E. Kahn, L. Kleinrock, D. C. Lynch, J. Postel, L. G. Roberts, and S. Wolff. 2009. Brief History of the Internet. *Internet Society.* http://www.internetsociety.org/internet/internet-51/history-internet/brief-history-internet

Lessig, Lawrence. 1999. *Code and Other Laws of Cyberspace.* New York: Basic Books.

Lessig, Lawrence. 2001. *The Future of Ideas.* New York: Random House.

Lessig, Lawrence. 2006. *Code: version 2.0.* New York: Basic Books.

Levi-Faur, David and Jordana, Jacint. 2005. The Rise of Regulatory Capitalism: The Global Diffusion of a New Order. *The Annals of the American Academy of Political and Social Science* 598(1), pp. 200–17.

Levin, K., B. Cashore, Steven Bernstein, and G. Auld. 2009. Playing it Forward: Path Dependency, Progressive Incrementalism, and the 'Super Wicked' Problem of Global Climate Change. IOP Conference Series: Earth and Environmental Science 6(50): 502002. doi:10.1088/1755-1307/6/50/502002.

Levinson, Nanette. 2008. The Internet Governance Ecosystem Assessing Multistakeholderism and Change. Paper prepared for delivery at the 2008 Annual Meeting of the American Political Science Association, 28–31 August.

Levinson, Nanette. 2015. A Tri-Decennia View of Knowledge Transfer Research: What Works in Diffusion & Development Contexts. *Journal of International Communication* 21(2), pp. 153–68.

Levinson, Nanette and Meryem Marzouki. 2015. Internet Governance Institutionalization: Process and Trajectories. In *Global Governance Facing Structural Changes*, edited by Rioux, Michele and Kim Fontaine-Skronski, pp. 17–35. Berlin and New York: Springer.

Licklider, Joseph C. R. 1965. *Libraries of the Future.* Cambridge, MA: MIT Press.

Litman, Jessica. 2000. The DNS Wars: Trademarks and the Internet Domain Name System. *Journal of Small and Emerging Business Law* 4(1), pp. 149–66.

Liu, Jiefei. 2018. China Internet Report 2018: Chinese internet giants are expanding and so is government regulation. *Technode*, 10 July. https://technode.com/2018/07/10/china-internet-report-2018/

Livingstone, Sonia. 2013. Online Risk, Harm and Vulnerability: Reflections on the Evidence Base for Child Internet Safety Policy. *ZER: Journal of Communication Studies* 18, pp. 13–28.

Livingstone, Sonia, John Carr, and Jasmina Byrne. 2015. One in Three: Internet Governance and Children's Rights. https://www.unicef-irc.org/publications/795-one-in-three-internet-governance-and-childrens-rights.html

Lohr, Steve. 2018. Microsoft emerges as clear no. 2 in cloud computing. *New York Times.* 19 July. https://www.nytimes.com/2018/07/19/technology/microsoft-earnings-cloud-computing.html

Lukasik, Stephen. 2011. Why the Arpanet was Built. *IEEE Annals of the History of Computing* 33(3), pp. 4–20.

Lynn, Stuart. 2002. President's Report: ICANN—The Case for Reform: ICANN. https://archive.icann.org/en/general/lynn-reform-proposal-24feb02.htm

Lyotard, Jean-François. 1979. *La condition postmoderne: rapport sur le savoir*. Paris: Minuit.

McCarthy, Daniel R. 2015. *Power, Information Technology, and International Relations Theory*. Basingstoke: Palgrave Macmillan.

McCarthy, Kieren. 2016. Happy 30th Birthday, IETF: The Engineers Who made the 'Net Happen. *The Register*. 16 January. https://www.theregister.co.uk/2016/01/16/happy_30th_birthday_ietf_now_what_you_going_to_do_with_your_life/

MacKenzie, Donald A. and Judy Wajcman. 1999. *The Social Shaping of Technology*. Buckingham: Open University Press.

McLean, Donald. 2005. A Brief History of the WGIG. In *Reforming Internet Governance: Perspectives from the Working Group on Internet Governance*, edited by Drake, William, pp. 9–24. New York: United Nations.

Majone, Giandomenico. 1996. *Regulating Europe*. London, New York: Routledge.

Malcolm, Jeremy. 2008. *Multistakeholder Governance and the Internet Governance Forum*. Sydney: Terminus Press.

Malkin, G. 1993. The Tao of the IETF: a guide for new attendees of the Internet Engineering Task Force. RFC 1391. https://tools.ietf.org/html/rfc1391

Markoff, John. 2012. Killing the computer to save it. *New York Times*, 30 October. https://www.nytimes.com/2012/10/30/science/rethinking-the-computer-at-80.html

Marsden, Christopher. 2011. *Internet Co-Regulation: European Law, Regulatory Governance and Legitimacy in Cyberspace*. Cambridge: Cambridge University Press.

Mathiason, John. 2009. *Internet Governance: The New Frontier of Global Institutions*. London: Routledge.

Meeker, Mary. 2015. Internet Trends 2015—Code Conference. http://kpcbweb2.s3.amazonaws.com/ files/90/Internet_Trends_2015.pdf?1432738078

Milan, Stefania. 2013. *Social Movements and their Technologies: Wiring Social Change*. Basingstoke: Palgrave Macmillan.

Mockapetris, Paul. 2009. HistoryHeard: Paul Mockapetris. 5 April. YouTube video. https://www.youtube.com/watch?v=VLahF1zwAog

Moran, Michael. 2002. Understanding the Regulatory State. *British Journal of Political Science* 32(2), pp. 391–413.

Morozov, E. 2013. *To Save Everything, Click Here: The Folly of Technological Solutionism*. New York: Public Affairs.

Mueller, Milton. 1999. ICANN and Internet Governance: Sorting through the Debris of Self-Regulation. *Info* 1(6), pp. 497–520.

Mueller, Milton. 2004. *Ruling the Root*. Cambridge, MA: MIT Press.

Mueller, Milton. 2006. The Forum MAG: Who are these People? http://www.icannwatch.org/article.pl?sid=06/05/18/226205

Mueller, Milton. 2010. *Networks and States*. Cambridge, MA: MIT Press.

Mueller, Milton. 2013. Are We in a Digital Cold War? Presentation delivered at the GigaNet workshop 'The Global Governance of the Internet: Intergovernmentalism, Multistakeholderism and Networks', Graduate Institute, Geneva, Switzerland (17 May).

Mueller, Milton, Andreas Schmidt, and Brenden Kuerbis. 2013. Internet Security and Networked Governance in International Relations. *International Studies Review* 15(1), pp. 86–104.

Mueller, Milton, John Mathiason, and Hans Klein. 2007. The Internet and Global Governance: Principles and Norms for a New Regime. *Global Governance* 13(2), pp. 237–54.

Musiani, Francesca, Derrick L. Cogburn, Laura DeNardis, and Nanette Levinson. 2015. *The Turn to Infrastructure in Internet Governance.* New York: Palgrave Macmillan.

National Research Council. 1999. *Funding a Revolution: Government Support for Computing Research.* United States: National Academies Press.

Neumann, Iver and Ole Jacob Sending. 2010. *Governing the Global Polity: Practice, Mentality, Rationality.* Michigan: University of Michigan Press.

Nilekani, Nandan. 2018. Data to the people: India's inclusive internet. *Foreign Affairs.* September/October issue. https://www.foreignaffairs.com/articles/asia/2018-08-13/data-people

Noble Umoja, Safiya. 2018. *Algorithms of Oppression: How Search Engines Reinforce Racism.* New York: New York University Press.

Nolke, Andreas and Jean-Christophe Graz. 2008. *Transnational Private Governance and its Limits.* Routledge/ECPR Studies in European Political Science. Hoboken: Routledge.

Nonaka, Ikujirō and Hirotaka Takeuchi. 1995. *The Knowledge-Creating Company.* New York: Oxford University Press.

NSF. n.d. The Launch of NSFNET. https://www.nsf.gov/about/history/nsf0050/internet/launch.htm

NSI. 1995. Domain dispute resolution policy statement. https://www.lectlaw.com/files/inp08.htm

NTIA. 1998. *Management of Internet Names and Addresses* (Statement of Policy No. 980212036-8146-02). Washington, DC: US Department of Commerce. https://www.ntia.doc.gov/federal-register-notice/1998/statement-policy-management-internet-names-and-addresses

NTIA. 2005. U.S. Principles on the Internet's Domain Name and Addressing System. https://www.ntia.doc.gov/other-publication/2005/us-principles-internets-domain -name-and-addressing-system

NTIA. 2016. NTIA Finds IANA Stewardship Transition Proposal Meets Criteria to Complete Privatization. https://www.ntia.doc.gov/press-release/2016/iana-stewardship-transition -proposal-meets-criteria-complete-privatization

Nye, Joseph S. 2011. *Future of Power.* New York: Public Affairs.

Nye, Joseph S. 2014. The Regime Complex for Managing Global Cyber Activities. Belfer Center for Science and International Affairs.

OECD. 2001. *Understanding the Digital Divide.* Paris: OECD.

Olufuye, Jimson. 2018. The evolving face of 'Enhanced Cooperation'. What is next after WGEC 2.0? *The Guardian.* 27 April. https://guardian.ng/technology/the-evolving-face-of-enhanced-cooperation-what-is-next-after-wgec2-0/

O'Reilly, Tim. 2005. What is Web 2.0. *O'Reilly Network.* 30 September. https://www.oreilly.com/pub/a/web2/archive/what-is-web-20.html

Orsini, Amandine, Jean-Frederic Morin, and Oran Young. 2013. Regime Complexes: A Buzz, a Boom, or a Boost for Global Governance? *Global Governance* 19(1), pp. 27–39.

Osborne, David and Ted Gaebler. 1992. *Reinventing Government*. Reading, MA: Addison-Wesley.

Palfrey, J., C. Chen, S. Hwang, and N. Eisenkraft. 2003. Public Participation in ICANN. A Preliminary Study. Cambridge, MA: Berkman Center for Internet & Society at Harvard Law School. http://cyber.law.harvard.edu/icann/publicparticipation

Parker, Edwin. 2000. Closing the Digital Divide in Rural America. *Telecommunications Policy* 24(4), pp. 281–90.

Parker, Geoffrey, Marshall van Alystyne, and Sangeet Paul Choudary. 2016. *Platform Revolution: How Networked Markets are Transforming the Economy—and How to Make Them Work for You*. New York: W. W. Norton & Company.

Pasquale, Frank. 2015. *The Black Box Society: The Secret Algorithms That Control Money and Information*. Cambridge, MA: Harvard University Press.

Pattberg, P. H. 2005. The Institutionalization of Private Governance: How Business and Nonprofit Organizations Agree on Transnational Rules. *Governance* 18(4), pp. 589–610.

Pattberg, P., R. Duffy, D. Compagnon, M. Hoffmann, D. Levy, H. Bulkeley, L. Andonova, et al. 2012. Governing Climate Change Transnationally: Assessing the Evidence from a Database of Sixty Initiatives. *Government & Policy* 30(4), pp. 591–612.

Pauwelyn, Joost, Ramses Wessel, and Jan Wouters. 2013. *Informal International Lawmaking*. Oxford: Oxford University Press.

Peters, Guy. 2007. Forms of Informal Governance: Searching for Efficiency and Democracy. In *The Role of Committees in the Policy-Process of the European Union*, edited by Christiansen, Thomas. Cheltenham: Edward Edgar.

Pierre, Jon. 2000. *Debating Governance: Authority, Steering, and Democracy*. Oxford: Oxford University Press.

Pierre, Jon and Guy Peters. 2005. *Governing Complex Societies*. New York: Palgrave Macmillan.

Post, David G. 1997. Governing Cyberspace. *Wayne Law Review* 43, pp. 155–73.

Post, David G. 2002. Against 'Against Cyberanarchy'. *Berkeley Technology Law Journal* 17(4), pp. 1363–85.

Post, David and Danielle Kehl. 2015. *Controlling Internet Infrastructure*. http://papers.ssrn.com/sol3/papers.cfm?abstract_id=2636417

Postel, Jon. 1994. RFC 1591: Domain name structure and delegation. Network Working Group. https://datatracker.ietf.org/doc/rfc1591/

Pouliot, Vincent. 2010. *International Security in Practice*. Cambridge: Cambridge University Press.

Pouliot, Vincent. 2016. *International Pecking Orders: The Politics and Practice of Multilateral Diplomacy*. Cambridge and New York: Cambridge University Press.

Powers, Shawn and Michael Jablonski. 2015. *The Real Cyber War: The Political Economy of Internet Freedom*. Champaign: University of Illinois Press.

Prassl, Jeremias. 2018. *Humans as a Service: The Promise and Perils of Work in the Gig Economy*. Oxford: Oxford University Press.

Puchala, Donald J. and Raymond F. Hopkins. 1982. International Regimes: Lessons from Inductive Analysis. *International Organization* 36(2), pp. 245–75.

Raboy, Marc, Normand Landry, and Jeremy Shtern, eds. 2010. *Digital Solidaries, Communication Policy and Multi-Stakeholder Global Governance.* New York: Peter Lang.

Radu, Roxana. 2012. The Monopoly of Violence in the Cyberspace: Challenges of Cybersecurity. In *Power in the 21st Century: International Security and International Political Economy in a Changing World,* edited by Fels, E., J-F. Kremer, and K. Kronenberg, pp. 137–50. New York: Springer.

Radu, Roxana. 2013. Power Technology and Powerful Technologies: Global Governmentality and Security in the Cyberspace. In *Cyberspace and International Relations: Theory, Prospects and Challenges,* edited by Kremer, Jan-Frederik and Benedikt Müller, pp. 3–20. Berlin: Springer.

Radu, Roxana. 2017. Event report: Current Internet governance challenges: what's next? *Digital Watch.* 14 November. https://dig.watch/resources/current-internet-governance-challenges-whats-next

Radu, Roxana and Jean-Marie Chenou. 2015. Data Control and Digital Regulatory Space(S): Towards a New European Approach. *Internet Policy Review* 4(2). https://policyreview.info/articles/analysis/data-control-and-digital-regulatory-spaces-towards-new-european-approach

Radu, Roxana, Jean-Marie Chenou, and Rolf H. Weber. 2014. *The Evolution of Global Internet Governance: Principles and Policies in the Making.* Berlin: Springer.

Radu, Roxana, Nicolo Zingales, and Enrico Calandro. 2015. Crowdsourcing Ideas as an Emerging Form of Multistakeholder Participation in Internet Governance. *Policy & Internet* 7(3), pp. 362–82.

Radunovic, Vladimir. 2017a. Cyber-armament: a growing trend (Part I). DiploFoundation blog. 20 February. https://www.diplomacy.edu/blog/cyber-armament-growing-trend-part-i

Radunovic, Vladimir. 2017b. Cyber-armament: diplomatic initiatives (Part II). DiploFoundation blog. 20 February. https://www.diplomacy.edu/blog/cyber-armament-diplomatic-initiatives-part-ii

Raustiala, Kal and David G. Victor. 2004. The Regime Complex for Plant Genetic Resources. *International Organization* 58(2), pp. 277–309.

Raymond, Mark and Laura DeNardis. 2015. Multistakeholderism: Anatomy of an Inchoate Global Institution. *International Theory* 7(3), pp. 572–616.

Rhodes, R. A. 1994. The Hollowing Out of the State: The Changing Nature of the Public Service in Britain. *The Political Quarterly* 65, pp. 138–51.

Rioux, Michele. 2014. Competing Institutional Trajectories for Global Regulation—Internet in a Fragmented World. In *The Evolution of Global Internet Governance: Principles and Policies in the Making,* edited by Radu, Roxana, Jean-Marie Chenou, and Rolf H. Weber, pp. 37–56. Berlin and New York: Springer.

Risk Placement Services. 2018. Data Break QuickView Report. Year End 2017. https://www.rpsins.com/media/2884/mc_0000634a-yearendreport.pdf

Risse, Thomas. 2006. Transnational Governance and Legitimacy. In *Governance and Democracy—Comparing National, European and International Experiences*, edited by Benz, A. and I. Papadopoulus, pp. 179–99. Abingdon: Routledge.

Rosenau, James. 1992. Governance, Order and Change in World Politics. In *Governance Without Government: Order and Change in World Politics*, edited by Rosenau, James and Otto Czempiel. pp. 1–29. Cambridge: Cambridge University Press.

Rosenau, James and Otto Czempiel. 1992. *Governance without Government*. Cambridge: Cambridge University Press.

RT. 2017. Whoever Leads in AI Will Rule the World: Putin to Russian Children on Knowledge Day. 1 September. https://www.rt.com/news/401731-ai-rule-world-putin/

Ruggie, John. 2004. Reconstituting the Global Public Domain—Issues, Actors, and Practices. *European Journal of International Relations* 10(4), pp. 499–531.

Russell, Andrew L. 2014. *Open Standards and the Digital Age*. New York: Cambridge University Press.

Ryan, Johnny. 2010. *A History of the Internet and the Digital Future*. London: Reaktion Books.

Schmidt, Andreas. 2014. Open Security. Contributions of Networked Approaches to the Challenge of Democratic Internet Security Governance. In *The Evolution of Global Internet Governance: Principles and Policies in the Making*, edited by Radu, Roxana, Jean-Marie Chenou, and Rolf H. Weber, pp. 169–87. Berlin and New York: Springer.

Schmitter, Philippe C. 2010. Governance Arrangements for Sustainability: A Regional Perspective. *The International Journal of Business in Society* 10(1), pp. 85–96.

Selwyn, Neil. 2004. Reconsidering Political and Popular Understandings of the Digital Divide. *New Media & Society* 6(3), pp. 341–62.

Sharrock, Lisa M. 2001. The Future of Domain Name Dispute Resolution: Crafting Practical International Legal Solutions from within the UDRP Framework. *Duke Law Journal* 51(2), pp. 817–49.

Shah, Rajiv and Jay Kesan. 2007. The Privatization of the Internet's Backbone Network. *Journal of Broadcasting and Electronic Media* 51(1), pp. 93–109.

Shapiro, Elmer B. 1967. Computer Network Meeting of 9–10 October . http://web.stanford.edu/dept/SUL/library/extra4/sloan/mousesite/Archive/Post68/ARPANETMeeting1167.html

Shields, Stuart, Ian Bruff, and Huw Macartney. 2011. *Critical International Political Economy*. Houndsmills: Palgrave Macmillan.

Sil, Rudra and Peter J. Katzenstein. 2010. Analytic Eclecticism in the Study of World Politics: Reconfiguring Problems and Mechanisms Across Research Traditions. *Perspectives on Politics* 8(2), pp. 411–31.

Singh, J. P. 2009. Multilateral Approaches to Deliberating Internet Governance. *Policy & Internet* 1(1), pp. 91–111.

Sismondo, Sergio. 2010. *An Introduction to Science and Technology Studies*. 2nd edn. New York: Wiley-Blackwell.

Slaughter, Anne-Marie. 2011. A New Theory of the Foreign Policy Frontier: Collaborative Power. *The Atlantic*. http://www.theatlantic.com/international/archive/2011/11/a-new-theory-for-the-foreign-policy-frontier-collaborative-power/249260/

Smith, Graham J. H. 2002. *Internet Law and Regulation*. 3rd edn. Suffolk: Sweet & Maxwell.

Smith, Roger K. 1987. Explaining the Non-Proliferation Regime: Anomalies for Contemporary International Relations Theory. *International Organization* 41(2), pp. 253–281.

Smyrnaios, Nykos. 2018. *The Internet Oligopoly: The Corporate Takeover of Our Digital World*. Bingley: Emerald Publishing.

Solum, Lawrence. 2009. Models of Internet Governance. In *Internet Governance: Infrastructure and Institutions*, edited by Bygrave L. A. and J. Bing, pp. 48–91. Oxford: Oxford University Press.

Sommer, Peter, Ian Brown, and OECD International Futures Programme. 2011. *Reducing Systemic Cybersecurity Risk*. Paris: Organisation for Economic Co-operation and Development.

Starosielski, Nicole. 2015. *The Undersea Network*. Durham, NC: Duke University Press.

Stoker, Gerry. 1998. Governance as Theory: Five Propositions. *International Social Science Journal* 50(1), pp. 17–28.

Stone, Diane. 2013. *Knowledge Actors and Transnational Governance*. Non-Governmental Public Action. Basingstoke: Palgrave Macmillan.

Strange, Susan. 1996. *The Retreat of the State. The Diffusion of Power in the World Economy*. Cambridge: Cambridge University Press.

Strange, Susan. 1983. Cave! Hic Dragon: A Critique of Regime Analysis. In *International Regimes*, edited by Stephen D. Krasner, pp. 337–54. Ithaca, NY: Cornell University Press.

Swidler, Ann. 2001. What Anchors Cultural Practices. In *The Practice Turn in Contemporary Theory*, edited by Cetina, Karin Knorr, Theodore Schatzki, and Eike von Savigny, pp. 74–91. London: Routledge.

Sylvan, David. 2014. Governance without Governors. In *The Evolution of Global Internet Governance: Principles and Policies in the Making*, edited by Radu, Roxana, Jean-Marie Chenou, and Rolf H. Weber, pp. 23–36. Berlin and New York: Springer.

Tarjanne, Pekka. 1997. *Internet Governance: Toward Voluntary Multilateralism*. Keynote address, Meeting of Signatories and Potential Signatories of the Generic Top-Level Domain Memorandum of Understanding. Geneva: ITU. 29 April–1 May.

Taub, Amanda and Max Fisher. 2018. Where Countries are Tinderboxes and Facebook is a Match. *New York Times*. 21 April. https://www.nytimes.com/2018/04/21/world/asia/facebook-sri-lanka-riots.html

Thiemeyer, Guido. 2013. The 'Forces Profondes' of Internationalism in the Late Nineteenth Century: Politics, Economy and Culture. In *The Nation State and Beyond: Governing Globalization Processes in the Nineteenth and Early Twentieth*

Centuries, edited by Löhr, Isabella and Roland Wenzlhuemer, pp. 27–42. Berlin and New York: Springer.

Thies, Cameron. 2002. A Pragmatic Guide to Qualitative Historical Analysis in the Study of International Relations. *International Studies Perspectives* 3(4), pp. 351–72.

Touré, Hamadoun. 2012. Statement from Dr Hamadoun I. Touré, Secretary General of the ITU [online], 13 December. http://www.itu.int/en/wcit-12/Pages/statementtoure.aspx

Townes, Miles. 2012. The Spread of TCP/IP: How the Internet Became the Internet. *Millennium—Journal of International Studies* 41(1), pp. 43–64.

UNGA. 2013. The right to privacy in the digital age, resolution A/C.3/68/L.45/Rev.1. November. http://www.un.org/ga/search/view_doc.asp?symbol=A/C.3/68/L.45/Rev.1

van Eeten, Michel and Milton Mueller. 2013. Where is the Governance in Internet Governance? *New Media & Society* 15(5), pp. 720–36.

van Eeten, Michel, Milton Mueller, and Nico van Eijk. 2014. *The Internet and the State. A Survey of Key Developments.* The Hague: Netherlands Council for Societal Development.

Vogel, David J. 2005. Is There a Market for Virtue? The Business Case for Corporate Social Responsibility. *California Management Review* 47(4), pp. 19–45.

Waldrop, M. Mitchell. 2001. *The Dream Machine: J.C.R. Licklider and the Revolution that Made Computing Personal.* New York: Viking.

Webb, K. Government, Private Regulation, and the Role of the Market. In *Law, Regulation and Governance*, edited by MacNeil, M., N. Sargent, and P. Swan. Don Mills, Ontario: Oxford University Press.

Weber, Rolf H. and Shawn Gunnarson. 2012. A Constitutional Solution for Internet Governance. *Columbia Science & Technology Law Review* 14. http://stlr.org/download/volumes/volume14/WeberGunnarson.pdf

Weick, Karl. 1988. Enacted Sensemaking in Crisis Situations. *Journal of Management Studies* 25, pp. 305–17.

Weinberg, Jonathan. 2011. Non-state Actors and Global Informal Governance: The Case of ICANN. In *International Handbook on Informal Governance*, edited by Christiansen, Thomas and Christine Neuhold, pp. 198–218. Cheltenham: Edward Edgar.

Weiss, Thomas G. 2000. Governance, Good Governance and Global Governance: Conceptual and Actual Challenges. *Third World Quarterly* 21(5), pp. 795–814.

Weiss, Thomas G. and Rorden Wilkinson. 2014. Rethinking Global Governance? Complexity, Authority, Power, Change. *International Studies Quarterly* 58(1), pp. 207–15.

Wenger, Etienne. 1998. *Communities of Practice: Learning, Meaning, and Identity.* Cambridge: Cambridge University Press.

WGIG. 2005. *Report of the Working Group on Internet Governance.* Geneva: United Nations.

White House. 1997. Framework for global electronic commerce. https://clintonwhitehouse4.archives.gov/WH/New/Commerce/

Whitman, Jim. 2005. *Limits of Global Governance*. London: Routledge.

WIPO. 2015. *Innovation Index*. http://www.wipo.int/econ_stat/en/economics/gii/

WIPO. 2018. China Drives International Patent Applications to Record Heights; Demand Rising for Trademark and Industrial Design Protection. Press release, 21 March. http://www.wipo.int/pressroom/en/articles/2018/article_0002.html

WSIS. 2003a. Geneva Plan of Action. Geneva: United Nations. http://www.itu.int/wsis/documents/doc_multi.asp?lang=en&id=2266|2267

WSIS. 2003b. Geneva Declaration of Principles. Geneva: United Nations. http://www.itu.int/wsis/documents/doc_multi.asp?lang=en&id=1161|0

WSIS. 2005a. Tunis Agenda for the Information Society. Tunis: United Nations. http://www.itu.int/wsis/documents/doc_multi.asp?lang=en&id=2266|2267

WSIS. 2005b. Tunis Commitment. Tunis: United Nations. http://www.itu.int/wsis/documents/doc_multi.asp?lang=en&id=2266|0

Young, Oran. 1982. Regime Dynamics: The Rise and Fall of International Regimes. *International Organization* 36(2), pp. 277–97.

Zehle, Soenke. 2012. New World Information and Communication Order. In *The Wiley-Blackwell Encyclopedia of Globalization,* edited by Ritzer, George. Hoboken: John Wiley & Sons.

Ziewitz, Malte and Christian Pentzold. 2014. In Search of Internet Governance: Performing Order in Digitally Networked Environments. *New Media & Society* 16(2), pp. 306–22.

Zittrain, Jonathan. 2009. *The Future of the Internet and How to Stop It.* London: Penguin.

Zook, Matthew. 2008. *The Geography of the Internet Industry: Venture Capital, Dot-Coms, and Local Knowledge*. Hoboken: John Wiley and Sons.

Index